Thomas O'Neill Russell

Beauties and Antiquities of Ireland

Being a Tourist's Guide to its most beautiful Scenery and an Archaeologist's Manual

for its most interesting Ruins

Thomas O'Neill Russell

Beauties and Antiquities of Ireland
*Being a Tourist's Guide to its most beautiful Scenery and an Archaeologist's Manual for its
most interesting Ruins*

ISBN/EAN: 9783337185572

Printed in Europe, USA, Canada, Australia, Japan

Cover: Foto ©Lupo / pixelio.de

More available books at **www.hansebooks.com**

BEAUTIES AND ANTIQUITIES
OF IRELAND

BEING

A TOURIST'S GUIDE TO ITS MOST BEAUTIFUL
SCENERY & AN ARCHÆOLOGIST'S MANUAL
FOR ITS MOST INTERESTING RUINS

BY

T. O. RUSSELL
AUTHOR OF "DICK MASSEY," "TRUE HEART'S TRIALS," ETC.

LONDON
KEGAN PAUL, TRENCH TRÜBNER & CO. Ltd.
1897

PREFACE

To describe all the beauties and antiquities of Ireland, an encyclopedia, instead of a volume the size of this one would be required. As one of the objects of this book is to show that Irish history is as generally interesting as Irish scenery is generally beautiful, few places are noticed that are not historic; but in a volume of the size of this, all the historic places could not be mentioned. Many books have been published during the last three-quarters of a century that treat on Irish scenery and antiquities. Some of them are very voluminous and copiously illustrated. They were, for the most part, written by persons utterly unfitted for the task they undertook. Their remarks on Irish scenery may be of some value; they may have thought Killarney more beautiful than the Bog of Allen; but wherever they touch on matters connected with history and antiquities, they are so often incorrect and misleading that the books they have published may, for the most part, be said to be useless. It is not too much to say that many of these works would be actually increased in value if the printed matter were torn out of them and nothing left but the illustrations and covers. The people who wrote them were totally unfitted to treat of Irish history and antiquities. They knew little about the history of ancient Ireland, and nothing of the Irish language or its literature. They could hardly be justified to treat of Irish architectural remains, because they were ill-equipped to do so, and were unsympathetic with the race that raised them.

If there is any country in Europe about the scenery and antiquities of which an interesting book could be written, it is Ireland. In no other country are scenery and antiquities so closely allied, for the finest remains of her ancient ruins are generally found where the scenery is most weird, most strange, or most beautiful. In no other country, perhaps, can so many places be identified with historic events, or historic personages, as in Ireland. It contains more relics of a long vanished past than any other European land. Great Britain seems a new country compared with Ireland. In spite of the wanton and disgraceful destruction of her ancient monuments that has been going on for centuries, more of such can be found in a single Irish county than in a dozen in

Great Britain. Although Stonehenge is the finest
druidic monument known to exist, the quantity
of druidic remains is much greater in Ireland than
in England. In the latter country we miss the
dun, the *rath*, the *lis*, the round tower and the
sepulchral mound, some of which are found in
almost every square mile of Ireland. And coming
down to later times, when men began to erect
structures of stone, we find the remains of castles
and keeps in such extraordinary numbers that we
wonder for what purpose so many strongholds were
erected. Counting *raths*, *duns*, *lises*, *cromlechs*,
round towers, crumbling castles, and deserted fanes,
Ireland may be called a land of ruins beyond any
other country in Europe. To make these multitudinous monuments of a far-back past still more
interesting, it will be found that mention is made
of most of them even in the remnant of Gaelic
literature that by the merest chance has been
preserved.

The place names of Ireland are as interesting
and as extraordinary as her antiquities, and to
some are even more fascinating than her beauties.
The bewildering immensity of Irish place names is
one of the most remarkable things connected with
Ireland; but like her ancient monuments, they are
every day disappearing—fading away with the

language from which they were formed. Even still, there are, probably, as many ancient place names in a single Irish province as in the whole of Great Britain. If it is not absolutely true when speaking of Ireland to say that, "No dust of hers is lost in vulgar mould," it can at least be said that there is hardly a square mile of her surface where some hoary relic of the past or some beautiful object of nature can be met with that is not mentioned in history, enshrined in legend, or celebrated in song.

T. O. R.

CONTENTS

CONTENTS

KILLARNEY

KILLARNEY is famed and known all over the civilized world; but there are places in Ireland where isolated scenes can be found as fair as any in Killarney. Much has been written about this "Eden of the West," but most of those who have attempted to describe it have omitted to mention its chief charm—namely, diversity of scenic attractions within a small compass. Almost everything that Nature could do has been done within a tract of country hardly ten miles square.

Except some favoured spots in Switzerland, there is no spot of European soil more famed for beauty than Killarney. Its very name is beautiful, as any one can know who has heard Balfe's grand song, "Killarney." No sounds more harmonious or more fitted for a refrain could be uttered by the organs of speech. The name signifies in Gaelic the church of the sloe or wild plum-tree. The real name of the lake, or chain of lakes, which is one of the charms of Killarney, is Loch Lein, but the latter name is now almost obsolete.

Before attempting to describe Killarney, it will

be well to give the reader an extract from
Macaulay's "History of England." The passage
is a masterpiece of prose. It is a sketch of the
scenic characteristics of that part of Ireland where
the famous lakes are situated :

"The south-western part of Kerry is now well
known as the most beautiful tract in the British
Isles. The mountains, the glens, the capes stretching far out into the Atlantic, the crags on which
the eagles build, the rivulets branching down rocky
passes, the lakes overhung by groves in which
the wild deer find covert, attract, every summer,
crowds of wanderers sated with business and the
pleasures of great cities. The beauties of that
country are often, indeed, hidden in the mist and
rain that the west wind brings up from the
boundless ocean. But, on rare days, when the
sun shines out in his glory, the landscape has a
freshness and warmth of colouring seldom found
in our latitude. The myrtle loves the soil; the
arbutus thrives better than in Calabria; the turf
has a livelier hue than elsewhere; the hills glow
with a richer purple; the varnish of the holly and
the ivy is more glossy, and berries of a brighter
red peep through foliage of a brighter green." *

Macaulay, in spite of his Celtic name, was not

* "History of England," vol. iii., p. 107.

a lover of Ireland and the Irish, and there is no reason to suppose that this most wonderful word-painting was evoked by any liking for the land it describes. He had seen Killarney, and it must have inspired him to write the greatest descriptive passage he ever penned.

Those who expect to find in Killarney the grandeur of the Alps, the Rocky Mountains, or even of the Scottish Highlands, will be disappointed. It is too small to be sublime, for it could be ridden round in a day. The most wonderful of its many wonders is variety of scenery in a small compass. In this respect few parts of the known world can compare with it. Almost every possible phase of Nature, almost everything she could do with land and water, can be found in Killarney, and found on a little spot of earth hardly larger than the space covered by London. Mountains, lakes, rivers, rocks, woods, waterfalls, flowery islands, green meadows and glistening strands, almost exhaust Nature's materials for forming the beautiful. But all are found at Killarney. Man, who mars Nature so often, has helped her here, for the castles and abbeys he raised of yore still stand, and their ivy and flower-decked ruins, tenanted only by the bat and the bee, put the finishing touch on this

earthly Eden, and make it one of the scenic
wonders of the world. If Killarney had glaciers
and eternally snow-clad peaks, it would have everything that Switzerland has.

Another wonderful thing about Killarney is the
admirable proportion its scenic features bear to
one another. If the mountains were any higher
they would be too high for the lakes, and if the
lakes were any bigger they would be too big for
the mountains. Even the rivers and waterfalls
are almost in exact proportion to the other phases
of Nature. The monstrous Mississippi or the
thundering Niagara would spoil such a miniature
paradise; but the limpid Laune and O'Sullivan's
babbling cascade suit it exactly. Killarney is the
most perfect effort of Nature to bring together
without disproportion all her choicest charms.

Small as Killarney is, it would take at least a
week, or perhaps two weeks, to see it and know
all its loveliness. It is only on foot and without
hurry that its beauties can be seen in perfection.
Its mountains may be ascended, and glorious views
of sea and craggy heights obtained; but the charm
of Killarney is not grandeur, but beauty. There
are mountain views in Scotland finer than can be
had from the summits of Mangerton or Carn
Thual. It would be something like waste of time

to climb those hills. Let the tourist rather wander
in the hundreds of shady lanes or paths that skirt
the lakes, or take a boat and navigate that most
picturesque river, for its length, in the world, the
Long Range, that connects the upper with the
lower lake. Let him mark the wondrous luxuriance
of grass, leaf, weed and flower. The arbutus grows
so large that it becomes a tree. Ferns of such
gigantic proportions may be found in shady nooks
that they seem to belong to some far-back geo-
logical age. Softness, freshness, luxuriance and
beauté riante are the real glories of Killarney. In
these it has no rival.

There are two drawbacks to Killarney; there is
the guide nuisance and the rain nuisance. The
nuisance of guides is probably no greater than in
many other places of tourist resort, and, by a strong
effort of the will, can be got rid of. But the rain is
a more serious matter and must be borne patiently.
Some years come when not a dozen dry days occur
throughout the entire summer, but generally there
is less rainfall than on the west coasts of Scotland
or England. There have been quite as many wet
days in Liverpool during the three last summers as
there usually are in Killarney. It does, however,
too often happen that tourists are confined to the
hotel for four or five days at a time owing to the

rain. It must be borne in mind that this excessive moisture of atmosphere is what has given the south-west of Ireland, and England too, their exquisite charm of verdure and wild flowers. When a fine day comes after rain in summer or autumn all Nature seems to laugh. Flowers of all hues open their petals, birds in multitudes begin to sing, and wild bees and hosts of insects make the air musical with their hum. The American tourist need have no fear when insects are mentioned, for the mosquito is unknown in Killarney. Midges are the only insect plague, but they never enter houses, and are troublesome only before rain, early in the spring or late in the autumn.

Most tourists go to Killarney early in the summer. June and July are favourite times for Americans to visit it. As it lies almost in the direct route between New York and Liverpool, they generally visit it before going to England or the Continent of Europe. But the time to see Killarney is in the autumn—it is then in all its glory. It should not be visited before the 15th of August; from then until the 1st of October it is the most beautiful place, perhaps, on the earth, provided always that the weather is not wet. There is only one thing that mars the weather in the south of Ireland—namely, rain. Cold, in the general sense of the word, is almost unknown. Every day that is not wet must be fine. There is, it must be confessed, rather more probability of having dry weather in Killarney in the spring or early summer than in the autumn, but, by visiting it in the spring, the tourist would gain nothing, and would lose the wild-flower feast of autumn. No American, or even native of England, no matter from what part of his country he comes, can form the faintest conception of what a Killarney mountain is in September, if the weather be fine. The wild-flower that is the glory of Ireland is the heath. It blossoms only in the autumn. Next in glory to the heath comes the furze. Both furze and heath are indigenous in the whole of the south-west of Europe, but, owing to the mildness and moistness of the climate of Ireland, they grow and blossom there with a luxuriance unknown in any other country. When a great mountain becomes a mighty bouquet of purple and gold, a sight is revealed which surpasses anything on earth in floral beauty. Almost every mountain round about the "Eden of the West" is clothed from base to summit in a vast drapery of heath. Some of the Killarney mountains are wooded for a few hundred feet up their sides, but most of them are entirely covered with heath interspersed with furze. When

a fine autumn occurs, tens of thousands of acres of
mountain and moorland gleam in the sunlight, an
ocean of purple heath and golden furze. Not only
do the heath and furze blossom in the autumn, but
myriads of other wild-flowers appear only at that
time of year, or blossom most luxuriantly then.
Even white clover, which rarely blossoms in other
countries except in the spring or early summer,
open its flowers widest and sends out its most
fragrant perfume in an Irish autumn. The air is
heavy with fragrance of flowers, the mountains are
musical with the hum of bees, and

> " Every wingèd thing that loves the sun
> Makes the bright noonday full of melody."

Killarney in a fine autumn becomes not only en-
trancing, but overpowering in its loveliness.

The whole country round Killarney is a wonderland. Macaulay's description of it is true to the
letter. In all his works nothing can be found of a
descriptive character equal to the passage quoted
from him. He had a great subject, and he handled
it as no other writer of the English language could.
He has described one of the loveliest regions in the
world in a few lines that will stand for ever as
one of the greatest efforts of a great writer. His
description is a brilliant gem of composition, just

as the place it describes is a brilliant gem of nature.

No one should visit Killarney without visiting Glengariff. It is only about twenty miles from Killarney, and can be reached by a sort of low-backed car peculiar to Ireland. This car is a very curious sort of conveyance. The occupants sit back to back, with their sides to the horses. In fine weather there is no pleasanter mode of travelling than on a low-backed car, but when it rains one is anything but comfortable. Glengariff is thought by some to surpass even Killarney in beauty. It is a deep glen surrounded by mountains of the most fantastic shapes, clothed with a wealth of foliage that would astonish any one who had not seen Killarney. The lake that is seen at Glengariff is sea-water, and opens into Bantry Bay. The tourist will find an excellent hotel there, and no matter how he may be satiated with the beauty of Killarney, he will see other and more striking beauties in Glengariff.

Killarney is well supplied with hotels. There are four or five, and they are all good. Most of them are situated in sequestered places, where a view of some enchanting scene spreads before the door. The village of Killarney is about a mile from the lake; it is a place of no interest at all, but there is a very good hotel in it, and many

tourists stop there, for it is just at the railway
terminus. Hotel expenses at Killarney in the
tourist season are not so high as at some of the
fashionable Continental summer resorts. Guides
are not much wanted, unless mountains are to be
ascended. Then they are indispensable, for mists
may suddenly come during the very finest day,

ROSS CASTLE.

and the tourist without a guide would run a chance
of spending a night on a bleak mountain or being
drowned in a lake or bog-hole. Ponies of a most
docile character can be hired cheap. Pony-back
travelling is a favourite mode of "doing" Killarney,
especially with ladies and lazy men, but no one
into whose soul the charm of Killarney really enters

would think of travelling through such lovely
scenes on horseback. On foot or in a boat is the
way to see Killarney.

There are ruins of the most interesting kind in
Killarney. Muckross Abbey is not so large as some
of the ruined shrines of England, but it is a venerable and imposing building. It was built by one of
the MacCarthys, chiefs of the district, in 1340.
Ross Castle is another imposing ruin. It is situated
on a green promontory that juts into the lake.
There is some doubt as to the exact time when it
was erected, but it could hardly have been before
the fourteenth century. The most interesting ruin
near Killarney, and by far the most ancient, is the
monastery on the supremely beautiful island of
Inisfallan. It was founded by Saint Finian in the
sixth century. It was there the yet unpublished
"Annals of Inisfallan" were compiled. Hardly
any of the walls of the old monastery remain.
The arbutus and the hawthorn are growing where
once were cloisters, and are fast completing the
ruin of what was one of the first of the ancient
churches that were erected in Ireland.

TARA

THE supreme attraction of Tara is its antiquity. It must not, however, be thought that a visit to this famous hill reveals no beauties. It is not situated among mountains ; hardly a lake is visible from its summit : yet the view from it is so fine that if there was no historic interest attached to it, the tourist in search of the beautiful alone would have his eyes feasted with as fair a scene from one of its grassy ramparts as could be gazed on in any part of Ireland. Eastward the view is obstructed by the hill of Screen, but on every other side it is superb. Westward the eye ranges over the fairest and most fertile part of Ireland, the great plain of Meath and West Meath, anciently called *Magh Breagh*, or the fair plain. And fair indeed it is in summer time, one great green sea of grass and wild flowers, reaching to the Shannon, sixty miles away. But it is southward that the view from Tara is most striking. The Dublin and Wicklow mountains are more imposing when seen from Tara than from any other place. They rise in a vast, blue rampart, and seem so colossal as to appear thousands of feet higher than they are. Those old, barbaric Irish kings and chieftains must have been lovers of the beautiful, for they almost invariably fixed their strongholds not only in the fairest parts, but in places commanding the fairest prospects. There are hardly two other places in Ireland the surroundings of which are more beautiful than those of Tara and Uisneach, or from which fairer prospects are to be seen. They were, from far-back antiquity, the seats of those by whom the country was *supposed* to be ruled, for it often happened that he who was styled chief king had but little control over his vassals.

There is no other spot of European soil the records of which go so far back into the dim twilight of the past as do the records of Tara. Before the first Roman raised a rude hut on the banks of the Tiber, when the place where the Athenian Acropolis now stands was a bare rock, kings, whose names are given in Irish history, ruled in Tara. When one gazes on those grassy mounds, that are almost all that remain of what our ancient poets used to call "the fair, radiant, City of the Western World," he can hardly believe that such a place could ever have been the abode of royalty, the meeting-place of assemblies, and

the permanent home of thousands. Other desolated strongholds of ancient royalty and dominion
bear ample evidence of their former greatness.
Ruined columns of Persepolis yet remain. The
site of Tadmor is marked by still standing pillars
of marble, and vast piles of decomposed bricks
tell of the greatness of ancient Babylon; but
green, grassy mounds and partially obliterated
earth-works are almost all that remain of Tara.
It is so ruined that it can hardly be ruined any
more. Time may yet destroy even what remains
of the bricks of Babylon, but time can hardly
change what remains of the ruins of Tara.

No other spot of Irish earth can compare with
Tara in historic interest or in antiquity. Emania
and Rathcroghan are little more than places of
yesterday compared with it. It is over three
thousand years ago since the first king reigned in
Tara. Some may say that it is only bardic history
that tells of what took place in Ireland in those
very remote times, and that it is unworthy of
credence. It is true that there is a great deal of
fiction mixed with the early history of Ireland, as
there is with the early history of all countries;
but the ancient Irish chroniclers did not attempt
much more than a mere sketch of the salient points
of Irish history of very remote times, say from

beyond the third century B.C. Some of the facts
they mention have been verified in remarkable ways
by what may be called collateral evidence. This
evidence is found in place names, and in the names
of persons and things. One of those proofs of the
general correctness of what is related in Gaelic
literature about far-back events of Irish history is
so remarkable that it deserves special mention.
One of the kings who ruled in Tara considerably
over a thousand years B.C. was named Lugh, or in
English, Lewy or Louis. He established the games
that were held annually at Tailtean, near Kells, that
were regularly celebrated down to the time of the
Anglo-French invasion, in honour of his mother,
whose name was Tailte. Those games were held
in the first week in August, and from them the
Irish name for the month of August is derived; it
is *Lughnasa*. This is the only name known in
Gaelic to the present hour for the month of August,
except a periphrastic one meaning "the first month
of autumn." This name for August is known in
every part of Ireland and Scotland where the old
tongue still lives, but it has been corrupted to
Lunasd in the latter country. The meaning of the
word *Lughnasa* is, the games or celebrations of this
same Lugh or Lewy, who lived and reigned centuries before Rome was founded, and before a stone

of the Athenian Acropolis was laid. It seems almost impossible to conceive that the Gaelic name for the month of August could have had any origin other than that given above on the authority of one of the most learned of ancient Irish ecclesiastics, Cormac MacCuillenan, Archbishop of Cashel, in the ninth century.

The descriptions of Tara given in ancient Gaelic writings have been verified in the most remarkable manner by the researches of modern archæologists. Dr Petrie's great work, "The Antiquities of Tara Hill," would go far to remove the prejudices of the most bigoted despiser of Irish historic records. He was one of the most learned and scientific investigators of antiquities that ever lived, and was not only a good Gaelic scholar himself, but had the assistance of the greatest Gaelic scholar of the century, John O'Donovan. Those two gentlemen translated every mention of Tara that they could find in prose or verse in ancient Irish manuscripts; they compared every mention they could find of the monuments of Tara with what remains of them at present; and they found such a general agreement between ancient descriptions of those monuments and the existing remains of them as proved what is said in Gaelic manuscripts about the extent and splendour of Tara in Pagan times to be well worthy

of credence. Every one who visits Tara, and who
is in any way interested in archæology, should have
Doctor Petrie's map of it, which will be found in his
minute and elaborate work on the "Antiquities of
Tara Hill." That map is reproduced here. The
book is very scarce, as only a small edition of
it was printed, but it can be found in the "Transactions of the Royal Irish Academy." Armed
with Petrie's map a visit to Tara would be one of
the most interesting and enjoyable excursions that
could be made from Dublin. Kilmessan Station
can be reached from the Broadstone terminus in an
hour, and less than two miles of a walk through a
beautiful country brings one to the summit of "the
Hill of Supremacy," as it was called of old when he
who ruled in Tara ruled Ireland. No matter how
confirmed an archæologist he may be who stands
for the first time on this celebrated hill, his first
feeling will be of joy at the beauty of the prospect
that is spread before him. To know how beautiful
Ireland is, even in those places that are not on the
track of tourists, and that are seldom mentioned in
guide books, one should see the view from the hill
of Tara.

It would be hard to find any other hill in Ireland
so well adapted for a place of assembly or for the
dwelling of a ruler as Tara. Uisneach, in West-

meath, is, perhaps, the only hill in Ireland that possesses all the advantages of Tara. In ancient times, when war was the rule and peace the exception, it was imperative that a stronghold should be on a height. Athens had its acropolis and so had Corinth. Tara had the advantage of extent as well as of height, and could be made a permanent dwelling-place as well as an acropolis, for there are fully a hundred acres on what may be called the summit of the hill. It is unfortunate that some of the hill has been enclosed, planted with deal trees, and a church erected on the very track of some of the most ancient monuments. This plantation and church have terribly interfered with the picturesqueness and antique look of Tara. Planting deal trees and erecting a modern church amid the hoariest monuments, and on the most historic spot of European soil, was little less than sacrilege. If there had been a proper national spirit, or a due veneration for their past among the Irish, they never would have allowed a church or any modern building to be erected on the most historic spot on Irish soil; and even now they ought to have the church removed, the wall torn down, and the plantation uprooted. All Greece would rise up in indignation were any one to erect a church or chapel amid the ruins of the Athenian Acropolis.

MONUMENTS ON TARA HILL.
(*After Petrie's Map.*)

The most interesting and best preserved of the
antiquities of Tara is the track of the banquetting-
house. It must have been an enormous building,
for it was about 800 feet long and about 50 wide.
It is wonderful how perfectly plain and well-de-
fined the track of this once great structure appears
after nearly fourteen hundred years, and in spite of
the way this historic spot has been uprooted and
levelled. But not a vestige of stone-work or of
stones is to be seen near the ruins of the banquet-
ting-house. It seems absolutely certain that there
were no buildings of stone in Tara when it was at
the height of its grandeur, and that seems to have
been about the middle of the third century, during
the reign of Cormac MacAirt. It must not be
thought that buildings cannot be fine unless they
are of stone; but buildings of stone were very rare
in northern countries until comparatively recent
times. Moore, in his "History of Ireland," says,
speaking of wooden buildings and of Tara—
" However scepticism may now question their
architectural beauty, they could boast the admiration of many a century in evidence of their
grandeur. That those edifices were of wood is
by no means conclusive either against the elegance
of their structure or the civilisation of those who
erected them. It was in wood that the graceful

forms of Grecian architecture first unfolded their beauties." So the absence of stone buildings in Tara in no way proves that it was not a place of grandeur as well as of beauty; and the tenth century Gaelic poet may have been justified in saying of it,

> " World of perishable beauty !
> · Tara to-day, though a wilderness,
> Was once the meeting-place of heroes.
> Great was the host to which it was an inheritance,
> Though to-day green, grassy land."

Every mention of Tara in the vast remnant of Gaelic manuscripts of the ninth, tenth, eleventh, and twelfth centuries that still exists shows it to have been, beyond all comparison, the most important place in ancient Ireland. Oengus the Culdee, author of the longest poem in ancient Gaelic, the famous Félire, recently translated by Mr Whitley Stokes, speaks thus of this renowned but now ruined spot :

> " Tara's mighty burgh hath perished
> With its kingdom's splendour ;
> With a multitude of champions of wisdom
> Abideth great Ardmagh."

The poet contrasts the desolation into which the strongholds of the Pagans had fallen with the then flourishing condition of the centres of Christian teaching. Tara was the political as well as the social centre of ancient Ireland. It is in connection with it that the only mention made of roads having names is found in ancient Gaelic writings. Five great roads, as will be seen by the annexed map, led from Tara to the extremities of the Island. The Slighe Dala went southward; the Slighe Asail went north-west; the Slighe Midhluchra, went north-east; the Slighe Cualann went south-easterly; and the Slighe Mór went in a south-western direction. Traces of those roads may still be seen by the practised eye of the archæologist.

One of the most interesting things connected with Tara is the Lia Fail, or Stone of Destiny. It was upon it the over-kings of Ireland had been inaugurated from far-back antiquity. It is said to have been brought by Fergus, brother of the then reigning chief King, to Scotland, in order that he might be crowned king on it over the part of Scotland he had conquered. It remained under the coronation chair of the Kings of Scotland down to the time of Edward the First, who seized it and brought it to Westminster, where it is now, and the sovereigns of England have been crowned on it ever since his time. Petric maintains that the Lia Fail is still in Tara, and that

the pillar stone that stands over the graves of
the men who fell in '98 is it. He adduces very
strong evidence from manuscripts of high authority
and of great antiquity to prove what he says.
There is, on the other hand, strong testimony to
prove that it was brought to Scotland by Fergus.
The question will probably never be finally settled.
The principal virtue supposed to be possessed by
the Lia Fail was that it would bring political
power to the country in which it was, particularly
if its people were of Celtic stock. It is very
remarkable that soon after the stone supposed to
be the Lia Fail was taken out of Ireland, her
political power began to decline, her over-kings
lost a great part of their former authority, and in
the long run she lost her independence. Scotland's political power and national independence
vanished not long after she had lost the Lia Fail,
and in a few centuries after England had got it
she became one of the foremost nations in the
world. The English claim to be Saxons, but it
is now generally admitted that the Celtic element
preponderates in the island of Great Britain, so
that the prophecy attached to the Lia Fail seems
to be fulfilled.

The Lia Fail is certainly the most extraordinary
stone in Europe, if not in the world. The famous

Rosetta stone, covered as it is with archaic writing,
and verifying, as many suppose, the truth of Old
Testament history, is hardly more interesting than
the rude granite slab that lies under the coronation
chair in Westminster, unmarked with a single letter.
It is about 25 inches in length, about 15 in breadth,
and 9 in depth.   How such a rude, unshapely flag-
stone could have such a history, and have been an
object of veneration and interest for so many centuries, is what strikes with wonder those who see
it.   But if it is not the real Lia Fail, if it is a
sham, and if the stone still standing in Tara is the
genuine one, the wonder increases; for the fact of
a spurious article having become invested with
such fame and regarded with such veneration is
the greatest wonder of all.

Doctor Petrie says, in his "Antiquities of Tara
Hill," that "it is in the highest degree improbable
that to gratify the desire of a colony the Irish
would have voluntarily parted with a monument
so venerable for its antiquity and considered
essential to the legitimate succession of their
own kings."   He quotes verses from a tenth century poet, Kenith O'Hartigan, who says that the
Lia Fail is

"This stone on which are my two heels";
and he quotes from an ancient tract called the

Dinseanchus, another proof that when it was composed, and that time could not have been later than the tenth century, the Lia Fail was in Tara. It often happens, however, that Irish annalists and historians, so fond were they of looking backward to the past, make things appear as they had been, and not as they were when they wrote. The over-kings of Ireland were called Kings of Tara five hundred years after Tara had been abandoned, and when it was as waste and desolate as it is to-day. O'Dugan, in his topographical poem, written in the fourteenth century, tells of clans inhabiting the English Pale, when they had been banished westward by the invaders nearly two hundred years before he wrote. He prefaces his topographical poem by saying

"O'Maolseachlinn, chief King of Tara and Erin,"

but the last O'Maolseachlinn that was nominally chief King of Ireland and Tara had died three hundred years before O'Dugan wrote! Why those old Gaelic poets were so fond of describing things as they had been, and not as they were when they wrote, is hard to understand. They may have got their information from documents that were centuries old when they copied them. It seems a certainty that the men whose writings Petrie quotes to prove that the Lia Fail was in Tara in the tenth century, did what O'Dugan did in his topographical poem—that is, speak of things as they had been hundreds of years before. He never mentions the English at all. This partially accounts for Irish writers of the tenth century speaking of the Lia Fail being then in Tara. They intended to describe where it used to be, but not where it was. When Petrie says that the Lia Fail is spoken of by all ancient Irish writers in such a manner as to leave no doubt that it remained in its original situation at the time when they wrote, he makes a great mistake. Here is a quotation from the "Book of Leinster," a manuscript of the highest authority, compiled in the early part of the twelfth century, and mostly from writings of a much earlier date:—"It was the Tuatha De Danaans who brought with them the great *Fal*, that is, the stone of knowledge that *was* in Tara; from which [the name of] Magh Fail is on Ireland. He under whom it would roar was then [rightful] King of Ireland." *

There is another very strong proof brought to

* Is iat Tuata De Danaan tucsat leo in Fál mór ; i. in lia fis *bai* i Temraig; di atá Mag Fail for Erinn. In ti fo ngéised saide bari Erenn. " Book of Leinster," page 9.

light by the publication of "Silva Gadelica," by Mr Standish Hays O'Grady, that the Lia Fail was removed from Tara. In the tract called the "Colloquy," one of the speakers says: "This, then, and the Lia Fail, or stone of destiny, that *was* there (in Tara) were the two wonders of Tara. When Ireland's monarch stepped on it, it would cry out under him," . . . "And who was it that lifted that flag, or that carried it away out of Ireland?" asked one of the listeners. "It was a young hero of great spirit that ruled over" . . . Here, unfortunately, the tract ends abruptly. The "Colloquy," or "Agallamh na Seanorach," is a tract of respectable antiquity. Its language seems to be that of the fifteenth or perhaps the fourteenth century, but the version that has come down to us may be, and probably is, but a transcript of a much more ancient tract, the language of which was modernised.

If Doctor Petrie had known of the existence of those two proofs given of the Lia Fail having been removed from Tara, he never would have said that all ancient Irish writers spoke of it in such a way as to leave no doubt of its being there still. O'Reilly, author of Irish dictionary, says: "Lia Fail, the stone of destiny, on which the ancient Irish monarchs used to be crowned until the time of Mortogh Mac

Earc, who sent it into Scotland that his brother
Fergus, who had subdued that country, might be
crowned on it.   It is now in Westminster Abbey."
O'Reilly was the most learned Irish scholar and
historian of his day, and was a painstaking, con-
scientious man, who would hardly state any thing
for, which he did not have good authority.   It
must, however, be admitted that up to the
present no positive statement seems to have
been found in ancient Irish writings as to when
and by whom the Lia Fail was brought from
Tara to Scotland;   neither does it seem to
be known where O'Reilly got his information
about it.

When Petrie spoke of the improbability of the
Irish allowing such a venerated monument as the
Lia Fail to be taken out of Ireland, he should
have remembered that at the time when it is said
to have been taken, in the beginning of the sixth
century, Christianity had become established in
Ireland.   Paganism or Druidism may have sur-
vived among a few, but it had got its death-blow.
Pagan monuments of every kind had begun to
be disregarded.   The Lia Fail was essentially a
Pagan monument, and consequently an abhorrence
to Christians.   The fathers, or at least the grand-
fathers, of the men who allowed Fergus to take

it to Scotland, would probably have shed the last drop of their blood to keep it in Ireland. The disrepute into which everything connected with Paganism had fallen after the introduction of Christianity is plainly set forth in the "Book of Leinster" in the very page from which the Gaelic extract about the Lia Fail has been given :—"It happened that Christ was born not long after ; it was that which broke the power of the idols."* The Lia Fail was an idol that had lost its power and prestige, so that the people would not be likely to have any objection to its being removed to Scotland or anywhere else.

But there are still other even stronger objections for accepting Petrie's theory that the Lia Fail is still in Tara. The pillar stone that is there is not a *lia*, and never would have been called such by the ancient Irish. *Lia* means a stone of any kind in its general sense ; but the pillar stone in Tara would not be called a *lia*, but a *coirthe*. *Lia* is always applied to a flag-stone, both in ancient and modern Gaelic. The stone under the coronation chair in Westminster is a real *lia* or flag-stone ; the one in Tara is a *coirthe*, or pillar stone, for, judging from its height above the ground, it

* Ecmoing ni hed fota acht Crist do genemain ; is sed ro bris cumachta nan idal. "Book of Leinster," p. 9.

cannot be much less than eight feet in length; it is very nearly round, and was evidently fashioned into its present shape by man. If the stone in Tara is the real Lia Fail, how did it come to lose its original name and be known even still by an Irish name that connects it with Fergus, the person by whom the real Lia Fail is popularly believed to have been brought to Scotland? This loss of an original name, and its substitution by a new one, could hardly have occurred in the case of such a famous monument as the Lia Fail. If the superstitious reverence with which it had been regarded before the introduction of Christianity had vanished, its original name would have remained. There are many place names in Ireland that have not changed during twenty centuries, and it is almost impossible to conceive how the name of the most venerated monument in all Ireland could have changed had the monument itself remained in the country. Another strong objection against the pillar stone in Tara being the real Lia Fail is its shape. The real Lia Fail was intended to be stood upon by the chief king at his inauguration; but the most flat-footed monarch that ever ruled Ireland would have considerable difficulty in standing steadily on the *coirthe* in Tara, even if it were prostrate,

for it is round and not flat. Standing steadily
on it would be nearly as difficult a performance
as "rolling off a log" would be an easy one.

Taking everything into consideration, there seem
to be very strong reasons to believe that the Lia
Fail was taken from Tara to Scotland at the
time it is popularly believed to have been taken—
namely, about the year 503 of the Christian era;
that it was taken in order to have Fergus Mac
Earc inaugurated on it as king over that part of
Scotland which he had brought under his domination; that it was taken from Scone to Westminster
by Edward the First in the year 1296, and that
it is now under the coronation chair in Westminster
Abbey. It seems strange how a man of Doctor
Petrie's archæological knowledge could have been
led to believe that the pillar stone still in Tara,
for whatever use it may have been originally
intended, was the real Lia Fail, or Stone of
Destiny.

It would be most instructive and interesting if
a scientific examination was made of the stone
under the coronation chair. If it was proved to
be a meteoric stone, its fame and the reverence
with which it was so long regarded could be
easily understood. If an ancient tribe saw a
stone falling from heaven among them, they would

regard such a thing as a miracle, and think that the stone was sent to them for some special purpose. They would, if possible, take it with them wherever they went. If the Lia Fail was proved to be a meteoric stone, the esteem and honour in which it was so long held, and the power which it was believed to possess, would be easily accounted for.

The history of Tara is, to a great extent, the history of ancient Ireland of pre-Christian times. It was more of a political centre than London or Paris is at present. The event that above all others left a permanent mark as well as a blot on Irish history may be said to have had its origin in Tara. The horrible Leinster Tribute and Tara are closely connected.

In the first century of the Christian era, an over-king called Tuathal, from whom the common Irish surname O'Tool, or Tool, seems to have originated, reigned in Tara. He had two daughters, famed for their beauty. We are told in the "Book of Leinster" that they were "fairer than the clouds of heaven." Their names were Fihir and Darine. A king of Leinster named Eochy married Fihir, the elder of the two sisters. He got tired of her after a short time, went to Tara, told Tuathal that Fihir was dead, and that he wanted to marry her sister Darine. Tuathal consented, and Eochy took his new wife home to his *dun*, which was in the western part of the present county of Wicklow. Darine had been only a short time in her new home when she met her sister Fihir, who she had been told was dead. Darine was so overwhelmed by shame that she died, and Fihir was so shocked at the death of her sister that she died of grief. So Tuathal's two beautiful daughters were dead, and were buried in the same grave. When Tuathal heard of their deaths he summoned his vassals, the kings of Ulster and Connacht; his army and theirs invaded Leinster, defeated and killed its king, ravaged it, and imposed the celebrated Tribute on the unfortunate province—namely, fifteen thousand cows, fifteen thousand sheep, fifteen thousand pigs, fifteen thousand silver chains, fifteen thousand bronze or copper pots, and fifteen thousand linnen (?) cloaks, together with one great cauldron into which, *Hibernicè*, "twelve beeves and twelve pigs 'would go,' in the house of Tara itself." This was, indeed, a prodigious pot that could boil four-and-twenty quadrupeds of the sort, for Ireland was always famous for its large pigs and beeves. Such a cauldron having been used, shows that however poorly the inhabitants of other

parts of Ireland may have fared in ancient times,
the people of Tara lived well. When it is remembered that ancient Leinster was little more than
half the size of the modern province, such a
tribute appears enormous. Ancient Leinster, or,
to speak more correctly, the Leinster of the time
of Tuathal, went no further north than a line
running from Dublin to Athlone. The counties
of Meath, Westmeath, Longford, and Louth
belonged to the province of Meath that had been
carved out of parts of the four old provinces
by Tuathal himself. The Tribute was to be paid
every year, but it was not, for, as the Leinstermen's own great Chronicle says, " It never was
paid without a fight"; and sometimes when they
succeeded, as they very often did, in licking the
combined armies of all the other provinces, it
used not to be paid for many years. It was,
however, paid on and off for over five hundred
years, and to forty over-kings. It was remitted in
the seventh century ; but many attempts were subsequently made to re-impose it on the unfortunate
Leinstermen, who paid more dearly for the
treacherous act of one of their kings than any
other province or nation mentioned in history.
One of their poets has said in a yet untranslated
poem in the " Book of Leinster " :

> "It is beyond the testimony of the Creator,
>   It is beyond the word of supplicating Christ,
> All the kings of the Irish
>   That make attacks on Leinstermen!" *

It is not to be wondered at that the Leinster Tribute totally denationalised the province on which it was levied, and made its harried inhabitants side with the Danes and with the Anglo-Normans against their own countrymen. But what is most astonishing about the Tribute is its enormousness. That part of Leinster which was the ancient province could hardly pay such a tax to-day. This matter seems to show that ancient Ireland, in spite of a state of almost continual intestine warfare, was far richer and more populous than is generally supposed.

The most horrible act recorded in Irish history was committed at Tara—that is, the slaughter of 3030 women by the Leinstermen in the year 241. Here is what the Four Masters say of it under that year:—"The massacre of the girls at Cloonfearta at Tara, by Dunlang, King of Leinster. Thirty royal girls was the number, and

---

* Is dar timna in Dulcman, is dar
  ˎbrethir Crist chaingnig
  Do cech rig do Gaedelaib do beir
  amnus for Laignib.
                          " Book of Leinster," p. 43.

a hundred maids with each of them. Twelve
princes of the Leinstermen did Cormac put to
death in revenge of that massacre, together with
the exaction of the Borumha ('Tribute) with an
increase after Tuathal." The Cormac here spoken
of was the celebrated Cormac Mac Airt, one of
the best over-kings that ever ruled ancient Ireland.
This horrible massacre of maidens in Tara is so
often mentioned in ancient Irish history and
annals, and the same number of victims so invariably given, that there cannot be any doubt
whatever about its having occurred. But particulars about it seem wanting. There was probably some pagan festival to be celebrated in
Tara, at which the children of the upper classes
only attended. The ladies may have arrived
from the different parts of the country before
the men, and when the harried Leinstermen
made a raid on Tara, they found it unguarded
save by women, and killed them and burned
Tara to the ground at the same time; or it may
have been that the women tried to help the
few men that happened to be there in protect-
ing the place, and Dunlang made an indiscrimi-
nate massacre of every one he found in it.
This horrible act was caused by the imposition
of the Leinster Tribute. It is to be presumed

that there were no Leinster girls among those who were slaughtered.

Those interested in Irish history, or in ancient history in general, should read the tract called the *Borumha*, or Tribute, in the "Book of Leinster." Translations of it have been recently made in the *Revue Celtique* and in *Silva Gadelica*. There is not in any ancient or mediæval literature anything to excel it in general interest. It is an historic gem that has been forgotten or overlooked for centuries. The indifference which the educated classes of the Irish people have heretofore shown about the ancient literature of their country was one of the most shocking, sickening symptoms of national degradation ever shown by any civilised people. They are latterly beginning to take more interest in it; but it is greatly to be feared that they have been induced to turn their attention to it more by the example shown them by foreigners than by any change of opinion originating among themselves. Much as O'Donovan, O'Curry, and Stokes have done to call the attention of the cultured classes of the Irish people to the study of Celtic literature, it is doubtful if they would have succeeded if the scholars of Continental Europe had not taken an interest in it. The *renaissance* of Celtic studies which seems to have taken place owes a large part of its origin to the Germans and the French.

Many valuable gold ornaments of antique and beautiful design and workmanship have been found in Tara and its immediate vicinity, but very few of them have found their way to the Kildare Street Museum in Dublin, one of the greatest, if not the very greatest, collection of ancient weapons, implements, and ornaments to be seen in Europe. Most of the gold ornaments found in Tara have been melted down. If one is to believe what the peasantry living in its vicinity say, the quantity of gold ornaments found there was very great. The famous Tara Brooch, preserved in the Dublin Museum, and considered the most beautiful piece of metallurgy, either ancient or modern, that is known to exist, was not found in Tara, but on the seashore about three miles from Drogheda, and nine or ten from this famous hill. It was found by an old woman, who is said to have sold it to a shopkeeper in Drogheda for ninepence. The Royal Irish Academy paid £500 for it. Many think that a regular, scientific exploration of Tara Hill ought to be made, such an exploration as Schlieman made of the site of Troy. If this were done under government surveillance, or by some responsible and skilled antiquarian, there is hardly a doubt but that many and precious ornaments in gold, and implements and weapons in bronze, would be found, especially the latter, for there seems every reason to believe that Tara was the seat of government long before iron was known, and long before the bronze age came to

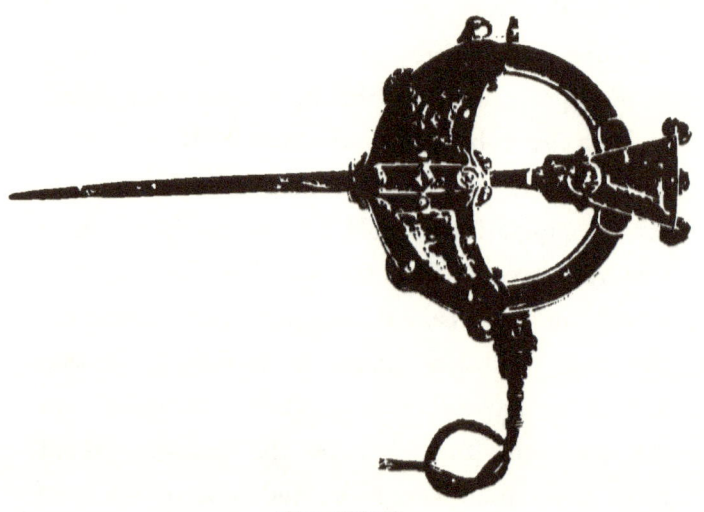

TARA BROOCH.

an end. It would, however, be a tremendous task to uproot several hundred acres merely on speculation. But the quantity of antique gold ornaments that has been found in Ireland was immense, more, it is thought by some, than has been found in all the rest of Europe. They are being found almost every year. Nearly £300

worth of golden fibulae was found in the County
Waterford in 1894. They are now to be seen in
the Dublin Museum.

The many things that are told about Tara in old
Gaelic books would fill a large volume. They are
all interesting. They may be incredible, grotesque,
or funny, but they are never common-place : it is
this uniqueness that is the great charm of ancient
Irish literature. What could be more unique
than this account of the burial of Laoghaire,
the chief king who was cotemporary with St
Patrick, but of whom the Saint never succeeded
in making even a half decent Christian. It is
taken from the book of .the Dun Cow. When
Laoghaire was killed by "the elements," by
lightning probably, "his body was taken from
the south and was buried with his warrior
weapons in the outward (?) south-eastern rampart
of the Kingly Rath Laoghaire in Tara, and its
face to the south against the Leinstermen [as if]
fighting with them, for he had been an enemy of
the Leinstermen when alive." The idea of facing
his enemies with his dead body, for Laoghaire
must have given orders as to how and where he
should be buried, could only have entered into
the brains of ancient Irish kings, for they were
grotesque or original in almost everything.

It is strange how long political memories last. The enmity between Leinster and Meath has not even yet quite died out. Meath, as the seat of the over-kings, represented Ireland, and was also the place from which the hateful Leinster Tribute originated. This is not yet forgotten, for whenever wrestling matches, or athletic sports of any kind, are held near Dublin by the people of adjoining counties, the counties of Dublin, Kildare, and Wicklow, are always pitted against Meath. Dubhthach Mac U Lugair, one of the first converts St Patrick made in Ireland, tells us, in a poem of his in praise of his native province of Leinster, that its war cry was "The magnification of Leinster, the destruction of Meath." Dubhthach may have been a good Christian, but there are good grounds for thinking that he was a better Leinsterman; for he says in the same poem that—

"Except the host of Heaven round the Creator
    There never was a host like Leinstermen round
        Crimhthan."

Crimhthan was a king of Leinster, who is said to have had a stronghold in Howth, where the Bailey Lighthouse now stands.

Although few traces of cultivation are to be seen on the Hill of Tara, there can be no doubt that it has been very much defaced and uprooted. The great *rath* of King Laoghaire, who was co-temporary with St Patrick, has almost entirely disappeared. Its earthen rampart must have been of a good height, when it served as a sepulchre for Laoghaire with his body in an erect position, with its face turned southward, against the Leinstermen. Laoghaire was never a Christian ; or if he was such at one time, there seems strong reason to think that he re-lapsed into paganism towards the end of his career. At all events it is evident that he was not a favourite of St Patrick's or of the early Irish Christians, and it is quite likely that when Tara was abandoned, his *rath* was uprooted, and his body, or what remained of it, consigned to some unmarked grave. But from whatever cause, this *rath* has certainly been almost entirely ob-literated. It must have been considerably over two acres in area, if one can judge by the small segment of it that can still be traced.

The following story is told in the life of St Patrick in the Leabhar Breac. Mr. Whitley Stokes says in his translation of the lives of the Saints from the "Book of Lismore," that it so disgusted Thomas Carlyle that it caused him to give up the study of Irish history :

"Then three of Ui Meith Mendait Tire (a tribe that were located in the vicinity of Tara) stole and ate one of the two goats that used to carry water for Patrick, and came to swear a lie. Whereupon the goat bleated from the stomachs of the three. 'By my good judge,' said Patrick, 'the goat himself hides not the place where he is.'" It is hardly to be wondered at that a story like this, that would make any right-minded man laugh, only disgusted a hypochondriacal crank like Carlyle.

The last chief king who lived in Tara was Dermot MacCarroll, who died in the year 565. He was evidently only half a Christian, for it has been fully proved that Druidism lingered in Ireland for many years after the death of St Patrick. Dermot got into a dispute with the clergy because they sheltered a man who had done something that displeased him. The end of the dispute was that St. Ruadhan, one of the prominent ecclesiastics of the time, cursed Tara, and it was forever abandoned as the seat of royalty. It is almost certain that the real cause of the cursing of Tara by the clergy was that druidical or pagan rites continued to be practised in it after the bulk of the people had become Christians; for it had been for untold centuries the seat of paganism as well as of royalty. It has to be admitted, however, that great a benefit

to the true faith as the abandonment of Tara as a
political centre undoubtedly was, it was disastrous
to the authority of the chief kings, for they appear
to have lost much of their authority over the provincial rulers when they abandoned Tara and made
their abodes in various places in Meath, Westmeath,
and Donegal.

The vast antiquity given to Tara cannot be
reasonably considered as the mere invention of
Irish bards or chroniclers. It is inconceivable that
they would invent the names of forty or fifty kings,
most of whom ruled there over a thousand years
before the Christian era. The Irish annalists who
wrote about the very remote historical events of
Irish history lived and wrote long before Ireland
came under English domination. They would have
no object in inventing historic falsehoods. The
Tuatha de Daanans and Firbolgs, who possessed
the country before the Milesians, had vanished
more than a thousand years before the most ancient
annals we possess were written. What object
could men who claimed to be Milesians have in
inventing historic falsehoods about races who
possessed the country before them? Besides, the
general correctness of Irish annalists in recording
purely historic events is now admitted by all those
capable of forming an opinion. The men who

wrote the oldest chronicles that we possess of
events in the very far-back past of their country,
evidently wrote what had been handed down to
them, either in writing or by tradition.   They
would have had no object in becoming fabricators.

So far, then, Tara with its glamour of greatness
and antiquity, its uprootedness, its ruin, and its
utter desolation.

LOCH REE

Of all the great lakes of Ireland there is none so little known to tourists or the public in general as Loch Ree. It is the fourth in size, Loch Neagh, Loch Erne, and Loch Corrib being the only Irish lakes of greater extent, but none of them exceeds Loch Ree in beauty. Loch Erne is a noble sheet of water, and is adorned with many beautiful islands, but owing to its peculiar shape, one cannot take in all its charms from any point on its shores; but there are dozens of places on the banks of Loch Ree from which all its great expanse of water, and most of the charming features of the country that surrounds it, can be taken in at a single glance. If the shores of Loch Ree were mountainous it would be one of the most beautiful lakes, not only in Ireland, but in the world. It is strange that it is not more generally known, and it lying almost in the geographical centre of Ireland, and surrounded by some of the richest land and most beautiful *paysage* scenery to be found anywhere. People rush to Killarney, Connemara, Achill and

47

many other places, and almost totally neglect this noble expanse of the king of Irish rivers, the Shannon. It is the unfortunate commercial state of Ireland that has caused the scenery of the Shannon to be so little known. If there were dozens of thriving and populous towns on its banks, as there would be if it flowed through any other country than Ireland, large and commodious steamers would be plying on its waters, and the beauties of Loch Ree and Loch Dearg would be as well known as those of Windermere or Killarney. Nothing can more plainly show how fast Ireland is retrograding from even the very mediocre trade she enjoyed half a century ago than the fact that the passenger steam-boats that used to ply almost daily in the summer season between Carrick-on-Shannon or Lanesboro' and Killaloe have long ceased to run, and are now rotting somewhere on the Lower Shannon. The decline in the population, and the consequent decline in trade, became so great that it was found that the money taken did not pay more than seventy per cent. of even the working expenses of those steamers, and they had to stop running. The writer travelled in one of them more than thirty years ago between Athlone and Killaloe. They were large side-wheel steamers that would carry over one hundred passengers, and on which excellent meals could be obtained at a moderate price. There is probably not in Europe a more generally interesting river than that from Athlone to Killaloe, but it is now practically closed, not only to tourists, but to the public in general, for a passenger steamer has not traversed the Upper Shannon for well-nigh thirty years. It is no wonder, then, that the glories of Loch Ree, with its almost countless islands, and the glories of Loch Dearg, with its mountain-girded shores, are now nearly as unknown to tourists and to the Irish public in general as are the reaches of the Congo or the Niger. It is simply heartrending to think that decline of population and general decay have made the mighty waters of the Shannon, that runs almost from one end of Ireland to the other, an almost lifeless stream, for the few little row-boats and sailing smacks one sees on it would not, all told, hold more people than the life-boats of a single Atlantic steamer. Bad as things are, they seem to be getting worse, for there is hardly a single town or city on the Shannon that is not declining in trade and population. At the rate things are going on, a turf boat will soon be the only sort of craft to be seen on the waters of Ire-

land's greatest river! It is, however, cheering to
be able to state that there is good reason to believe
that steps are being taken to re-establish a line of
passenger steam-boats on the Upper Shannon.

The tyranny and folly of man may mar towns
and turn fields into wildernesses, but they cannot
mar nature. If no steam-boats plough the waters
of Loch Ree, and if men have given place to cattle
and sheep on its banks, it is still as beautiful as
ever. Its sinuous shores are still as fair to the eye
as they were fifty years ago, when a teeming popula-
ation lived on them, and when twenty thousand
people might be seen at the annual regatta that
used to be held every autumn on its waters.
Nothing less than an earthquake could destroy
the beauty of Loch Ree. It has every element
of scenic beauty save mountains, but such are its
general beauties that mountains are hardly missed.
Loch Dearg is almost surrounded by mountains,
but it is not nearly so fair to look upon as Loch
Ree. The former lake is almost entirely islandless,
but Loch Ree is studded with them. In traversing
its entire length, from Lanesboro' to Athlone, a
distance of twenty miles, islands are ever in view.
Hare Island is the most beautiful island in the
lake; seen from the waters or from the mainland
it seems a mass of leaves. The trees grow on it so

thickly that they dip their branches into the water almost all round it. Lord Castlemaine has a charming rustic cottage on Hare Island, and the pleasure grounds attached to it are laid out with very great taste and skill. It is one of the most beautiful sylvan island retreats in Europe. Hare Island contains nearly a hundred acres. Inchmore is still larger, but not so well wooded. Then there are Inchbofin, Inis Cloran, Inchturk, Saints' Island, Hag's Island, Carberry Island, and many others, the names of which would be tedious to mention. The islands of Loch Ree are of almost all sizes, from a hundred acres to a square perch. Except in the vast St Lawrence alone, with its famed thousand islands, there are few river expansions in the world that contain so many islands as Loch Ree. Its shores are fully as beautiful as its islands. It would be hard to conceive anything in the way of shore scenery more beautiful than the shores of Loch Ree for eight or ten miles on the Leinster side of the lake between the mouth of the river Inny and Athlone. The shores are so irregular and cut up into so many promontories and headlands that, to follow the water's edge from Athlone to where the Inny enters the Shannon, a distance of not more than ten miles as the crow flies, would involve a journey of over fifty. Every headland is

tree-crowned, and every promontory rock-girded.
Very little of the shores of this beautiful lake are
swampy; they are generally as rocky as those of a
Highland tarn, with deep, blue water ever fretting
rock and stone into thousands of fantastic shapes.
So rocky are most parts of the shores of Loch Ree,
that those æsthetic persons living near it who wish
to form rock-works in their pleasure grounds find
abundance of water-worn stones on the shores of
Loch Ree to make rock-work of any shape
required.

The shores of Loch Ree, particularly the Leinster
shore, are more adorned with gentlemen's seats
than the shores of perhaps any other lake in
Ireland. From Athlone to nearly the head of
the lake there is a succession of gentlemen's
seats. Many of them are kept with great care
and taste, and are in themselves well worth a
visit. The house in which Goldsmith spent his
early youth is about two miles from Loch Ree,
and about two-and-a-half from the village of
Glassan. The house is a ruin, but a well-pre-
served one. When it was built seems unknown,
but from what can be gathered from the old men
living in its vicinity, it seems to have been built
about the year 1700. The walls are still intact.
It was two storeys high, and must have contained

seven or eight apartments. The name Auburn is still applied to the townland on which the house stands; but the name seems to have originated with Goldsmith himself, for the place does not appear to have been so called before his time. Lissoy is its Irish name, but Auburn does not seem to be an Irish name at all. The "Jolly Pigeons" public-house still exists. It is about a mile from Auburn. There never was a village called Auburn in the locality. The nearest place to Goldsmith's house that could be called a village is Glassan.

Loch Ree is not void of considerable historic interest. There are many noble ruins on its shores; among them Randown Castle is the most remarkable. It was one of the earliest Norman-French keeps erected in Ireland. It is situated on a bold promontory jutting into the lake on the Connacht side, about ten or twelve miles north of Athlone. It is now generally called St John's Castle. At *Blein Potog*, or Pudding Bay, took place in the year 999 one of the most important events in Irish history—namely, the surrender of the sovereignty of Ireland to Brian Boramha by Malachy the Second. The Munster king came up the Shannon with a large army in a flotilla of boats, and Malachy met him there and surrendered to him. Many think that it was, in a political point of view, one of the most disastrous events of Irish history, for the usurpation of the chief sovereignty by Brian caused such weakness and confusion after his death, that each provincial ruler wanted to be chief king, and created such wars and political chaos that no chief king that succeeded possessed complete sway over the country, the so-called chief kings that succeeded being kings only in name. For a full account of the treaty of Blein Potog, the reader is referred to the "Wars of the Gaels and the Galls," translated by the late Rev. Dr Todd. The site of the treaty is some ten miles north of Athlone, on the Leinster shore of Loch Ree.

Athlone is one of the most picturesque and interesting inland towns in Ireland. Its situation is simply superb,—in the almost exact geographical centre of Ireland, at the foot of one of the most beautiful of lakes, and on the banks of a noble river, deep and wide enough to carry ships on its waters.

Athlone is one of the few towns—perhaps the only one—on the Shannon that is not decaying at present. For many years after the famine it decayed rapidly, but some thirty years ago a

woollen factory was established; now there are
two woollen factories and a saw-mill that give
employment to some hundreds of hands, consequently Athlone has been saved from decay. But
comparatively prosperous as it is, it is not one-
fourth as prosperous as it ought to be considering
its splendid situation and the fertility and beauty
of the country that surrounds it. It has recently
become a great railway centre; one can go by
rail from Athlone to almost any part of Ireland.
But all the railways and all the fertility of all
the world cannot bring real prosperity to any
country in which the population is declining.
The decline of the population in Athlone itself
and in the country surrounding it has, during the
last fifty years, been something frightful, and can
only be fully realised by those who remember
what it was in former times. A market day in
Athlone now is very different from a market day
there half a century ago. The writer recollects
having been at a market in Athlone when a
small boy, about the year 1841 or '42, and saw
more people there in one market than could be
seen in twenty markets there now. The town
was too small to contain much more than half
of them; they flowed out into the fields surrounding it. The crowds in the streets were so

dense that it would take hours to jostle one's
way from one end of the town to the other,
and, what will hardly be credited by those whose
memories do not go back fifty years, there were
certainly three persons speaking Irish for one
who spoke English. One might attend markets
in Athlone now every week in the year and not
hear a word of any language but English. Irish
has completely died out of the country surrounding Athlone, save in the south-western corner of
the county Roscommon, where some old people
still speak it. There is something inexpressibly
sad in the fading away of any form of National
speech, but, above all, in the fading away of a
tongue so old and once so cultivated as Irish.
It seems to forebode not only the death of all
real National aspirations, but the death of heart
and soul. It seems to show that Philistinism is
rapidly driving away sentiment from the Irish
people. But the life of the Irish peasant has
been so long such a battle for mere existence
that it is no wonder that he came to look with
contempt on everything that did not administer
to his mere animal wants. He is rapidly improving since he has had a barrier put between
him and the generally cruel treatment he was
wont to receive from his landlord. None but

those who remember what his position was fifty
years ago, and who see what it is now, can fully
understand all the advance he has made. In
spite of the awful decline of population in the
rural districts of Ireland during the last fifty years,
there is much to be seen in them to gladden
the heart of the philanthropist. Small farmers'
cottages, that would formerly be a disgrace to a
Zulu or an Esquimaux, are now not only generally
clean, but sometimes beautiful. Flowers in pots
in the windows and evergreens creeping up the
walls of a peasant's cottage would have caused
him to be laughed at by his neighbours fifty years
ago, but now they cause him to be respected
instead of being laughed at. He will become
again what he once was, one of the most soulful
and un-Philistine of beings ; it is probable he
will become such when better laws and freer
institutions shall have raised him from the slough
of poverty and despondency in which he has been
steeping for centuries.

Tourists and the travelling public in general will
find good accommodation at the Prince of Wales
Hotel in Athlone, in which town boats can be
hired by those going either up or down the
Shannon.

Two miles west of the city of Armagh lies an earthen fort known as the "Navan Ring." This is all that remains of the renowned palace of the Pagan Kings of Ulster, the real name of which was Emain Macha, which has been Latinised Emania, and corrupted into Navan.

After Tara, Emania is the most historic spot of Irish soil. No other place in all Ireland, Tara only excepted, is so often mentioned in the historic and romantic tales that have been preserved in such abundance in ancient Gaelic. Emania is the great centre of that wondrous cycle of legend, history, and song known as the Cuchullainn cycle of Celtic literature. Every tale and legend in it refer more or less to Emania. It is curious that while hardly any of the treasures of ancient Irish manuscript literature we possess were compiled in Ulster, there is hardly a page of them, no matter in what province they were originally composed, that does not mention this now almost obliterated stronghold of the Ulster kings. The "Book of Leinster" was compiled in Kildare or in Glendoloch, and for

58.

nearly a thousand years, or from the imposition of
the Leinster Tribute early in the second century
down to the time of Brian Boramha, Leinster and
Ulster were inveterate enemies, yet the "Book of
Leinster" teems with mention of Emania. Even in
the great manuscript books compiled in Connacht
and Munster, the name of Emania occurs next in
frequency to that of Tara.

So far as can be gathered from the most authentic
sources, the palace of Emain Macha, or Emania,
was erected by the over-king Cimboath, about
five hundred years before the Incarnation. It continued to be the seat of the Ulster kings down to .
A.D. 331, when it was destroyed by the three
Collas, chieftains of the race of the over-kings of
Ireland from a hostile province, that made war on
Ulster. The destruction of Emania is recorded by
the Four Masters under the year 331, when Fergus,
King of Ulster, was defeated and slain by the
three Collas. Emania was burned, and the ancient
dynasty that had so long ruled the province of
Ulster was destroyed. Emania may be said to
have been a desolation since then; for though we
are told that one of the O'Neill's built a house
within the ruins of the fort in 1387, no vestige of
it now remains, and it is not probable that it was
long in existence.

None of the ancient palaces or great *duns* of ancient Ireland shows such utter desolation, or bears evidence of having been so uprooted as does Emania. The great fosse by which it was once surrounded is entirely obliterated save on the west side, where it is nearly twenty feet in depth. Much as Tara has been obliterated, its monuments are more easily traced than are those of Emania. The county Meath seems to have been a grazing country almost from time immemorial. This saved Tara from being entirely uprooted; but the country round this ancient seat of the Ulster kings is essentially agricultural; it is mostly in the possession of small farmers owning from ten to twenty acres; consequently they have levelled most of the great circular embankments that formerly enclosed an area of nearly a dozen acres, and have filled up most of the deep fosse which, if we can judge by the small part of it that still remains, must have been, when Emania was in its glory, between twenty and thirty feet deep. So potatoes are growing and corn is waving over a large extent of the inside of the fortress, where vast wooden buildings once stood, and where mirth and revelry and clash of arms once resounded.

Mons. Darbois de Jubainville, the eminent French archæologist and Celtic scholar, made an

exhaustive examination of Emania some years ago.
He found that the area within the original
enclosure was four and a half hectares, or between
eleven and twelve English acres in extent, and
that the space enclosed was nearly circular. Like
Tara, the buildings in Emania must have been
almost entirely of wood. Some of them may, like
many of the wooden houses in America, have been
built on stone foundations, and there are some
traces of stone-work still to be seen. There is a
magnificent passage in the Féilere of Oengus the
Culdee, written about A.D. 800, in which the
greatness and glory of the Christian cities of
Ireland are contrasted with the state of utter
desolation into which the strongholds of the Pagan
kings had fallen. Speaking of Emania he says—

> "Emain's burgh hath vanished
> Save that its stones remain;
> The Rome of the western world
> Is multitudinous Glendaloch."

There is no doubt that the ruins of Emania
were in a much better state of preservation when
Oengus wrote, nearly eleven hundred years ago,
than they are in at present, and it is certain that
many of its stones have been carried away to
build walls and houses. But it is also quite certain
that neither in Ireland, Great Britain, or in any

northern country, were stone buildings general in ancient times, and we may be sure that when Emania was at the height of its splendour its best and largest buildings were of wood.

The area of eleven or twelve acres that was once surrounded by a deep fosse and high embankment, and within which all the buildings of Emania were erected, is not quite circular, nor is its surface level. Considerable inequality of surface evidently existed in it before it was chosen for the site of palace or *dun*. The highest part within the enclosure is a good deal removed from its centre, and it was evidently on it that the citadel stood. There was a dun within a dun, as there generally was in all ancient Irish fortresses of any great extent. The citadel having been on the highest ground within the enclosure, commanded a view of the surrounding country for a considerable distance. Emania, when at its best, with its vast surrounding fosse and high earthen rampart, capped with a strong fence of wood, might, if properly provisioned and manned, defy almost any army that could be brought against it in ancient times when firearms were unknown.

It is for the antiquarian rather than for the seeker of the picturesque that Emania will

ever have the most attraction. There is nothing
very striking from a scenic point of view in its
environs. Its present shockingly uprooted condition, and the almost total lack of interest the
peasantry living in its immediate vicinity take
in it, have a depressing effect on anyone interested in Irish literature, history, or antiquities.
During the writer's last visit to this historic spot
he met a small farmer whose potatoes were
planted over part of the obliterated fosse and
rampart of this famous stronghold of Ulster. He
had never heard of King Connor MacNessa, of
Connall Carnach, of Cuchullainn, or of the Red
Branch Knights. He knew no more about them
than about the heroes of ancient China. He said
that he " ever an' always hard that the Navan
Ring was built by the Danes." This man had
been born and bred in the locality, but he took
no more interest in the historic spot that had
given him birth than if he were a Hottentot
instead of an Irishman. Anglicisation has indeed
been carried to an extreme pitch in most parts
of Ireland, and is rapidly turning the Irish peasant
into the most generally uninteresting, prosy, and
least *spirituel* of mortals. As a rule, the more
Anglicised he becomes the more intolerable he
is. If the peasantry living round Emania had

preserved their native language, while at the same time knowing English, if they were bilingual, like millions of their class in different European countries, many things connected with the history of this celebrated place would be known to them ; but having lost the link that bound them to the past, they are like a new race in a new country. It is well known that the masses of the Greek peasantry, notwithstanding that a large percentage of them are illiterate, know more about the history and traditions of their country than any Irishman, save a specialist, knows about the history and traditions of Ireland. In very few European countries will such a knowledge of its past be found among the masses as in Greece, and principally because the Greeks have preserved their language.

Although Tara is more ancient and more historic than Emania, the latter place is connected with the most pathetic, the most dramatic, and most generally beautiful tale in all the vast mass of ancient Gaelic literature — " The Fate of the Children of Uisneach." It was in Emania that their betrayer and murderer, Connor, King of Ulster, lived; it was there that they themselves were killed, and it was there that Deirdre died. The tale appeared almost a century ago in a book brought out by a Gaelic Society that then existed in Dublin. The Irish text was given, with a translation by Theopholus O'Flanagan. It was thought by some that he had no ancient copy of the tale, and that he might have embellished it, for he did not say from what manuscript he had taken it. The story, as given in the "Book of Leinster," while agreeing in the main with O'Flanagan's version, is not nearly of such literary value as his, and is not more than one quarter the length. But all doubts as to the existence of an ancient version of the story given by O'Flanagan have been removed, for an ancient copy of it, supposed to be of the fourteenth century, was found some years ago in the Advocates' Library, Edinburgh, and has been edited and translated by Mr. Whitley Stokes. It may be seen in Windische's *Irische Texte*. It agrees almost exactly with the version given by O'Flanagan. It would be hard to give a clearer proof of the utter neglect with which Celtic literature has heretofore been treated, than by a statement of the fact that there are not probably a hundred persons living, at least of the literary class, who have read this wondrously beautiful tale of the Children of Uisneach. For pathos, dramatic power, and pure poetry it would be hard to get anything in the way of romance

E

superior to it. If such a literary gem existed in
the literature of any European language but Irish,
if such existed even in Arabic or Persian, it would
be known to literary people almost all over the
world. But how can people of other nations be
blamed for their ignorance of Gaelic literature
when the Irish themselves are more indifferent
about it than the Germans or the French? A
text and translation of the "Fate of the Children
of Uisneach" is sorely wanted—not merely as a text
for scholars, but for the people at large. When
such appears it will make a visit to Emania
infinitely more interesting; for, after reading such
a pathetic tale, he would indeed be hard-hearted
and unsympathetic that would not, if he could
find where she was buried, shed a tear over the
grave of Deirdre. The very fine poem by the
late Doctor Robert Dwyer Joyce, published in
Boston, America, in 1877, was the only attempt
ever made to popularise the story of the Children
of Uisneach and the fate of the unfortunate but
true and noble Deirdre.

The country in the vicinity of Emania, while
containing no striking objects of scenic interest,
is, at the same time, picturesque and beautiful.
Southern Ulster, even where it is not mountainous, is usually most varied and interesting in

its general features. It is essentially a land of
hills and valleys; but the hills are never so
high that they cannot be cultivated, and the best
land is sometimes found on their very tops. The
country round Emania is extremely broken, hill
and valley are on every side. It is generally,
like most parts of Ulster, well cultivated. There
are many antiquarian curiosities in the neighbourhood of this ancient fortress. Some of the most
perfect Druid circles in Ireland are in its vicinity.
There is a very remarkable one about a mile
from it which a thrifty farmer has turned into
a haggard. It encloses about quarter of an acre
of ground. The stones of which it is composed
stand about four feet over the surface, and must
average nearly a ton each in weight. But vandalism is strong in the vicinity, for it is only a
short time since another splendid Druid circle,
nearly as large as the one mentioned, was torn
down, and its stones broken to mend roads withal.
Thus are many of the relics of ancient Erin disappearing before the march of denationalisation.

Those who live in the vicinity of Emania tell
many stories about the finding of treasure-trove
close to and in this ancient fortress. According
to them, gold ornaments of great value were found
by some persons many years ago who suddenly

became rich, much to the surprise of their neighbours. Those ornaments were, of course, melted down, and like hundreds of thousands of pounds worth of similar articles found in almost every part of Ireland, never found their way to any museum, and are lost to the country for ever. There can hardly be any doubt that some very valuable articles in gold have been found near Emania.

One of the most interesting instances of the long survival of a place name is to be found adjacent to this celebrated spot. Most Irish persons have heard of the Red Branch Knights. Moore has immortalised them in his exquisite lyric, "Let Erin Remember the Days of Old." Few believe that such an institution as the Red Branch Knights ever existed. It is generally looked on as a bardic fable; but there is a townland close to Emania which is still called Creeve Roe, in correct orthography, *Craobh Ruadh*, which means Red Branch. The preservation of this place name for nearly two thousand years cannot be regarded as an accident. It goes far to prove that the Red Branch Knights did exist, and that the townland took its name from them. This extraordinarily long survival of a place name, the historic fame and antiquity of the locality, lend a supreme interest to this ruined stronghold, which, centuries after its glories had vanished, Gaelic bards used still to call "Emania the Golden."

Ardmagh is so near Emania, only two miles from it, that one place could hardly be described without saying something about the other. Its ancient name was Ardmacha, meaning the height of Macha. This Macha was queen, or at least ruler, of that part of the country in far-back pagan times. It was also from her that Emain Macha, or Emania, was named. Ardmagh was founded by St Patrick in the year 457. A man named Daire, chief of the district, is said, in the "Annals of the Four Masters," to have given Patrick the site on which the city is built. Patrick appointed twelve men to build the town, and ordered them to erect an archbishop's city there, and churches for the different religious orders. It seems strange that the saint should have chosen Ardmagh for the site of the chief religious establishment in Ireland. Emania had been ruined and desolated in the previous century, but it is evident that it was the fame of the ancient stronghold of Ulster that induced Patrick to choose its immediate vicinity as a site for his new Christian city, because Emania had been for so many centuries previous the political centre of the province, and, next to Tara, the chief political centre of Ireland. Of the old ecclesiastical buildings of Ardmagh, not a vestige remains. Some of its new ones, are, however, magnificent. The new Catholic cathedral is the finest building of its kind in Ireland. It is hardly to be wondered at that none of the ancient buildings of Ardmagh should remain, for of all towns in Ireland, it was burned, plundered, and razed the oftenest. In the course of the two centuries and a half ending in 1080, it was plundered and wholly or partially burned *twelve times* by the Danes. No other city in Ireland seems to have suffered so much from the Northmen. Turgesius, the Danish king, captured it and lived there for some years. The present city is one of the most picturesque towns of its size in Ireland, but it is not growing much. It once had a good linen trade, but since the introduction of cotton fabrics, its linen trade has entirely ceased.

QUEEN MAB'S PALACE

RATHCROGHAN, about two miles from Tulsk, in the county Roscommon, is one of the most celebrated places in Irish history, legend, and song. It was there that Queen Mab, spelt Medb in old Irish, and Meave at present, had her palace, and it was there she was buried. That she was a real historic personage, and not a myth or a fairy, there can be no doubt at all, and that she was a very extraordinary woman cannot be doubted either. She was Queen of Connacht, and was cotemporary with Cleopatra; but if the Egyptian queen is mentioned in history she is forgotten in legend, while Mab has lived in legend for more than eighteen centuries. It is remarkable that the myths and legends about her should have been more prevalent during the sixteenth and seventeenth centuries in England than in Ireland. There are few legends about her in Ireland; she is simply an historic personage there, but in England she became a fairy. There is hardly a popular English writer of the two centuries referred to that has not said some-

thing about Queen Mab; and it is very probable that none of them knew that she was a
reality in Irish history. Shakespeare, Spenser,
Drayton, and other English writers contemporary
with them, speak of her as a fairy, and even
Shelley considers her a sprite; but she is rarely,
if ever, mentioned as such by the Gaelic writers
of any epoch. Why legends about Queen Mab,
or, as we call her at present, Meave, should be
so rare in Ireland is probably owing to the fact
that she belongs to what is known as the
Cuchulainn cycle of Irish history and legend.
That cycle is almost forgotten by the people,
and has been for many centuries. It has been
eclipsed by the greater popularity of the Finn
cycle, which is some centuries more recent. For
the one legend existing in the most Gaelic-
speaking parts of Ireland and Scotland about
Cuchulainn or his cycle there are a score about
Finn, Oisin, Caoilte, and others of their contemporaries. It may have been that the introduction of Christianity had much to do in stereo-
typing the legends of the Finn cycle in the
memories of the masses, for Finn is said to have
lived so long that he saw St Patrick, and held
converse with him. One of the most remarkable
literary productions in Irish, the "Dialogue of

the Sages," consists of converse between the Saint and Finn, and others belonging to the same cycle.

There could hardly be a stronger proof of the high civilisation that existed in Ireland in ancient times as compared with that which existed in England than the fact that the remembrance of Irish historic personages continued widely spread in England in spite of so many changes, not only in government, but in race and language. There is no traditional remembrance in Ireland of any English historic personage contemporary with Queen Meave, or of any such that lived for many centuries after her time. That a knowledge of her and Lir, the Lear of Shakespeare, should have existed among the ancient Britons is not to be wondered at, for they were kin to the Irish, and must have spoken the same, or nearly the same, language; but that this remembrance of Irish historic personages should have continued to exist in England under Roman, Saxon, Dane, and Frenchman, is very remarkable. If it was knowledge obtained through books it would be less to be wondered at; it was knowledge transmitted by legend, and like all legendary knowledge, it had a tendency to go astray. The legends that existed in England about Meave and Lir did go astray, for they made a little fairy of

the one and a King of Britain of the other. But
Meave was not a little fairy, but a very fine woman
of flesh and blood; and Lir was not King of
Britain, but an Irish pirate whose principal
stronghold appears to have been the Isle of Man.
It is called after him, for his full name was
Mananan Mac Lir. It seems more than probable
that both Dunleer and Liverpool are also called
after him, for the latter place is written "Lyrpul"
in the earliest known document in which the name
occurs, and it is Lyrpul still in Welsh. It is
probable that Lir had possessions in England as
well as in Ireland and the Isle of Man.

Medb or Meave, Queen of Connacht, was
daughter to Eochy Fayloch, over-king of Ireland.
She lived about half a century before the Christian
era. Keating says, in his "History of Ireland,"
that she reigned ninety-eight years. This very long
reign is doubted by some Irish historians, but it is
generally admitted by them that her reign, as well
as her life, was remarkably long. She had more
husbands than even the woman of Samaria is
credited with. It was evidently her extraordinary
long life and reign that caused her to be ultimately
believed to be something supernatural, and to be
regarded as a fairy. She was, however, no fairy,
but a bold, bad, and warlike woman. She, even

more than Cuchulainn, is the central figure of the greatest prose epic in the Irish language, the *Tain Bo Chuailgne*, or Cattle Raid of Cooley. By lies and bribes she persuaded the other provincial rulers to join her in a totally unjustifiable war on Ulster, so that she was able to invade that province with a great army of fifty-four thousand men. She carried off a great prey from Ulster, but not without suffering some defeats and losing some of her bravest warriors. It is said that Mr Ernest Windisch is engaged in translating this great epic into German, but it seems not yet finished. Meave, like most of the prominent people of her day, met with a violent death. She had many enemies, especially in Ulster. One of them, a son to the king of that province, killed her by a cast from a sling as she was about taking a cold water bath in Iniscloran, an island in Loch Ree. She must have been considerably over a hundred years old when she was killed, but she appears, even at that great age, to have been the admiration of every one that saw her on account of the great beauty of her face and figure. Perhaps it was her cold water baths that were the chief means of preserving her youth and good looks, for we are told in the "Book of Leinster" that she was under *geis*, or bonds, not to let any morning pass by without taking a bath.

It is no wonder that such a person should have in
the long run passed into the realm of fairie, and
have been thought something supernatural. It is,
however, a wonder that the Four Masters do not
mention the name of Meave, although they do
mention the name of her father; but there are
many similar strange omissions in their annals.
Meave is, however, mentioned in the Annals of
Clonmacnoise, in which many hard things are said
of her.

The fort, as it is generally called, of Rathcroghan, upon which Queen Meave's palace must
have stood, is unlike any other place of its kind
known to the writer. Strictly speaking, it is not
a fort at all, and it is impossible to conceive how
it ever could have been used for purposes of
defence, or for any purpose other than to build
some sort of habitation on. It is nothing but a
raised circular elevation, an English acre in area,
in a perfectly level field, without a vestige of the
fosse or rampart that usually surrounds the ruined
strongholds of Celtic chiefs and kings. Long ago
as it is since Rathcroghan was the seat of kings
or queens of Connacht, some traces of the surrounding ramparts would almost certainly be yet
visible had they ever existed. Queen Meave seems
to have depended more on her soldiers to defend

her than on ramparts of stone or earth. She seems
to have relied on "castles of bones" rather than on
castles of stones; for her palace, so far as can be
judged from existing remains, seems to have been
without defending ramparts of any kind. There
are many references in old Gaelic manuscripts to
the splendour of Queen Meave's palace. It is said
to have been built of pine and yew, and to have
contained beds enough to accommodate a small
army. It was probably an immense round wigwam
that covered all or nearly all of the raised platform
that still remains. That platform is about eight or
nine feet above the level of the field on which it
stands, and has two entrances into it, one exactly
opposite the other. If the vast circular wooden
building that stood on it was roofed, as it almost
certainly was, the walls would have to be fifty feet
or more in height to give it anything of an imposing
appearance. It may have been that the entire
raised platform was not covered by the wooden
structure, but the descriptions of its great size given
in old books would lead one to think that it was.

Rathcroghan does not appear to have been a
place of residence of any of the rulers of Connacht
since the time of the celebrated Queen Meave. If
it was, the writer has not been able to find trustworthy evidence of the fact. It may, however,

have been used as a place for assemblies in comparatively recent times. *Relig na Riogh*, or the cemetery of kings, at Rathcroghan, was one of the great burial places of the Pagan Irish Kings. It is a circular enclosure, about half a mile from the platform on which Queen Meave's palace stood. It bears all the marks of extreme antiquity, and has suffered much from the ravages of time. It covers between two and three acres, and at first sight appears nothing more than a piece of ground of very broken surface, for the mounds that marked the graves of kings and chiefs have become nearly obliterated. But it was here that many of the kings and heroes of ancient Ireland were buried, and it is here that the bones of Queen Meave rest, that is, if we are to believe the most trustworthy records of Irish history. It is thought by some that she was buried under the vast cairn of stones that crowns the summit of Knocknarea, near Sligo, for it is called to this day *Moisgan Meabha*, literally Meave's butter-dish; but by extension it probably means Meave's heap or cairn. There is no historic evidence to prove that she was interred under the cairn on Knocknarea, however it came to be called by its present Irish name; and according to the late Sir Samuel Ferguson, her name, or a name closely resembling it, has been found written in Ogam characters on a stone in *Reilig na Riogh*.

That there was such a person as Queen Meave there cannot be any doubt whatever. History and legend never yet existed about a fabulous personage, and Meave figures in both. Whatever impossible things may be related about her in legend, history says nothing about her that cannot be easily believed, her great age and length of reign excepted. It must, however, be remembered that the ancient Irish were a very long-lived people. This fact is so apparent in so many places in ancient Gaelic literature that it has to be believed. We have as strong proof as can be afforded by history that in comparatively modern times Henry Jenkins lived to be over a hundred and sixty, and Old Parr to be over a hundred and fifty years old, and why could not Queen Meave have lived to as great or even a greater age? She was an extraordinary woman, and her name sheds a halo of romance round the place where she lived, and where her remains rest in peace after her long and stormy career. It was also in *Reilig na Riogh* that Dathi, the last pagan Irish Chief King, was buried. His mound is marked by a pillar stone, and O'Donovan, one of the most cautious and least impulsive investigators of Irish

history and antiquities, saw no reason to doubt
that the pillar stone marks his grave.

It may be said that no proof has been given
that the Connacht Queen Medb or Meave was
the prototype of the Mab of Shakespeare, Drayton,
Spenser, and other English poets. True, no absolute proof has been given, and probably never
will; but there is that which may be called
negative proof, which in such a case is very
strong. The negative proof, if it can be called
such, that the Connacht queen was the prototype
of the Queen Mab of English poets and English
legend, is found in the complete silence of history
and of tradition as to how else the legend of Queen
Mab originated, for it must have originated somewhere and from some one. We are, then, and in
a great measure by the total lack of any other way
to account for the origin of the legend of Queen
Mab being queen of the fairies, forced to come to
the conclusion that the Connacht queen is the only
person known to history who furnishes the prototype for her. But there is something more. It has
been stated that the old Irish form of the name
was *Medb*. It is well known to Celtic savants
that what is now called " aspiration," or the
change in sound, and sometimes the entire suppression of certain consonants in pronunciation,

did not take place nearly so often in old Irish as in the modern language; so that the name *Medb* would in ancient times be pronounced *Mab*, or something very like it. It is curious that in Drayton's poem, "The Nymphadia," Queen Mab, though a fairy, is remarkable for those things for which her Irish prototype was also remarkable—namely, her chariots, her amours, and her beauty.

A very strong proof that Queen Meave was an historic personage and not a myth is to be found in the name of the island in Loch Ree where she was killed. It is usually pronounced and written Iniscloran; but Inis Clothran is how it ought to be spelled, and how it is invariably spelled in the "Annals of the Four Masters" where the name frequently occurs, the island having been the seat of more than one church in early Christian times, and therefore often mentioned in annals. Meave had a sister named Clothru who lived in Iniscloran, and who was Queen of Connacht before Meave. Here is a translation from the "Book of Leinster," page 124: "It was there that Clothru used to explain the laws of Connacht in Inis Clothran in Loch Ree." The island was evidently called after Clothru (Clothran in the genitive), sister to Meave. This preservation of a place name connected with the name of an historic personage for

F

two thousand years is most remarkable, and shows
that Irish history is more truthful than is generally supposed.   It is thought that Meave had
Clothru killed, in order that she herself might
become Queen of Connacht.

The country around Rathcroghan abounds in
antiquities of far-back ages. Sepulchral mounds,
ruined raths, tortuous caves, and weather-worn
cromlechs are to be found on almost every side.
It is a spot where the antiquarian might revel
for weeks and find something every day to interest him.   It is a beautiful country also, not a
plain, in the strict sense of the word, and yet
not hills, but what an American would call "rolling," and a Frenchman "accidenté."   It is the
"Magh Aoi" of Queen Meave's time, and "Ma-
chaire Chonnacht," or plain of Connacht, of later
days.   It is part of the celebrated Plains of Boyle,
and is considered to contain some of the best grass
land in Ireland.   No fairer spot could be found in
Connacht for the dwelling of a potentate who dealt
largely in cattle than the green eminence on which
Queen Meave had her palace, and both history and
legend say that her flocks and herds were well-nigh
innumerable. She made her home in the centre
of the fairest and richest part of the province she
ruled ; and long as that home has been desolate, it

has not been forgotten in history or in song, for that noble melody which Moore has made immortal —"Avenging and Bright Fall the Swift Sword of Erin"—was first known as "Croghan na Veena," or "Croghan of the Heroes"; and the incident to which it refers—the murder of the children of Uisneach—occurred when Queen Meave was at the height of her splendour, when Rathcrogan was in its glory, and when it was really the dwelling-place of heroes.

There are many mentions of Rathcroghan in ancient Gaelic writings, and all of them speak of it as one of the most important places in Ireland in Pagan times. Oengus, the Culdee, whose poem has been already referred to, says of it—

> " Rathcroghan hath vanished
>   With Ailill, offspring of victory ;
>   A fair sovranty above Kingdoms
>   Is in Cluain's city."

The Ailill mentioned was one of Qeeen Meave's many husbands, and "Cluain's City" means Clonmacnois.

The nearest railway station to Rathcroghan is Castlerea, from which it is about eight miles distant. Its long distance from a railway and the want of good accommodation for tourists in its vicinity have helped to cause this celebrated place to be so neglected and forgotten.

THE HILL OF UISNEACH

UISNEACH is one of the most historic hills in Ireland, yet there are probably not five per cent. of the people of Ireland that have ever heard of it, and not one per cent. of them that has ever seen it. Apart even from its historic interest, it is well worth seeing, for it is not only a beautiful hill, but it affords from its summit one of the most extensive and lovely views in Ireland. The hill of Uisneach is in the Barony of Rathconrath, County Westmeath, and only about four Irish miles from Streamstown Station on the Midland Great Western Railway, so that it is easily reached. There is, unfortunately, no hotel where tourists could be accommodated nearer to it than Moat, which is about eight Irish miles from it; and Mullingar is about the same distance. The village of Ballymore is five miles from the hill, but as there is no hotel there, Moat and Mullingar are the only towns within any moderate distance of it where tourists could get either lodgings or meals. It is not certain if even a car could be hired at Streamstown or near it, consequently those wishing to visit Uisneach should either have a private conveyance or make up their minds to "do it" on foot.

Uisneach is one of the most peculiarly-shaped hills in Ireland. It is only six hundred feet in height—a fair elevation in a part of the country where there are no mountains—but no matter from what side it is approached, it cannot be seen until one is almost at its base. The country immediately around it is so broken and so cut up by many hills and hollows of almost all shapes, that Uisneach, the highest of all the hills near it, can hardly be noticed until one is just at it. A public road runs close to its base, so there is no difficulty in reaching it, and the ascent is by no means steep. It is not until one is on the top of Uisneach that he finds out how high it is, for the view from its summit is extensive and beautiful almost beyond power of description. The country on every side of it consists of some of the richest pasture lands, not only in Ireland, but in the world. No matter in what direction one looks, a vast, undulated expanse of green meets the eye. If the view from Uisneach is seen in autumn, when the too few and far between grain-fields are turning yellow, it is as fair a sight as human eye ever gazed on.

The country for scores of miles on every side is so rich, so green, and so varied with hill, dale, wood, and water, that the Biblical phrase that is applied to parts of Palestine, "the garden of the Lord," might well be applied to the land round this hill. But it is safe to say that no Israelite ever gazed from Gilboa or Carmel on so fair a prospect. The vast extent of the view from this hill seems out of all proportion with its moderate height. On a clear day one can very nearly see from the Irish Channel to Galway Bay. The Wicklow hills seem close by. The mountains, not only of Cavan, but of Leitrim, are distinctly visible. On every side, save the south-west, the prospect is what some would be tempted to call boundless. On the south-west the view is obstructed by the hill of Knock Cosgrey, an eminence slightly higher than Uisneach, and one of the most beautiful hills in Ireland. It is about four miles south-west of Uisneach. Unlike Uisneach, however, it is, seen from a distance, both striking and bold. It has the misfortune to be called by so many different names, or rather, its name is pronounced in so many different ways, that strangers are often sadly puzzled what to call it. It is called Kunna Kostha and Kruck Kostha by the peasantry, and by the gentlefolk

generally Knock Ash. But its proper name is
Cnoc Cosgraigh, and is so written by the Four
Masters, who are, undoubtedly, the highest
authority we possess on place names. Seen from
the road from Moat to Ballymahon, Knock Cosgrey is one of the most charming sights imagin-
able. It is nearly a mile from top to base, and
forms a green pyramid of almost perfect symmetry. Its surface is entirely under grass; for
this part of Ireland has been largely turned into
pastures; and sometimes one may drive for six
miles and not see a field of grain. "The bold
peasantry" of whom Goldsmith speaks in his
"Deserted Village" have become so few in these
parts that miles may be travelled at mid-day
through as fine a country as there is in the world
without meeting a human being. Sheep and
cattle, and not men and women, seem the prevailing living creatures. Knock Cosgrey is not
only higher than Uisneach, but more near the
true geographical centre of the island; but it
possesses hardly any historic interest from the
fact that its summit was too narrow to allow the
ancient Irish either to build or assemble on it.
Uisneach, with its over a hundred acres of nearly
level land on its top, was therefore chosen, for
a hundred thousand men could find space on it.

It became, for that reason, one of the most historic, and in ancient times one of the most celebrated, hills in Ireland.

There is probably not another hill in Ireland so well adapted both for a place for assemblies and a site for building as Uisneach. Its summit is extensive. There are springs of the purest water on it. Plenty of stones of almost every size abound, and the soil, even in the most elevated parts, is of great fertility. In the troublesome times of yore, Uisneach possessed advantages that were most important in its elevation, and the extensive view it commanded; for they made it impossible for an army to approach it from any side without being seen by the watchers on its top. From the many advantages that this beautiful and extraordinary hill possesses, it seems strange that it was not chosen by the ancient Irish for a place of central government. It would have been even better suited for such a purpose than Tara. It probably would have been the chief seat of ancient Irish sovereignty if it had not been that the mistake made in selecting Tara instead of it, occurred so far back in what may be called prehistoric times, and antiquity had given Tara such a prestige that it continued to be the most important place in Ireland until it

was abandoned as a seat of government in the
sixth century. But Uisneach was also used as a
place of residence by the Irish over-kings. That
they sometimes resided there can be proved from
ancient Gaelic writings. It was supposed to be
the geographical centre of Ireland, and before the
formation of the province of Meath by the over-
king, Tuathal, in the early part of the second
century, the four provinces met at Uisneach Hill.
It is curious what a close guess the ancients
made to locate the exact centre of the island.
They seem, however, to have placed it four or
five miles too far to the north-east, for, according
to the most recent surveys, the hill of Knock
Cosgrey is in the exact geographical centre of
Ireland. In far-back ancient times, before the
province of Meath had been formed by taking
parts of the four original provinces, the hill of
Uisneach was in Connacht. This almost exact
quaternal division of Ireland into provinces, and
their meeting at a point that was supposed to be
the exact centre of the island, is a very curious
and interesting feature in ancient Irish polity.
In other countries, provinces seem to have originated by mere accident, some being big, and some
little; but in Ireland they seem to have been laid
out by line and rule, for the four provinces that

met at Uisneach must have been very nearly of
equal area. The celebrated Cat Stone on the hill
of Uisneach was known from remote antiquity
as *Ail na Mireann,* or "the rock of the divisions,"
because the four provinces met at it. This rock
was known by this name among the peasantry of
the neighbourhood up to recent times, until Irish
became a dead language in this part of the
country.

Ail na Mireann, or, as it is now called, the
Cat Stone, is the greatest curiosity on Uisneach
Hill. It is not on the top of the hill, but on its
side. It is, perhaps, the most puzzling rock in
Ireland, for it is hard to say whether it was
placed in its present position by an iceberg in
the glacial age, or whether it was placed there
by human agency, and intended for a rude cromlech. Here is what the eminent scholar and
antiquarian, John O'Donovan, says about it in
his yet unpublished letters when he was on the
Government Survey of Ireland in 1837 :—"The
huge rock on this hill of Uisneach, a part of
which was split and formed into a cromlech, is
now called the Cat Stone, from a supposed re-
semblance to a cat sitting and watching a mouse."
If this stone is a cromlech, or Druid's altar, it is
unlike anything of the kind found elsewhere in

Ireland or other countries, for the four upright stones which usually support the flat one, are not to be seen here. The weight of this enormous mass of stone can hardly be less than twenty tons, and if it was put in its present position by human agency, it is by far the most extraordinary thing of its kind in Ireland. But a majority of those who see it think that it is merely a boulder of peculiar shape. If it is a boulder it is a very extraordinary one, and if it is a cromlech it is a more extraordinary one still.

It was on Uisneach Hill, or in its immediate vicinity, that the ecclesiastical synod met in the year 1111. This great meeting is mentioned in almost all Irish annals. It was attended by fifty bishops, three hundred priests, and upwards of three thousand students, and by the nobles of the southern half of Ireland, with Muircheartach O'Briain, King of Munster, at their head. We are told that the synod was convened to regulate the manners and mode of living of both clergy and laity. It does not seem to have done much good on account of the then chaotic political state of the country, caused by almost constant wars between the aspirants for chief kingship.

There are many interesting things besides the cromlech to be seen on the vast undulated summit

of Uisneach. There is a hollow known as St
Patrick's bed, and there are the remains of the
walls of large stone buildings on the most elevated part of the hill. There is also one of the
finest raths in Ireland, which must have been a
place of great strength, for the embankments are
still of immense height, and are overgrown with
hawthorn bushes of great size. This rath, unlike
the generality of such structures, is not round,
but oblong. It encloses a space of nearly an
acre in extent.

Apart from antiquarianism, the hill of Uisneach
is well worth seeing, for it is as strange in shape
as it is beautiful in verdure. It is only a few
miles from a railroad; it is easy to ascend, for
a carriage might be driven to its summit. The
longest summer day might be passed on it, and
some new curiosity of antiquity or some fresh
beauty of scenery be continually discovered. The
surface of the hill is so broken, and is of such
great extent, that to explore it thoroughly, and
to enjoy all the varied prospects to be seen from
it, even a long summer day would hardly be long
enough.

When treating of hills and of the country in
the vicinity of Uisneach, it may be interesting
to say something about the most beautiful and

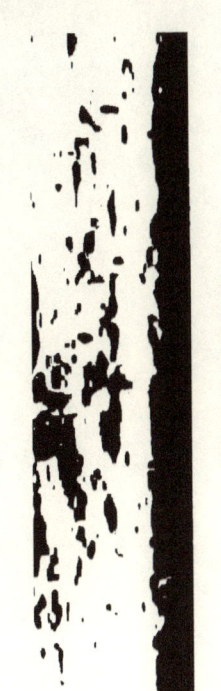

MOUNT OF BALLYLOCHLOE.

perfect *artificial* hill in Ireland—namely, the Moat
of Ballylochloe. It is about nine miles west of
Uisneach, and three north-west of Moat. It was
evidently erected for a sepulchral mound, but
seems to have also been used as a place of defence. A ridge of sand-hills has been cut, and
a most perfect and symmetrical *moat* has been
formed. It cannot be less than a hundred and
fifty feet in height. When seen from the road
approaching it from the east, it is almost Alpine
in appearance, and looks like a small mountain.
Neither history nor legend throws much light on
the origin of this gigantic mound. We are told,
however, that in the time of Queen Meave, about
the year 50 B.C., there was a terrible battle in a
place called Cloch Bruighne, now called Cloch
Brian, some two miles from where the moat now
stands, in which battle a wealthy farmer called
Da Choga was killed, and his house burned.
His wife, whose name was Lucha, died of grief,
and was buried, it is said, near Loch Lucha,
which seems to have been called after her. In
Irish, the name of this place is *Baile Loch
Lucha*. From the fact of the name of the wife
of the farmer, or *bruighe*, being contained in the
name of the stead, the late Mr W. M. Hennessy,
an excellent authority on such matters, thought

that the mound was erected over the remains of the woman Lucha.   In former times, there was a small lake at the foot of the moat, hence the modern name Ballylochloe.

This beautiful artificial hill is well worth seeing. It is only three miles from the railway station at Moat.

CLONMACNOIS

THE ruins of Clonmacnois form by far the most
interesting architectural remains on the Shannon.
Their situation is unique—on a sandy knoll overlooking the winding river, as it flows in great
reaches among marshy meadows of apparently
illimitable extent. Thousands of acres of them on
both banks of the Shannon are spread before one's
gaze when standing at the base of any of the
ruined shrines of this ancient seat of piety and
learning. The ecclesiastics of ancient Ireland seem
to have been gifted with an extraordinary amount
of appreciation for the beautiful and unique in
nature. The wilder and the more beautiful a
place was, the more it seems to have attracted
them. Cashel's solitary Rock, Glendaloch's
gloomy vale, and this barren sandhill overlooking the most peculiar scenery in all the
island, were the places in which they reared
their most cherished fanes and most beautiful
buildings. The situation of Clonmacnois cannot be said to be beautiful, but it is strange
and weird to the last degree — more strange

and weird, perhaps, than any other place in
Ireland.

The best and most agreable way to reach
Clonmacnois is from Athlone. It is twelve
English miles from Athlone by road, and ten
by river. By river is not only the cheapest
way but the most interesting. Sails can be
used on this part of the Shannon almost as well
as on Loch Ree, for the banks are so low that
every breeze that blows can be fully utilised; and
the river is so crooked, that no matter from what
quarter the wind comes it can sometimes fill the
sail. The Shannon here is no tiny stream like
the Liffey, but a wide river, never less than from
150 to 200 yards in breadth, and generally deep
enough to float a small ocean steamer. The
current is, however, not rapid.

The first thing that strikes the stranger who sees
Clonmacnois for the first time is the extraordinary
view from it over the largest extent of callow
meadows to be seen in any part of Ireland. It
must not be thought that these meadows are mere
bogs, for some of the finest hay is raised on them.
The grass that grows on them must be of a fairly
good quality, for they let at from £5 to £6 per
Irish acre, the purchaser having to save the hay,
and run all the risk attending the making it in

land so liable to be flooded. Not infrequently, the taker of meadow on the vast flats that border the Shannon between Loch Ree and Loch Derg, will awaken some fine morning and find all his small cocks of hay afloat, sailing placidly southward, and more likely to find their way to Killaloe than to his haggard. The second thing that will strike the observant stranger in Clonmacnois is the small size of the churches. That it was one of the most important ecclesiastical establishments in ancient Ireland there cannot be any doubt, for it is more frequently mentioned in ancient Irish history and annals than any other place of its kind in the country. Yet the largest church in it, the ruins of which exist, would not, by any stretch of imagination, accommodate more than three or four hundred worshippers. There are the ruins of but three churches existing in Clonmacnois; the largest of them is called Cathedral, the two smaller ones can hardly be called churches. They must have been oratories, and would not combined contain over two hundred persons. When Clonmacnois was in its most prosperous condition —that was in the early part of the ninth century, or about the time when the Danish invasions were heaviest and most harassing—Ireland must have been a very populous country. There are so many

proofs of this in ancient Gaelic annals and literature that it may be regarded as a fact. How, then,
did it happen that the churches in Clonmacnois
were so small? This is a question that cannot
be answered fully. It may be that what now
remains of its churches is of comparatively
recent origin, and may not have been erected
until the decadence of the population had com-
menced at the time of the Danish invasions,
which decadence became more and more pronounced down to the latter part of the sixteenth
century. Or it may have been that there were
large wooden Churches in Clonmacnois in ancient
times, not a vestige or trace of which would be
found after fire had done its work on them.

The two round towers are by far the most interesting and beautiful buildings in Clonmacnois.
The larger one wants apparently twenty or thirty
feet of the top; whether it was struck by lightning,
or knocked off by cannon, no one seems to know.
The smaller tower is as perfect as it was when
its builder pronounced it finished a thousand years
ago. No more beautiful piece of architecture in
the way of a tower ever was erected. It seems
to be absolute perfection. The most skilled
modern artisan in stone could not find an im-
perfection in it. It is built entirely of cut stones.

ROUND TOWER, CLONMACNOIS.

The roof or dome is made of lozenge-shaped stones, fitted so closely and finished so well that time and weather seem to have passed over it in vain, for it is, as far as can be seen from the ground at its base, as perfect as it ever was. Of all round towers in Ireland, it is the most beautiful and perfect. The larger tower seems to have been built of stones similar to those of the smaller one, but as it wants its top its beauty is almost entirely spoiled. What remains of it seems about as perfect in its architecture as human hands could make it. The smaller tower appears to afford positive proof of Petrie's theory as to the post-Christian origin of the Irish round towers, for it and the little church or oratory at its base, and out of which it rises, were evidently built at the same time, for the walls of both are actually in some places one. Like some few of the existing round towers (the one near Navan, for instance), the smaller one at Clonmacnois has no opening in the roof by which the sound of bells could be emitted, showing clearly that it could never have been erected solely for a belfry ; for no matter how big a bell might be, its sound would not have been heard a hundred yards away, if rung under the windowless stone roof of this most perfect and beautiful of Irish round towers. That round towers were sometimes used as belfries seems very probable; but that their principal use, and the prime object for which they were erected, were to protect the clergy and the treasures of the churches from the marauding Northmen is the theory regarding them that is now most generally accepted.

Clonmacnois is not so rich in ancient crosses as some other places like it. There are only two to be seen there at present. They are not nearly so well carved and ornamented as many that still remain in other Irish cemeteries. There is not, so far as can be seen by the passer-by, a single inscription in the Irish language visible, though some scores of such inscriptions exist in it, every one of which has been faithfully copied and translated by Doctor Petric in his great work, "Christian Inscriptions in the Irish Language." The inscribed stones are, very properly, stowed away in a vault under lock and key where they are safe from the mischief of so many who would delight in marring and effacing any thing they could not understand. There are plenty of inscriptions in English to be seen in Clonmacnois, for it is still used as a place of interment. This takes away a great deal of its antique charm and general interest. It seems a sort of profanation

to erect a modern tomb with an English inscription on it at the very base of a hoary round
tower that was a wonder of art and beauty
when London was little else than a large village,
and when England itself was hardly civilised,
and as politically powerless as Saint Domingo or
Corea.

Clonmacnois has suffered as much from vandalism as any other place of its kind in Ireland.
It was taken and spoiled by the Danes when at
the height of its splendour in the ninth century.
But it was not the Danes that committed the
worst depredations in this wonderfully unique and
ancient place. They were committed by men who
used gunpowder, for it was evidently by it that
most of the old buildings of Clonmacnois were
destroyed. It is generally believed that it was
by one of Cromwell's captains who was stationed
with some troops at Athlone when the Royalist
cause had been lost that most of the destruction
at Clonmacnois was accomplished. The blowing
up of the magnificent castle erected here by Hugo
de Lacy in the twelfth century, is attributed to
Cromwell's troopers, as is also the demolition of
some thirty or forty feet of the larger of the two
round towers, known as O'Ruarc's tower.

There are the remains of only three churches

extant in Clonmacnois; but we know from authentic annals and history that there were nearly a dozen churches in it at one time. What became of them, or where they stood, cannot now be known. Many of them were, probably, wooden churches, and, when once destroyed, left no trace. The ruins of the ancient nunnery are distant nearly quarter of a mile from the church-yard, on the grounds of a gentleman named Charlton. It is only about thirty years ago since an attempt was made to clear away the rubbish in which they were buried, and to try if any of the sculptured stones could be recovered. The excavations were made under the supervision of the Protestant Bishop of Limerick. Sculptured stone-work of the highest order of art was dug up from many feet under the surface where the destroyers had buried it. Visitors to Clon-macnois will not have any difficulty in seeing the ruins of the nunnery, for Mr Charlton willingly permits visitors to see them. It is not only curious, but hopeful and pleasant, to find people of the same religious belief altering so much for the better as time rolls by. Whilom Protestant men and a whilom Protestant Government did all they could in the seventeenth century to turn Clonmacnois into a heap of ruins, almost as void and as shapeless as those of Babylon; but Protestant men and a Protestant Government in the nineteenth century have done everything in their power to save it from further decay, and to dig up its sculptured stones from the dust in which ancient Protestant fanaticism and bigotry had buried them.

Clonmacnois was founded by St Kieran, who died in the year 549. There are records of the erection of most of its ancient buildings to be found in Irish annals and history. According to the *Chronicon Scottorum*, a work of high authority, the Cathedral was built in the year 909. The Cathedral that existed when Turgesius the Dane obtained sway for some years over the greater part of Ireland, and when his wife used to issue her orders from that building, was probably of wood, for no trace of it appears extant. Doctor Petrie says that the larger round tower was erected in the tenth century, and the smaller one in the eleventh or early part of the twelfth. There is good authority to prove that the nunnery was erected and endowed by the too well-remembered Dearvorgil, wife of O'Ruairc, whose *liaison* with Dermot Mac Murrough, King of Leinster, is popularly believed to have brought about the Anglo-Norman invasion of Ireland.

One of the great curiosities of Clonmacnois is the powder-blown-up castle built by Hugo de Lacy in the latter part of the twelfth century, the remains of which stand on a hill about two hundred yards from the cemetery. It is generally known as the Prior's house, but it was evidently built as a place of defence. It was one of the strongest castles ever erected in Ireland. Although comparatively small, building and enclosure not covering more than half an acre, it was a place of immense strength, and before the invention of gunpowder could have defied a host. It is encompassed by a fosse in some places forty feet in depth, that descends sheer from the walls. The walls are of immense thickness and strength, from six to eight feet thick in many places, and so firmly are the stones embedded in grouting that to detach one of them from the powder-riven walls, or from the vast masses of blown-up masonry that lie scattered around, a hammer and chisel would be required. Huge heaps of the ruined walls, some of them tons in weight, have been tumbled into the deep fosse that surrounds the castle, but they are still almost as solid as rocks. If ever the art of building solid walls was brought to perfection, it was by those who reared this now ruined pile. To know the strength of gunpowder and the solidity of ancient masonry, one should see this ruined castle of Clonmacnois.

With all the beauties and diversity of scenery of the Shannon, on the banks of which stands all that remains of Clonmacnois, and with all the places of historic interest laved by its waters, it is a disgrace to Ireland at large that there is not a single passenger steam-boat on it above Limerick. It is nearly a hundred and fifty miles from Carrick-on-Shannon to Killaloe, and in all that vast distance of spreading lake and winding river there is not a passenger steam-boat to be seen! There may be said to be no obstacle to navigation in all that distance for boats drawing from five to six feet of water, and there are only four or five locks to pass through. No other river of equal length affords more variety of scenery than the Shannon. Sometimes the voyager passes by wooded banks, anon through apparently illimitable meadows, and then through great lakes like veritable inland seas,— island-studded or mountain-girded, — change of scene occurring in almost every mile. Let it be hoped that a line of passenger steamers will soon again be seen on the waters of this great and beautiful river, — this "ancient stream," as

its Gaelic name is said to mean,—that has on
its banks so many relics of the past—the grass-
grown rath, the hoary round tower, the crumbling
castle, and above all, the ruined fanes of Clonmacnois.

KNOCK AILLINN

AFTER Tara and Uisneach, Knock Aillinn is the most historic hill in Ireland—that is, if it was really the seat of the celebrated Finn, the son of Cumhail. It is a different hill from the hill of Allen, which is about nine miles north of it, and must not be confounded with it, although, as it will be shown further on, the confusion of the two hills seems to have taken place very long ago indeed. Knock Aillinn is some five or six miles south of Newbridge, in the County Kildare. Apart from its historic interest, it is well worth visiting, for it is situated in a rich and beautiful part of the country, and the view from its summit is one of the fairest and most extensive to be seen in any of the eastern counties. Eastward the view is obstructed by the Wicklow mountains, but on every other side it is very extensive, for Knock Aillinn is 600 feet high. So fine is the view from this hill that O'Donovan, the celebrated Gaelic scholar, was inspired by it to write a poem in Irish in praise of it, when he was employed on the Government Survey in 1837. The poem may

be seen in his unpublished letters in the Royal
Irish Academy. One verse of it, translated into
English, will show that it is a composition of more
than ordinary merit :—

> " Beautiful the view from the hill of Aillinn,
>   Over lofty hills and fair plains,
>   Over mountains wreathed in veils of cloud ;—
>   The view will remain in my memory for ever."

But beautiful and extensive as the prospect is
from Knock Aillinn, and greatly as the lovers of
the beautiful may enjoy it, the chief interest possessed by this hill is historic rather than scenic.
On its summit is to be seen the most gigantic of
all Irish raths. O'Donovan called it "prodigious."
The whole top of the hill is surrounded by a
mighty rampart of earth, four hundred yards in
diameter, that encloses over twenty acres. After
nearly two thousand years those earthen ramparts
are still of great height; and when, according to
the fashion of the times, they were topped with
a strong palisade of timber, Knock Aillinn might
be said to be an almost impregnable fortress. To
render it still stronger, the hill on which it is
placed is steep, and its ascent difficult. It was
on this hill that some think the renowned in
Celtic song and legend, Finn, the son of Cumhail,
had his stronghold; but others, and it must be

confessed that they are the most numerous, think that Finn's dun was on the hill of Allen, some eight or nine miles to the north.

That the vast *dun*, or enclosure, on Knock Aillinn was an ancient residence of the Kings of Leinster is generally admitted; and that it was erected long previous to the Christian era is also the opinion of those best acquainted with early Irish history and literature. Proofs of this can be obtained from the most reliable and ancient Gaelic writings. There is hardly a vestige of antiquity to be seen on the summit of Knock Aillinn save the vast earthen rampart. When one stands within it, and recalls to mind what it must have been in days long gone by, when a large population dwelt in it, and when armed multitudes issued from it, he will be tempted to exclaim with Byron :—

> "Shrine of the mighty ! can it be
> That this is all remains of thee ?"

He will wonder that no vast masses of ancient masonry are to be seen. But stone buildings of the kind that have been in use in these islands for nearly a thousand years were unknown when the vast earth-works on Knock Aillinn were erected. Walls built of dry stone have been used in Ireland as fortresses from the most remote antiquity; but the art of building with mortar was entirely unknown until after the introduction of Christianity.

The hill of Allen is the one on which, it is over and over again stated by the most ancient and trustworthy Gaelic documents extant, Finn, the son of Cumhail, had his palace. We are even told how, partly by force and threats, he obtained Allen from his grandfather, Tadg; that he went to live on it, and that it was his habitation as long as he lived. But here a great difficulty meets us—there is not a vestige of dun or fort on the hill of Allen. O'Donovan says in his unpublished letters, while on the Ordnance Survey of Ireland, that Knock Aillinn was, according to various ancient Irish authorities, one of the royal residences of the Kings of Leinster, and that it received the name of *Aillinn* from the *ail*, or stone which was placed in the mound of the rath. On speaking of the hill of Allen, where the celebrated Finn Mac Cool or Cumhail is said to have had his seat, he says, "There are no traces of forts nor any other monuments excepting one small mound called *Suidhe Finn*, or Finn's chair, which occupies the highest point of the hill. On every side of this mound there are faint traces of field works, but so indistinct that I could not with any certainty decide whether they are traces of forts or of recent cultivation, for the hill was tilled on the very summit. I travelled all the hill, but could find upon it no monument from which it could be inferred that it was ever a royal seat like Tara, Emania, Maistean, or any of the other places of ancient celebrity whose localities have been identified; and still in all Fingallian or Ossianic poems this hill (the hill of Allen) is referred to as containing the palace of the renowned champion, Finn Mac Cool, who seems to have been a real historical character, who flourished here in the latter end of the third century."

O'Donovan says also in the same unpublished letters that "The antiquary may draw his own conclusion from the non-existence of a dun on the hill of Allen at this day. It is possible that there were forts on it a thousand years ago, and that the progress of cultivation has effaced them; but it is strange that these alone should disappear, while those of Tara, Emania, Aileach, Naas, Maistean, and Raoirean remain in good preservation. . . . It is curious to remark that all the monuments mentioned in the *Dinnseanchus* and the authentic annals still exist, while no trace is to be found of Finn Mac Cool's palace on the hill of Allowin (Allen). . . . If he had such a palace as this on Aillinn, near Kilcullen, on his hill of Allowin, it would not disappear, because the labour of levelling it would be so great that no agriculturist would undertake to level it."

It would seem as if the two hills, Aillinn, or Knock Aillinn as it is now called, and Allen got confounded, and at an early date too. Allowing liberally for exaggeration and discounting tradition, one has to believe in the extent of Finn's house or palace, however rude and barbaric its arrangements may have been. He was the most powerful man in Ireland, more powerful even than the chief king. The fame of his household was spread abroad, not only over all Ireland, but all Scotland. This we know by the publication of the poems collected in the Highlands by the Dean of Lismore in the sixteenth century, and translated by the late Mr T. M'Lauchlan, and also from a host of other poems. They abound with allusions to Finn and his house and household, as does almost all the folk-lore of the Celtic-Scotch. One thing seems certain, that neither Finn nor his house or palace were myths; his house must have existed, and, like all places of

its kind in the days when it existed, it must
have been surrounded with an earthen rampart
no less high than that to be seen on Knock
Aillinn. But no vestige of house or rampart can
be traced on the hill of Allen. A still greater
difficulty meets one in the size of the summit of
the hill. It is not much over half an Irish acre
in extent, and where would there be room on
such a limited space for the vast household of
Finn? His residence was known from far-back
times as "Almhuin riogha leathan mór Laighean,"
the kingly, great-broad Allen of Leinster; but
no *dun* or habitation situated on the narrow
space on the top of the hill of Allen could be
"great-broad;" but the existing remains on Knock
Aillinn would suit the description almost exactly.
We may be sure that if any man in Ireland in
those days had a big house, it was Finn. The
names Allen and Aillinn are so much alike, and
both hills are so comparatively near each other,
and both seem to have been abandoned as
strongholds at such an early date, that confusion of one with the other could easily have
taken place; besides, Finn's name does appear
to be, in some measure at least, associated with
Knock Aillinn. Here is a passage from the
"Dinnseanchus" at page 162 of the "Book of

Leinster." Treating of Knock Aillinn, these lines occur :—

> "Faichthi ruamand ruamnad rinn
> Co failgib flatha for Fhind."

Irish scholars may interpret these lines as they like, but it would seem that the last word is a proper name, and that it relates to Finn.

But whether Finn lived in Knock Aillinn or in Allen, or whether he lived in both places off and on, is a matter of minor importance. The real wonder about him is the way he impressed himself not only on the age in which he lived but on every age since then. No other man in any age or country seems to have so fastened himself in the memories of the people of his own race and lineage. It may be safely said that neither Julius Cæsar nor Charlemagne have impressed themselves on popular imagination so much as Finn and those associated with him have. Those who have not studied the Celtic folk-lore of Ireland and Scotland can form but an incomplete idea of the overwhelming immensity of the folk-lore about Finn and his cycle that exists even yet. But with the decay of Gaelic speech it is rapidly fading away. It is hardly too much to say that when Gaelic was the language of the fireside all through Ireland and

a large part of Scotland, and that is only a few
centuries ago, there was not a parish from Kerry
to Caithness in which dozens of different stories
about Finn and his contemporaries did not exist;
and it is equally safe to say that not the tenth,
probably not the twentieth, part of them was
ever committed to writing. Finn, Ossian, and
Caoilte were the *dramatis personæ* of the most
extensive, if not the choicest, popular, unwritten
folk-lore that probably ever existed in any country.
But one of the strangest things connected with
the cycle of Finn and Ossian is that its folk-lore
hardly appears at all in really ancient Gaelic
literature. The Gaelic scribes of the tenth,
eleventh, and twelfth centuries took but little
notice of it; it was to the events of the Cuchulainn cycle that they gave almost their entire
attention. In the "Book of Leinster," the greatest
repertory of Gaelic literature that exists in one
volume, there is only one story that can be called
an Ossianic or Finnian one, while nearly half
the book is taken up with tracts and stories
relating to the cycle of Cuchulainn, which was
nearly three centuries earlier than that of Ossian
and Finn. But the Cuchulainn cycle, from whatever cause will probably be never known, seems
to have entirely failed to take hold of the popular

imagination. Folk-lore relating to the Cuchulainn cycle is rare. There are a few in which Cuchulainn is mentioned, and M'Pherson in his Ossian mixes the Ossianic and Cuchulainn cycles together, although they were three centuries apart. Of all the prominent names belonging to the Cuchulainn cycle, Queen Medb or Meave was one of the most prominent, but not a single story exists about her in the oral Gaelic folk-lore of Ireland or Scotland of which the writer has ever heard. She seems to have found her way into the folk-lore of England, but not into that of Ireland or the Gaelic-speaking parts of Scotland. She figures very prominently in Irish history and literature, but in folk-lore she does not figure at all. The reason of this may be that Finn, Ossian, and others of their "set" were supposed to have lived so long that they met St Patrick and were converted to Christianity by him; but there is no foundation for such a belief, for authentic Irish history says that Finn was killed in the year 283 at Ath Brea on the Boyne.

It is not easy to see clearly why Finn so impressed his memory and his cycle on the minds of his countrymen, for he does not appear to have been an altogether amiable personage. There are very many discreditable things told of him in the

multitudinous stories of which he is the central
figure. In one of them, the "Pursuit of Dermot
and Gráine," he plays the part of a revengeful,
unforgiving, bad man; while his great enemy,
Dermot O'Duibhne, is a bold, open-hearted hero,
the very opposite of his unrelenting pursuer. With
all the absurdities and impossibilities of the "Pursuit," the leading characters in it are sustained
with a consistency that would do credit even to
Shakespeare. Finn at the end of the story is just
what he was at the beginning, unforgiving and
bad; and Gráine, who is bad at the beginning is
bad also at the end; while Dermot, a hero at the
beginning of the story, is still a hero at its close.
It may interest some to know that most Irish historians and scholars think that Dermot O'Duibhne
was the person from whom the barony of Corcaguiney, in the County Kerry, is called. In correct
orthography it would be *Corc Ui Dhuibhne*, and
would be pronounced very nearly as the name of
the barony is written at present. If it be true that
Corcaguiney got its name from Dermot O'Duibhne,
and there seems no reason to doubt that it did,
another proof is given of the general correctness
of at least the salient points in Irish history. It
may also interest some to know that the Campbells
of Argyll are popularly believed, even in their own

country, to be descended from this same Dermot O'Duibhne. They have been known for centuries as the Clann Diarmid, or children of Dermot, as will be remembered by any one who has read Scott's "Legend of Montrose." The real name of the Argyll Campbells seems to be really O'Duibhne. It was so that they generally signed their names up to a comparatively recent date. Bishop Carsewell, who translated John Knox's Prayer Book into Gaelic in 1567, the first Gaelic book that was ever printed, dedicates it to the Duke of Argyll, whom he calls Gilleasbuig O'Duibhne.* Carsewell would hardly have dared to address his patron, and the most powerful nobleman in Scotland, by a false name or a sobriquet. The Campbells seem to have been called O'Duibhne down to the middle of the seventeenth century, for in the national manuscripts of Scotland there is a very fine Gaelic poem on the death of a Campbell, who is styled "O'Duibhne" in the Gaelic.

Translations that have been recently made from Gaelic manuscripts of high authority have thrown considerable light on Finn, and the events of his

---

* In Carsewell's Gaelic, *Giollaeasbuig van duibhne.* The *v* stands for *u;* the spelling was intended to represent *Ua n Duibhne.* *Ua* and *O* mean the same thing, grandson. The *n* before Duibhne would not now be used.

epoch. We are told in the tract called the "Boramha," or "Tribute," to which reference has been already made, that when Bresal, a king of Leinster, in the third century, was given his choice to pay the tribute or fight the rest of Ireland, he asked help from Finn. A person called Molling was sent to ask Finn to help the men of Leinster. Molling told Finn that he should not come with a small army to fight the chief king, who had the national army with him. The number of men that Finn had, was, we are told in the "Boramha," fifteen hundred chiefs, each having thirty men under him, making the total number of men that Finn brought to help Leinster forty-five thousand, a very large army in those days. They joined the Leinster men, inflicted a crushing defeat on the forces of the chief king, so that the tribute was not paid for many years after. Nine thousand of the "men of Ireland," as the "Book of Leinster" almost invariably calls the national forces, were slain in the battle.

The militia of which Finn was the Commander-in-Chief, and of which his father and grandfather had also been commanders, are the heroes of hundreds of Ossianic tales and poems. It would appear that they numbered twenty-one thousand men on a peace footing, but could raise their numbers to double that amount in time of need. They became so extortionate and arrogant in the long run, that the chief king, Cairbre, and it would seem all the provincial rulers except the King of Leinster, determined to crush them. So a great battle was fought at Garristown in the County Dublin in the year 290 or 296, and the militia of Finn was totally destroyed. It would seem that neither Knock Aillinn nor the hill of Allen has been since then inhabited.

It may not be out of place to state here that students of Gaelic are often puzzled on seeing the name of Finn spelt *Fionn*. It seems certain that *Finn* is the proper orthography. The name is invariably so spelt in all cases in the "Book of Leinster," one of the most correct of all the great Gaelic books; but the editor of "Silva Gadelica" makes it *Fionn* in all cases except in the genitive. It is difficult to understand why, when copying from a manuscript of such high authority as the "Book of Leinster," he did not follow its orthography. In the northern half of Ireland the name is pronounced according to its correct orthography, but in the south of Ireland it is pronounced as if written *Fyun*.

Those who visit Knock Aillinn and its mighty *dun* should also visit the hill of Allen. If there is nothing to be seen on it, there is a great deal to be seen from it, for the view is very extensive. If any one wanted to know how vast the bog of Allen is, he should ascend the hill of Allen, from which he will see a very large part of it. If he is in any doubt as to the exact place in which Finn had his dwelling and *dun*, he will at least be in the locality that has given birth to the most colossal folk-lore that perhaps ever existed,—stories that in the far-back past, before the world was tormented by newspapers and bewildered by politicians, beguiled many a tedious hour and delighted many a sad heart.

THOSE in search of the picturesque alone will not find very much to interest them in Kildare or its immediate vicinity. There may be said to be hardly any remarkable scenic beauties in its neighbourhood. There is the broad expanse of the Curragh not far from the town, one of the finest places for military manœuvres in the British Isles. It is strange why it is called a curragh—more correctly, *currach*—for the word means a marsh, a place that *stirs* when trodden on. There is only a very small part of the land to which the name is applied that is a marsh. It is almost all perfectly dry upland. However, it was called *Currach Life* from very early times, that is the marsh or swamp of the Liffy. It would seem as if the word *Life* meant originally the country through which the river Liffy flows, and that the river took its name from the country; for when King Tuathal wanted revenge on Leinstermen, for the death of his two daughters, who have been mentioned in the article on Tara, he says—

" Let them be revenged on Leinstermen,
   On the warriors *in* the Life."

It is thought that the name Liffy comes from the adjective *liomhtha*, meaning smooth, or polished, for part of the country through which the river flows is very smooth and beautiful.

Hardly a vestige of the ancient buildings of Kildare remain save the round tower. It is over one hundred and thirty feet in height, and therefore one of the highest in Ireland. It seems as perfect as it was the day it was finished. It is sad to say that it is the most completely spoiled—bedevilled would probably be a better word—of all the Irish round towers; for some person or persons whose memories should be held in everlasting abhorrence by every archæologist, have put an incongruous, ridiculous, castellated top on it that makes it look as unsightly and as horrible as a statue of Julius Cæsar would look with a stove-pipe hat on its head. The people of Kildare and its vicinity should at once raise funds and have a proper, antique roof put on their tower, for it is an absolute disgrace to them as it is at present. The top of the tower may have been destroyed by lightning, or, like many other round towers, it may have been left unfinished, and may never have had a top or roof on it. But whatever may

have happened to it, its present castellated roof
is a disgraceful incongruity.

The cathedral of Kildare is a modern and
rather plain building of mediocre interest. It is
supposed to be built in, or nearly in, the place
where the old church stood that was founded by
St Brigit in the sixth century. Kildare seems to
owe its origin to St Brigit, for the name means
the cell or church of the oak ; and as Brigit was
contemporary with St Patrick, hers must have
been the first Christian establishment founded at
Kildare. It is stated in the *Trias Thaumaturga*
of Colgan that when she returned to her own
district, a cell was assigned to her in which she
afterwards led a wonderful life ; that she erected
a monastery in Kildare, and that a very great
city afterwards sprang up, which became the
metropolis of the Lagenians, or Leinster folk.
It requires a great stretch of imagination to conceive how Kildare could ever have been a "very
great city," for it is now, and has for many years,
been a small, a very small country town, hardly
any more than a village. It seems strange that
Kildare is not larger and more prosperous, for if
not situated in a picturesque part of the island,
the country round it is very fair and fertile, and
beautiful as any flat country could be. There is,

however, a passage in the "Calendar of Oengus," written in the latter end of the eighth or the beginning of the ninth century, that goes far to prove that what is said in the *Trias Thaumaturga* about Kildare having been once a large place is true. Speaking of the fall of the strongholds of the Pagans, and the rise of Christian centres, Oengus says—

> "Aillinn's proud burgh
> Hath perished with its warlike host:
> Great is victorious Brigit:
> Fair is her multitudinous city."

The "multitudinous city" was, of course, Kildare. It is curious that Oengus should mention Aillinn, and not mention Allen, the supposed seat of Finn, for wherever he had his stronghold must have been, in his epoch, the most important place in Ireland, Tara alone excepted.

Kildare is famous and historic solely on account of St Brigit. Of all Irish Saints, she is the most to be loved. Her charity, her love for humanity, was so absolutely divine, that reading her life as narrated in the *Leabhar Breac*, we are moved to our very heart's depths. The miracles she is said to have performed are so wondrous, and show such a love for mankind, especially for the poor, that when we read them we long to be children again

I

in order that we might unhesitatingly believe such
beautiful fables.   It was in Kildare that that
wondrous lamp was which is said to have

"Lived through long ages of darkness and storm,"

without having been replenished by human hand;
and it was this legend that inspired Moore to com-
pose the noblest national lyric ever written, "Erin,
O Erin."   If he never wrote a line of poetry save
what is contained in that song, the Irish people
would be justified in raising a statue of gold to
his memory.   It is, beyond anything of the kind
known to humanity,

"Perfect music set to noble words";

yet, heart-sickening to think of, the masses of the
Irish people hardly know it at all!

When St Brigit is contrasted with St Patrick,
she appears very different from him.   The lives of
Ireland's three great Saints are in the *Leabhar
Breac*, an Irish manuscript compiled early in the
fourteenth century; but the greater part of it is
made up of transcripts from documents that were
probably many hundred years old when they were
copied into it.   The three Saints whose lives
appear in it are Patrick, Brigit, and Columba, or
Colum Cill, as he is generally called in Ireland.
These lives were translated some years ago by

Mr Whitley Stokes, the greatest of living Gaelic
scholars; but as only a few dozen copies were
printed for private circulation, the book is practically as unknown to the general public as if it
never had been printed at all. Extracts from it,
therefore, cannot fail to be interesting to the
readers of this book.

Brigit shines out a star of the first magnitude,
totally eclipsing the lesser two lights, Patrick and
Columba. Nothing shall be said about Columba
at present, but it has to be admitted that Patrick,
as he is represented in the *Leabhar Breac*, makes
a poor show when contrasted with glorious St
Brigit. Patrick is represented as spending a large
part of his time in cursing and killing, but St
Brigit spends most of hers in blessing and reliev-
ing. If St Patrick converts a great many, he is
represented as killing a great many; but St Brigit
kills nobody. The narrative of her life in the
Leabhar Breac is probably as wonderful a piece
of biography as ever was written. There is no
effort at style in it, and no attempt at book-mak-
ing. The narrative is simplicity in the true sense
of the word. One of the wonderful things about
it is the side light it throws both on the social
and political conditions of ancient Ireland; but,
curiously enough, no such light is thrown on the

state of the country by the lives of St Patrick
and St Columba, written in the same book and
probably by the same author.

St Brigit seems to have acted on some of the
precepts found in the "Ancient Mariner" fourteen
hundred years before the poem was written. She
seems to have known that—

> "He prayeth best
> Who loveth best
> All things both great and small,"

for we are told that her father, who at present
would be called Duffy, "sundered a gammon of
bacon into five pieces, and left it with Brigit to
be boiled for his guests. A miserable, greedy
hound came into the house to Brigit. Brigit,
out of pity, gave him the fifth piece. When the
hound had eaten that piece, Brigit gave another
piece to him. Then Duffy came and said to
Brigit, 'Hast thou boiled the bacon, and do all
the portions remain?' 'Count them,' saith Brigit.
Duffy counted them and none of them was wanting. The guests declared unto Duffy what Brigit
had done. 'Abundant,' said Duffy, 'are the
miracles of that maiden.' Now the guests ate
not the food, for they were unworthy thereof,
but it was dealt out to the poor and needy of
the Lord."

The following narrative shows St Brigit's love of animals in a still stronger light :

"Once upon a time a bondsman of Brigit's family was cutting firewood. It came to pass that he killed a pet fox of the King of Leinster's. The bondsman was seized by the King. Brigit ordered a wild fox to come out of the wood. So he came, and was playing and sporting for the hosts and for the King at Brigit's order. But when the fox had finished his feats, he went safe back to the wood, with the hosts of Leinster after him, both foot and horse and hounds."

This is simply beautiful. St Brigit, while she got the poor bondsman out of trouble, managed to do so without depriving the fox of his liberty.

Here is another extract that makes one wish that the life of St Brigit in the *Leabhar Breac*, instead of containing only about twenty octavo pages, contained a thousand :—

"Then came Brigit and her mother with her to her father's house. Thereafter Duffy (her father) and his consort were minded to sell the holy Brigit into bondage, for Duffy liked not his cattle and his wealth to be dealt out to the poor, and that is what Brigit used to do. So Duffy fared in his chariot, and Brigit along with him. Said Duffy to Brigit, 'Not for honour or reverence to thee art

thou carried in a chariot, but to take thee and sell
thee, and to grind the quern for Dunlang Mac Enda,
King of Leinster.' When they came to the King's
fortress, Duffy went in to the King, and Brigit
remained in her chariot at the fortress door. Duffy
had left his sword in the chariot near Brigit. A
leper came to Brigit to ask alms. She gave him
Duffy's sword. Said Duffy to the King, 'Wilt
thou buy a bondmaid, namely, my daughter?' says
he. Said Dunlang, 'Why sellest thou thine own
daughter?' Said Duffy, 'She stayeth not from
selling my wealth and giving it to the poor.' Said
the King, 'Let the maiden come into the fortress.'
Duffy went for Brigit, and was enraged against her
because she had given his sword to the poor man.
When Brigit came into the King's presence, the
King said to her, 'Since it is thy father's wealth
that thou takest, much more if I buy thee, wilt
thou take of *my* wealth and *my* cattle, and give
them to the poor.' Said Brigit; 'The Son of the
Virgin knoweth if I had thy might with all Leinster
and with all thy wealth, I would give them to the
Lord of the Elements.' Said the King to Duffy,
'Thou art not fit on either hand to bargain for this
maiden, for her merit is higher before God than before men.' And he gave Duffy for her an ivory-hilted
sword. So was St Brigit saved from bondage."

The idea of giving a sword to a poor crippled leper because she had nothing else to give could hardly have entered into the head of any saint but an Irish one.

The next extract from this marvellous biography is, perhaps, the most curious and interesting of all. In another interview that Brigit had with the King of Leinster, "a slave of the slaves of the King came to speak with Brigit, and said to her, 'If thou wouldst save me from the servitude wherein I am, I would become a Christian, and would serve thee thyself.' Brigit said, 'I will ask that of the King.' So Brigit went into the fortress and asked her two boons of the king, the forfeiture of the sword to Duffy, and his freedom for the slave. Said Brigit to the King, 'If thou desirest excellent children and a kingdom for thy sons, and heaven for thyself, give me the two boons I ask.' Said the King to Brigit, 'The kingdom of heaven, as I see it not, and as no one knows what thing it is, I seek it not; and a kingdom for my sons I seek not, for I shall not myself be extant, and let each one serve his time. But give me length of life in my kingdom, and victory always over the Hui Neill, for there is often war between us; and give me victory in the first battle, so that I may be trustful in the other fights.' And this was fulfilled in the battle

of Lochar which was fought against the Hui
Neill."

By the "Hui Neill' the people of the entire
north of Ireland, including Meath, were meant.
They represented the national party because the
chief kings, for some centuries previous, were of
the race of Niall of the Nine Hostages. Mr Stokes
says, speaking of the above extract in his preface
to the translation, "The conversation between
Brigit and Dunlang (King of Leinster) seems to
preserve the authentic utterance of an Irish pagan
warrior."

One extract more to show in a still stronger
light the angelic kindness and love for humanity,
especially for suffering humanity, that glowed in
the heart of this wonderful woman :

"Once upon a time the King of Leinster came
unto Brigit to listen to preaching and celebration
on Easter Day. After the ending of the form of
celebration the King fared forth on his way, and
Brigit went to refection. Lommán, Brigit's leper,
said he would eat nothing until the warrior
weapons, *arm gaisgedh*, of the King of Leinster
were given to him, spear, sword, and shield, that
he might move to and fro under them. A mes-
senger was sent after the King. From mid-day to
evening was the King going astray, and attained

not even a thousand paces, so that the weapons
were given by him and bestowed on the leper."

This instance of going to such trouble to please
a poor crippled pauper, for Lommān was evidently
such, and of working a miracle so that the King
of Leinster should lose his way, and not go so far
that he could not be overtaken, is one of the most
extraordinary instances of trouble taken to please
a pauper that is to be found in all the records of
benevolence and charity.

The "Annals of the Four Masters" say that St
Brigit was buried in Downpatrick, in the same
grave with St Patrick; but the learned editor
and translator of their annals says that she and
Bishop Conlaeth were buried, one on the right,
and one on the left of the altar, in the church of
Kildare, and he gives Colgan's great book, *Trias
Thaumaturga*, as his authority, and no authority
could be higher.

THERE are not many places in Ireland more interesting than this strange and weird glen. It can hardly be called beautiful. It is gloomy and grand; and there is something depressing about it even in the finest day in autumn when the sombre mountains by which it is surrounded on all sides but one are mantled in their most gorgeous crimson drapery of full-blooming heather. It is just such a spot as an anchorite like St Kevin would choose as a place for contemplation and prayer.

Glendaloch—it ought *not* to be spelled *Glendalough*—is very nearly in the centre of the romantic county of Wicklow. It is a good central point from which to make excursions to the many beautiful and interesting places in its vicinity, such as Glen Molur, the Glen of Imail, the Meeting of the Waters, and the Mountain of Lugnacuilla, the highest in Leinster. The interior of the County Wicklow may be said to be a vast wilderness of mountains, bogs, and glens. But its mountains have, with one exception, the defect of being

round-topped. They lack the boldness of the
hills of Connemara and Donegal. The mountain
that is the most bold and alpine in the county,
and that forms an exception to the general con-
tour of its hills, is the famous one called the

GLENDALOCH.

"Sugar-loaf," near Bray. The Dublin grocer, or
whoever he was that gave this beautiful hill such
an abominable name, should have his memory held
in everlasting contempt. Its real name is a grand
one, Sleeve Coolan, *rectè* Sliabh Cualann. But

in spite of the generally rounded outlines of the
Wicklow Mountains, there are some splendid alpine
views to be seen among them; and none finer than
from the Glen of Lugalaw, about seven or eight
miles from Bray.

But of all places in Wicklow, Glendaloch is the
most famous. It ought to be so, for there is
nothing like it in Ireland. There are many glens
as wild and as gloomy as it, but they lack the
historic interest and the legendary halo that make
Glendaloch dear to the archæologist, the poet, and
the dreamer. Its history goes back almost to the
beginning of Christian times. For five hundred
years it was one of the most important ecclesiastical and educational places in Ireland. Its name
constantly occurs in Irish annals and history; and
its history was for centuries as gloomy as itself, for
the Danes plundered it and burned it so often that
it seems strange that it was not abandoned many
centuries sooner. It was so near their great stronghold, Dublin, that it was harried by them on and
off for over two hundred years.

St Kevin's name is indissolubly associated with
Glendaloch, or the Seven Churches, as it is most
frequently called, for it is supposed that there
were seven churches in it at one time. St Kevin,
according to the best authority who ever wrote

on Irish history and archæology, the famous John
O'Donovan, came of a distinguished family in the
County Wicklow. His name, in correct orthography, *Coemhgen*, means "fair offspring." He
seems to have been predestined to be a Saint, for
many miraculous things are told of his infancy and
early youth. When he was a baby a white cow
is said to have come miraculously to supply him
with milk. The story about his having murdered
Kathleen, the girl with eyes of "unholy blue,"
by throwing her into that lake that the "Skylark
never warbles o'er," is a mere fable. It seems a
pity that the story upon which Moore founded his
very beautiful lyric, "By that Lake, whose gloomy
Shore," should have hardly any foundation in fact.
That a certain girl fell in love with him and caused
him a good deal of annoyance is quite true; but
he did not kill her or throw her into the lake.
He only administered a rather mild castigation, as
shall be seen. O'Donovan says that the following
extract, taken from the *Codex Killkenniensis*,
which, there are good reasons to believe, has never
yet been made public by translation, is the oldest
and most trustworthy account of the transaction
known to exist; and that the trouble between St
Kevin and the girl did not take place in Glendaloch, but in another place in the County

Wicklow. O'Donovan's translation of the story is
the one now given :—

"While the most holy Caemhgen (Kevin) was as
yet remaining in the house of his parents, the
Lord performed many miracles through him. . . .
The parents of Kevin observing so great a grace in
him, committed him to the care of the holy seniors,
Eoganus, Lochanus, and Enna, in order that he
might in their cell be brought up for Christ; and
St Kevin was sedulously reading with those saints.
When he was grown up in the first flower of his
youth, a young girl saw him out in a field along
with the brethren, and fell passionately in love
with him, for he was exceedingly handsome. And
she began to make known her friendship for him in
astute words. And she was always laying snares
for him in every way she could, by looks, by
language, and sometimes by messengers. But the
holy youth rejected all these allurements. On a
certain day she sought the opportunity of finding
him alone, and on a day when the brethren were
working in a wood, she passed by them, and
seeing St Kevin working by himself in the wood,
she approached him, and clasped him in her arms
with fondest embrace. But the soldier of Christ
arming himself with the sacred sign, and full of the
Holy Ghost, made strong resistance against her,

and rushed out of her arms in the wood; and
finding nettles, took secretly a bunch of them, and
struck her with them many times on the face,
hands, and feet. And when she was blistered with
the nettles, the pleasure of her love became extinct.
And she being sorrowful of heart, asked on her
bended knees pardon of St Kevin in the name of
the Lord. And the Saint praying for her to Christ,
she promised him that she would dedicate her
virginity to the Lord. The brothers finding them
discussing together, wondered very much; but the
virgin related to them what had passed; and the
brethren hearing such, were confirmed in their
love for chastity. And that little girl afterwards
became a prudent and holy virgin, and diligently
observed the holy admonitions of St Kevin."

The above translation has not, to the writer's
knowledge, ever been previously published. John
O'Donovan, the greatest authority on such matters
that ever lived, says in his unpublished letters,
while on the Ordnance Survey of Ireland, that the
above extract "is the oldest and only authority
for the story about St Kevin and the lady, and
shows clearly that the scene of it is erroneously
placed at Glendaloch by oral tradition and modern
writers. It will also be sufficient evidence that
this Saint did not murder the lady Kathleen, but

inflicted a somewhat mild punishment by flogging her with a bunch of nettles!"

So poor St Kevin's memory is cleared. It is a pity that Moore did not see the *Codex Killkenniensis* before he wrote the beautiful lyric that casts such a cloud on Wicklow's greatest saint. That the name of St Kevin was highly esteemed not only in Wicklow in ancient times, but all through Leinster, there is ample proof in ancient Gaelic literature. A poet named Broccan, writing in the tenth century in praise of his native province of Leinster and the great people it produced, said :

> "I never heard in any province,
>   Between earth and holy heaven,
> Of a nun like St Brigit
>   Or a cleric like Kevin." *

Glendaloch must have been founded in the latter part of the sixth century, for St Kevin died in 617, aged 120 years. There cannot be any doubt that it was he who founded Glendaloch. We are told that he sought the sombre valley for a retreat in which to contemplate and pray, and that before there were any buildings in it he lived for a long time in a hollow tree, and subsisted on wild fruit and water. The cave in the cliff overhanging the

---

* This poem is in the "Book of Leinster," and has not yet been translated.

lake, known as St Kevin's Bed, the entrance to
which is not only difficult but dangerous, seems
also to have given him shelter for a long time
before there were any habitations in the glen. It
is said that if *nouvelles mariées* succeed in getting
into this dark and dismal cavern, they are sure to
be blessed with large families. Why such a belief
should be current is not easy to understand,
because St Kevin, after whom the cavern is called,
not only had no children, but was a decided
woman-hater. If he did not drown Kathleen, he
at least whipped her with nettles, a thing that no
gallant man would think of doing to a girl who
loved him. It will, however, be the general
opinion of most of those who read this version of
the story, that St Kevin "served her right."

Glendaloch has been ruined and uprooted in a
shocking manner. Of all its edifices there are
only two that still stand—namely, the round tower
and the building known as "Kevin's Kitchen."
This latter is stone-roofed, and is considered to be
one of the oldest buildings of the kind in Ireland.
Archæologists are not agreed as to what particular
use it was originally intended, but that it was an
ecclesiastical edifice of some kind seems to be the
opinion of everyone. There are, it is said, the
remains of seven churches still to be seen in

K

Glendaloch. It appears to have been a walled city, and Petrie, one of the most painstaking and learned archæologists that ever Ireland produced, claimed to have traced the tracks of the walls in many places. That it contained a large population in the eighth and ninth centuries seems to admit of little doubt. Oengus the Culdee, whose verse in which Glendaloch is mentioned has been given in the article on "Emania the Golden," calls it "multitudinous Glendaloch," and "the Rome of the western world." Allowing for the exaggeration of which ancient Gaelic poets may have been rather too fond, it must be admitted that what they say cannot be entirely ignored; and it is more than probable that immediately before the Danes and other northern nations began their raids on Ireland, Glendaloch may have been, and probably was, a large monastic city, as cities were in those days. The Irish monasteries of the eighth and ninth centuries were probably the wealthiest in the world, if not in lands, at least in gold and silver. Where or how they got, or where or how the ancient Irish got, such quantities of the precious metals is a mystery that may never be solved; but that Ireland had an enormous amount of gold and silver in ancient times there can be no doubt at all. This would be sufficiently proved by the quantity,

not of coined money, for they had not any, but of
ornaments of almost every kind that have been
found in all parts of the country, more, it is said,
than have been found in the rest of Europe. There
is hardly a barony in Ireland, it might be said
hardly a parish, in which stories are not told of
people having become suddenly rich by finding, it is
naturally supposed, treasure trove in the shape of
gold ornaments, very few of which have been preserved, for they were generally melted down. Sir
Wm. Wilde mentions, in one of his catalogues of
articles in the Royal Irish Academy, a find of
£3000 worth of gold ornaments in the County
Clare some fifty years ago. It seems a well-ascer-
tained fact that two labourers found over £20,000
worth of gold ornaments when working on a railway in Munster some forty odd years ago. The
founder of one of the largest jewellery houses in
Ireland told a friend of the writer's that his first
"rise" in business was brought about by buying
antique gold ornaments, at sometimes not half their
value, from people who brought them to him from
the country.

When the marauding Northmen first raided
Ireland, they seem not to have had the most remote
idea of either conquering the country or making
permanent settlements in it. They may not have

despised Irish beef and mutton, but what they wanted above all was gold and silver. When Christianity was firmly established in Ireland, the monasteries became the great depositories of the wealth of the country, and the clergy may be said to have become its bankers. The monasteries, therefore, became, to a certain extent, what banks are now, and it was to the monasteries the Danes gave their first attention. It can hardly be proved from Irish history that the Danes ever tried to conquer Ireland but once, and that was at the battle of Clontarf. Even under Turgesius, when they succeeded in establishing themselves almost everywhere there was salt water or fresh water to float their ships, they played the part of raiders and not of conquerors, and never formed a permanent settlement out of sight of their galleys. In England and in France they acted quite differently. They conquered and kept all England and a considerable part of France. They went to England and France to establish themselves, but they went to Ireland to plunder. The question to be solved is, Why did the Danes act so differently in Ireland from the way they acted in England and in other countries? There seems to be no way to answer this question except by saying that there was so much more of the precious metals in Ireland, that to get them, and not to conquer the country or form permanent settlements in it, was their prime object. If history was absolutely silent about the doings of the Northmen in Ireland, we would, from a surer guide than history, know that plunder and not settlement was what they had in view. That guide is place names. There are more Scandinavian place names to be found in some parishes in the north-east of England than there are in all Ireland. There are hardly a dozen Scandinavian place names in Ireland, and they are *all* on the sea coast but *one*. That one is Leixlip, and it is only a few miles from the sea, on a river which the galleys of the Northmen could easily ascend. The only time at which a serious attempt seems to have been made by the Northmen to become possessed of Ireland was shortly before the battle of Clontarf, and that attempt seems to have owed its origin to that horrible but beautiful woman, Gormfhlaith, sister to the king of Leinster, and whose last of many husbands was Brian Boramha. That attempt utterly failed, and no other was ever made. If the Northmen cannot be said to have seriously contemplated the conquest of Ireland prior to the time immediately before the battle of Clontarf, it does not seem to have been from lack of men in the country, for Irish annals and history speak of their vast numbers in such a way as hardly leaves a doubt as to the awfulness of the scourge they were to the country at large. So great were their numbers at one time during the ninth century that we are told that it seemed as if the sea vomited them forth, and that there was hardly a harbour on the Irish coasts in which there was not a Danish or a Norwegian fleet. It has to be admitted that the Irish fought them with the most astonishing persistency and valour. In spite of the way the country was split into petty kingdoms, with chief kings, who were generally such only in name, the reception the Northmen got in Ireland was very different from that which they got in England. The Saxons often got rid of them by paying them to go away, but the Irish got rid of them only by the sword. Those who want to know what Ireland suffered from the raids of the Northmen should read the "Wars of the Gael and the Gaill." The book is generally believed to have been written by M'Liag, who was living when the battle of Clontarf was fought, and who was chief poet, or secretary, to Brian Boramha.

Although the Northmen were allies of Leinster for a long time, they plundered Glendaloch in the years 833, 886, and 982. It was so near Dublin and so near the sea that their alliance with Leinster did not prevent them from raiding it. It was one of the rich ecclesiastical establishments in Ireland, and one of those most exposed to the incursions of the Northmen. Its round tower was, therefore, in all probability, one of the first that was erected. It is now generally believed by those most competent to form an opinion that the round towers of Ireland were erected as places of security against the Northmen, and that they were sometimes used as belfries. Their Irish name, *cloigtheach*, means a bell house and nothing else; but it is quite clear that, although they sometimes served as belfries, the primary object of their erection was to secure a place of safety for the treasures of the church or monastery, close to which they were invariably erected. Of the hundred and eight round towers which are known to have been erected in Ireland, and of which remains exist, every one of them is known to have been erected close to where a church or monastery stood. More than half of them are in ruins; of some only a few feet of the walls remain; and of some others the foundations only remain. It may seem hard for some, in these days of far-reaching projectiles to imagine

how those slender towers, so chaste and beautiful
in their construction, could serve as places of
defence or security against the Danes. They
could not have served as such if the Danes had
come as conquerors to form permanent settlements,
but as they were only raiders the towers were
generally perfect defences against them. A dozen
men shut into a round tower, the door of which
was generally from ten to fourteen feet from the
ground, could laugh at an army of Danes who
had neither battering rams nor artillery of any
kind. There was only one way by which a round
tower could be taken or destroyed by men like
the plundering hosts of the Vikings, who did not,
and could not, take ponderous implements like
battering rams with them on their raids, and
that was by undermining it—digging its foundations so that it would fall. But this would have
been a very tedious business, for the foundations
of many of the round towers are six and even
ten feet below the surface. A few dozen resolute
men in a round tower might defy an army of
Danes, provided the besieged had enough of food
and drink in their stronghold. It must, however,
be admitted that the Northmen did sometimes
succeed in taking and plundering round towers,
but by what means we do not know.

Those who maintain that the round towers are pre-Christian structures, and that there is nothing said in Irish annals about their erection, have very little warrant for such an assertion. If they read Lord Dunraven's work on ancient Irish architecture, they will find copies of more than one allusion to their erection from the most authentic Irish annals known to exist. Here is one taken from the *Chronicon Scottorum*, a work of the highest authority and authenticity, compiled about the year 1124. "The great *Cloigtheach* (or belfry) of Clonmacnois was finished by Gillachrist Ua Macleoin and by Turloch O'Connor." This entry refers to the year 1120.

While speaking of the uses of round towers, the wealth of Irish monasteries, and of Ireland in general in ancient times, it may not be out of place to say that that very wealth proved a curse to the country, for if Ireland had not been so rich in precious metals, the Northmen would probably never have invaded and raided it; or if they did invade it, they would have done so with a view to subjugating it and forming permanent settlements in it, as they did in England and France, — things that might have been, and that probably would have been, of

benefit to the country. If Ireland had been conquered by the Northmen they would certainly
have destroyed the provincial kingdoms, and have
brought the whole island under the sway of one
ruler; and whether that ruler was Irish or Norse,
it would have been of immense benefit to the
country at large. Ancient Irish polity was very
good theoretically, but practically it was a frightful
failure. The Scandinavian invasions only added
to the political confusion of Ireland. They were
of benefit to England and France, for they brought
an infusion of fresh blood into those countries.
But to Ireland they brought destruction and ruin,
with only a slight infusion of fresh blood. They
made the political confusion of the country more
confounded. They robbed it of an immense
quantity of its wealth, but worse than that,
they destroyed a large part of its literature. The
monasteries were not only the repositories of wealth
but of books. It was impossible that monasteries
could be plundered and burnt without damage
being done to the books they contained. There
is positive proof in Irish annals that the Northmen
were in the habit of *drowning* the books they
found in the religious houses. Books were in
those days, as is well known, made of vellum,
or prepared leather, a material hard to burn;

they were consequently cast into the nearest lake
or river, from which very few of them were
probably ever recovered. If it had not been for
Scandinavian burnings and plunderings, mediæval
Gaelic literature would, even now, be so immense
that it would command the respect of the world
at large. Those who say that the bulk of
mediæval Gaelic writings has come down to
us — and there are those that have the un-
speakable hardihood to say so—must be classed
as very prejudiced, or very ignorant of Irish
history.

The last entry in the Four Masters relating
to Glendaloch occurs under the year 1163. It
appears to have been abandoned shortly after
that date; but why it was abandoned as an
ecclesiastical establishment when Danish raids
and plunderings had ceased does not seem to be
clearly known.

Glendaloch has been thus lengthenedly treated
on because it is the most interesting ecclesiastical
ruin in the province of Leinster, Clonmacnois only
excepted. Its strange and gloomy, yet romantic
situation, its antiquity, its sad history of burnings
and plunderings, the utter ruin that has overtaken most of its monuments, the halo of legend
and romance that is around it, give it a charm

even to the non-imaginative and the rude. For
the archæologist, the poet, the romancer, or the
dreamer, it has attractions and charms greater,
perhaps, than they could find on any other spot
of Irish soil.

NEXT to Emania and Ardmagh, Aileach is the most historic spot in the province of Ulster. It lies four miles west of the city of Derry, on a round, heath-clad hill, some eight hundred feet above the level of the sea. It is one of the most ancient cyclopean fortresses in Ireland, or, perhaps, in the world. There is no scenic beauty in the immediate vicinity of Aileach, but there is a view from the hill-top on which it is situated that for wildness and sublimity can hardly be equalled anywhere in the British Isles,—a view which will amply repay any one who sees it on a clear day. On the north the hills of Inishowen obstruct the view, but west and south-west it is sublime. The eye ranges over a wilderness of fantastic-shaped mountains, some shooting up sharp as arrows, others round and ridgy, separated by sinuous sea-lochs and glittering tarns,—a land of awful ruggedness and desolation,—of rock-bound shores cleft into myriad bays and fiords by the thundering almost ever restless northern sea that beats against them. If no hoary ruin crowned the hill on which the "Lordly Aileach" of Gaelic poets stands, the view from its summit would be worth a journey of a hundred miles to see, for most of the wildness and grandeur of "Dark Donegall" are spread before the eye. On the north-east and north-west the waters of Loch Foyle and Loch Swilly spread themselves almost beneath the feet of the gazer from Aileach. It stands on a hill that commands a view of both Loch Foyle and Loch Swilly; and the site of this ancient fortress was evidently chosen on account of the view it commands of those two sea-lochs, for no fleet could enter them for any distance without being seen by the watchers on the walls of Aileach.

The first thing that should be mentioned when speaking of Aileach is the noble work that has been lately accomplished regarding it. An article appeared about it some twenty years ago in the *Irish Times* of Dublin, calling attention to its antiquity, the historic and legendary renown of that ancient place; and a Mr Barnard of Londonderry became interested in Aileach and determined to make an effort to have the demolished fortress restored as far as was possible. He made a pilgrimage among the farmers living in the locality, and got promises of help in the way of men to work for so many days at the restoration of the fortress. The farmers kept their word, gave him the help of the men they had promised, and in a comparatively short time the walls of the ruined fortress, under the surveillance of Mr Barnard, once again crowned the hill of Greenan, after having been in ruins for well-nigh eight hundred years. Mr Barnard, and the farmers that gave him assistance in the good work, deserve the thanks of every one who is a patriot, or has any reverence for the ancient monuments of his country, or any respect for the hallowed past.

The early history of Aileach is "lost in the twylight of fable." It is a pre-historic building, almost as much so as a Pyramid of Egypt. It was used as a stronghold down to the beginning of the twelfth century; but when it was built, or by whom, cannot be said to be known from authentic history, for the many poems that exist about its origin in ancient Gaelic are legendary rather than historic. There may be, and there probably is, a great deal of truth in them, but they cannot be accepted as history.

Aileach is a circular, dry-stone fortress with walls nine feet thick. It was levelled down to the ground when Mr Barnard undertook its restoration. The history of its destruction is so

strange, so unique, and so Irish, that it must be
given. Let the Four Masters tell it. They say,
under the year 1101, that "A great army was led
by O'Brian, King of Munster, with the men of
Munster, Ossory, Meath and Connacht, across
Assaroe into Innishowen. . . . He demolished
Grianan Aileach in revenge of Kinncora, which
had been razed and demolished by Muircheartach
O'Lochlainn some time before. O'Brian commanded his army to carry with them from Aileach
to Limerick a stone of the demolished building for
every sack of provisions they had. In commem-
oration of which was said (by some unknown
poet)—

'I never heard of the billeting of grit stones,
  Though I heard of the billeting of companies,
  Until the stones of Aileach were billeted
  On the horses of the King of the West.'"

This is the only attempt at anything like humour
in all the dreary annals of the Four Masters.
Such quiet sarcasm would be a credit to Mark
Twain. But if the poet had said "King of the
South" instead of "King of the West," although
it might not have answered his Gaelic rhyme or
assonance quite so well, it would have been more
correct, for although Munster is west of Aileach,
it is more south than west. It can never be

known how high the walls of Aileach had been
before they were pulled down by O'Brien, because
we don't know how many cavalry he had, or how
many stones he carried to Limerick. Never before
was an army loaded with such impedimenta; but
that the story of the stones of Aileach, or at
least, stones similar to them, having been brought
to Limerick or its immediate vicinity, there cannot be much doubt, for they were found there.

The fortress of Aileach is nearly a hundred feet
in diameter in the inside. It is not known if it
was ever roofed, but it is probable that it was.
There were two lines of earthen ramparts round
it, but they have nearly disappeared. John
O'Donovan thought that the entire hill of Grianan,
on which the fortress stands, was once enclosed
by a vast rampart of earth, and that cultivation
has destroyed all but the faintest traces of it.
It seems probable that Aileach was intended
more for a stronghold than for a permanent
dwelling-place. It may have been inhabited only
when a siege or an invasion was expected. One
of its names, or rather the first part of one of
its names, "Grianan," would indicate that it was
intended only as a summer residence, like the
Dunsinane = *Dún soinine*, fine weather fortress,
of Macbeth. Those who could live in winter

on top of the wind-swept hill on which Aileach
stands without getting coughs or colds would
require constitutions of iron and lungs of brass.

O'Donovan says that if any reliance can be placed
on Irish chronology, the antiquity of Aileach must
be very great, no less than upwards of a thousand
years before the Christian era.   He says, also, that
the poet, part of whose poem on Aileach is given
below, in making the Tuata de Danaan King, Eochy,
generally known in Irish history and legend as the
Dagda, contemporaneous with the Assyrian King,
Darcylus, exactly agrees with the chronology of
O'Flaherty and Usher, who say that he reigned
1053 years before the Christian era.

There is a poem in the "Book of Lecan" on
Aileach by the poet to whom O'Donovan alludes,
that in language and *tournure* bears the marks of
extreme antiquity.   Even O'Donovan, great a Celtic
scholar as he was, had apparently extreme difficulty
in translating it.   It has never been published.
The first dozen or so lines are given here :—

"Aileach Fridreann, arena of mighty kings.   A
dun through which ran roads under heroes through
five ramparts.   Hill on which slept the Dagda.
Red its flowers.   Many its houses.   Just its spoils.
Few its stones.   A lofty castle is Aileach.   Fort of
the great man.   A sheltering *dun* over the lime

[white] schools. A delightful spot is Aileach. Green its bushes. The sod where the Dagda found the mound wherein rested Hugh."

But it is in more recent times that the history and records of Aileach become supremely interesting. It was from there that Muircheartach Mac Neill, styled the Hector of the west of Europe by old annalists, started on his celebrated "Circuit of Ireland" in the year 942. He was heir apparent to the chief kingship of Ireland, and wanted to show the provincial rulers that he was fit to rule *them*. So he determined to start on his circuit in the depth of winter, when it appears the ancient Irish seldom went on forays, and either make or persuade the provincial rulers to acknowledge his right to the throne when the then reigning chief king, Donacha, died. The way he is said to have chosen men for the expedition is very curious and very Irish. He caused a tent to be erected, keeping the cause of its erection unknown, and made his men to go into it at night. A fierce dog attacked every one that entered; and opposite to where the dog was, an armed man also attacked those that entered; both man and dog simultaneously attacking the intruder. If he who entered the tent flinched neither from dog nor man, but showed fight to both, he was chosen; but whoever showed the least sign of cowardice

was rejected.   Out of his whole army we are told
that Muircheartach could only get a thousand men,
and with that small army, protected by strong
leather cloaks, he started on his Circuit of Ireland
to force, intimidate, or coax the provincial kings to
acknowledge that he was their master, and that he
was to be their next suzerain.

Our principal source of information about the
Circuit comes from a poem of undoubted authority
and antiquity, written by one called Cormacan
Eigeas, who accompanied Muircheartach on the
expedition.   It is one of the most remarkable poems
of its age, not only in Gaelic, but in any language.
It was translated more than forty years ago, and
may be seen in the "Transactions" of the Royal Irish
Academy ; but it is not probable that even forty persons have ever read it, so little general interest has
heretofore been taken in Gaelic literature or Irish
history.   For these reasons it cannot be uninteresting
to give some extracts from it.   It commences :

" O Muircheartach, son of the valiant Niall,
   Thou hast taken the hostages of Inis Fail,
   Thou hast brought them all into Aileach,
   Into the stone-built palace of steeds !

" Thou didst go forth from us with a thousand heroes
   Of the race of Eoghan of red weapons,
   To make the great Circuit of Ireland,
   O Muircheartach of the yellow hair !

> The day thou didst set out from us eastwards
> Into the fair province of Connor,*
> Many were the tears down beauteous cheeks
> Among the fair-haired women of Aileach."

Muircheartach carried off the King of Ulster; and, as the old chroniclers tell us, keeping his left hand to the sea, he fared to Dublin, then the greatest stronghold the Danes had, not only in Ireland but in the west of Europe. He did not have to fight the Danes of Dublin, although he had often fought them before, for their king, probably thinking that "discretion was the better part of valour," surrendered himself a prisoner. And here one of these inconsequential incidents is related, which no one but an ancient Irish poet would dream of mentioning. Muircheartach seems to have had no objection to make love to a Danish maiden, often as he had fought Danish men. Cormacan, the poet, tells us that they

> " Were a night at fair Ath-cliath [Dublin] ;
> It was not a pleasure to the foreigners :
> There was a damsel in the strong fortress
> Whose soul the son of Niall was ;
> She came forth until she was outside the walls,
> Although the night was constantly bad."

Muircheartach then proceeded south-west from Dublin to Aillinn, and carried away the King of

---

* The eastern part of Ulster.

Leinster. He then made for Cashel, where the
King of Munster lived. But Callachan, that was
his name, showed fight, and Muircheartach's men
threw off their leather cloaks and prepared to
stand by him. However, seeing that things were
beginning to look serious, the King of Munster
yielded and was carried away prisoner with a
golden fetter on him. The leader of the Circuit
then turned northwards into Connacht, and carried
away the king of that province. So he had the
four provincial kings in his power, and also the
Danish King of Dublin. But he did them neither
hurt nor harm, for he seems to have been in a
good humour all the time he was "on circuit";
and we are told by his poet laureate that on
their halts the soldiers amused themselves in
many ways, especially by music and dancing, and
he says—

> "Music we had on the plain and in our tents,
> Listening to its strains, we danced awhile ;
> There, methinks, a heavy noise was made
> By the shaking of our hard cloaks."

The next three verses are magnificent. They are
full of dramatic power and naturalness. When the
triumphant army, but triumphant without having
shed a drop of blood, approach Aileach, a mes-
senger is sent forward to announce its arrival :—

"From the green of Lochan-na-neach
  A page is despatched to Aileach
  To tell Duvdaire * of the black hair
  To send women to cut rushes.

"'Rise up, O Duvdaire (*said the page*),
  There is a company coming to thy house;
  Attend every man of them
  As a monarch should be attended.'

"'Tell me (*she said*) what company comes hither
  To the lordly Aileach Rigreann,
  Tell me, O fair page,
  That I may attend them?'

"'The Kings of Erin in fetters (*he replies*),
  With Muircheartach, son of the warlike Niall.'"

The kingly prisoners were all brought to Aileach,
where they were feasted for five months; and the
following list of their bill of fare will show that
they lived well. Let the same poet tell it :—

"Ten score hogs—no small work,
  Ten score cows, two hundred oxen,
  Were slaughtered at festive Aileach
  For Muircheartach of the great fetters.

"Three score vats of curds,
  Which banished the hungry look of the army,
  With a sufficiency of cheering mead,
  Were given by magnanimous Muircheartach."

---

* Duvdaire was Muircheartach's wife. She was daughter
of the King or Chief of Ossory. Rushes in those days served
as carpets, as they did in England.

When the five kings were feasted—and it is to
be hoped fattened—for five months, Muircheartach
brought them to the chief king or emperor,
Donacha, and gave them up to him. The following extraordinary dialogue, taken from the
same poem, occurs between them. Muircheartach
says:

> "'There are the noble kings for thee.'
> Said Muircheartach, the son of Niall;
> 'For thou, O Donacha, it is certain to me,
> Art the best man of the men of Erin.'

> " *Donacha.*
> "'Thou art a better man thyself, O King,
> With thee no one can vie;
> It is thou who didst take captive the noble kings,
> O Muircheartach, son of the great Niall.'

> " *Muircheartach.*
> "'Thou art better thyself, O Donacha the black haired,
> Than any man in our land;
> Whoever is in strong Tara
> It is he that is monarch of Erin.'

> " *Donacha.*
> "'Receive my blessing, nobly,
> O son of Niall Glundubh, bright, pure;
> May Tara be possessed by thee,
> O Prince of the bright Loch Foyle!*

* A poetic name for Muircheartach, for his patrimony was
on the shores of Loch Foyle.

"'May thy race possess Moy Breagh,*
May they possess the white-sided Tara,
May the hostages of the Gael be in thy house,
O good son, O Muircheartach!'"

It is sad to know that this extraordinary poem, with its uniqueness, its dramatic power, and its raciness of the soil and of the time, notwithstanding the fact that it was translated and published in the Transactions of the Royal Irish Academy over forty years ago, is to-day hardly any more known than it was when it lay unheeded and unknown in the archaic Gaelic of the tenth century. It might, for all the notice that has been taken of it, as well not have been translated at all. No other people on earth would have treated such an archaic literary gem with such coldness and contempt. It would seem as if the Irish people were losing not only their soul but their brains. If such a poem were written in Finnish or in Ojibaway it could not have been more ignored than it has been by a people who call themselves intellectual.

In this poem the same anachronism may be noticed that led Petrie so much astray about

---

* Moy Breagh, or the fine plain, was the country round Tara. To possess Moy Breagh was the same as to possess Tara, and that was to be chief King. But Tara was as deserted in the time of the Circuit as it is now.

the Lia Fail having been in Tara in the tenth century. Muircheartach addresses Donacha as if he were living in Tara, although Tara had been abandoned four hundred years before, and was as waste and as desolate in the time of Donacha as it is to-day; the chief kings of his epoch and for centuries before it, lived usually in Westmeath or in Donegal.

That Muircheartach Mac Neill, though a sort of Rory O'More of the tenth century, was a great man can hardly be doubted. He seems to have contemplated the entire overthrow of the pentarchy and the union of all the provinces under one sole king, namely, himself. He could hardly have been ignorant of what had occurred in England in the century previous—how Alfred had broken up the Saxon heptarchy and made himself practically sole king in England. If Muircheartach had succeeded in destroying the wretched system of provincial nationality, and had made the country a political unit, the subsequent history of Ireland would probably be very different from what it has been. But Muircheartach was killed by his old enemies the Danes, the year after he made his famous circuit. They also killed his father, Niall Glundubh, at the battle of Killmoshogue, near Dublin, in the year 917. Here is what the Four Masters

say about him under the year 941 *: "Muirchear-
tach of the Leather Cloaks, Lord of Aileach, the
Hector of the west of Europe in his time, was
slain at Ardee (in Louth) by Blacaire, the son of
Godfrey, Lord of the Foreigners, on the 26th of
March. In lamentation of him it was said—

> "'Vengeance and destruction
>   Have descended on the race of Conn for ever;
> As Muircheartach does not live, alas!
>   The country of the Gael will always be an orphan.'"

* This date is thought to be two years too early, and that
943 was the year in which Muircheartach was killed.

THE situation of three of the most historic and remarkable ecclesiastical establishments in Ireland, namely, Clonmacnois, Glendaloch, and Cashel, is very peculiar. The first is on a barren sand-hill surrounded by the most strange and unique scenery in Ireland, consisting of almost illimitable meadows interspersed with bogs. The second is in one of the gloomiest and weirdest glens in the island; but Cashel is on a towering rock amid some of the richest land, not only in Ireland but in the world, and overlooking as goodly a country as human eye perhaps ever gazed on. Ancient Irish monks and churchmen must have been peculiarly gifted with an appreciation of the strange, unique, and beautiful in nature, or they would not have fixed their retreats in such peculiar places. If ancient Irish kings loved to place their strongholds on hills such as Tara, Aileach, Knock Aillinn, and Uisneach, ancient Irish ecclesiastics seemed not to have cared whether their churches were on hills or in hollows, provided they were somewhere that was strange, weird, or beautiful.

172

The situation of Cashel is not only beautiful but superb. There is no other place of its kind in Ireland situated like it. Its situation is as peculiar as that of Glendaloch or Clonmacnois. It is, perhaps, the most imposing pile of ecclesiastical ruins in Europe. Mont St Michael in

BUILDINGS ON THE ROCK OF CASHEL.

France can hardly compare with Cashel in commanding beauty of situation. One overlooks the chilly sea, but the other overlooks as warm, as fair, and as fertile a country as there is in the world.

Cashel has inspired many poets; but, unfortun-

ately, none of the great English masters of song
has made it a theme; and it is strange that our
own Moore, who has celebrated Glendaloch, the
Vale of Avoca, and other famous places, never
composed a lyric on Cashel. No other place in
Ireland could have given him a grander theme to
write poems of the kind in which he delighted,
and in the composition of which he was such an
acknowledged master. It is indeed strange that
so few of those who may be called our minor
poets have written about Cashel, and so seldom
taken it as their theme. There exists, however, a
short poem on Cashel of the class usually known
as sonnets, and it is probable that neither Moore,
nor any of the other great masters of song, could
have written anything superior to it. It is by the
late Sir Aubry de Vere. It first appeared in the
Dublin Penny Journal some sixty years ago; but
it has so long been partially forgotten that it can
hardly be out of place to reproduce it here:

"Royal and saintly Cashel! I could gaze
 Upon the wreck of thy departed powers,
 Not in the dewy light of matin hours,
 Nor the meridian pomp of summer's blaze;
But at the close of dim autumnal days
 When the sun's parting glance thro' slanting showers
 Sheds o'er thy rock-throned pediments and towers
 Such awful gleams as brighten on Decay's

Prophetic cheek ;—at such a time methinks
  There breathes from thy lone courts and voiceless aisles
A melancholy moral, such as sinks
  On the worn traveller's heart amid the piles
Of vast Persepolis on her mountain stand,
Or Thebes half buried in the desert's sand."

It is strange that Cashel has not inspired more poets; but it is stranger still that the once soulful people of Ireland would have allowed it to be defaced by any modern building erected on the rock on which stands its hallowed and ruined piles. Some gentleman named Scully has erected a brand new round tower almost in the very centre of the hoary monuments that are so sanctified by antiquity. The new tower is not shown on the annexed plate, because of the horrible picture it would make. It is strange that those living near Cashel did not prevent, if they could have done so, the marring of one of the most striking, beautiful and soul-inspiring ruins not only in Ireland but in Europe. It may be that Mr Scully thought that by erecting a new monument of antique type there would not be any incongruity manifested by it, and that by having his name written on it in the Irish language and in Irish characters he would atone for the error he committed. If he thought so, he made a great mistake, for *anything* new, whether a round tower, a cross, or a brick-

built grocery, would destroy all the antique charm
of such noble ruins as those on the rock of Cashel.
It may be willingly granted that it is a pity there
are any ruins at all in the world, and that buildings
cannot last new for ever. It should be remembered, however, that nothing can last always; and
that when buildings become ruined by time, and,
above all, when they have become historic like
those on the rock of Cashel, and when they serve
to show either the piety or the civilisation of those
who have passed away, it becomes absolute barbarism to mar them and mock them by erecting
anything new in their immediate vicinity. A
modern church on the Hill of Tara is bad enough,
but a new building on the Rock of Cashel is little
else than a profanation.

Cashel was a seat of the kings of Munster from
a time so far back in the dim past, that one almost
shudders to think how long ago it is. Long before
a Christian edifice crowned the Rock of Cashel,
the barbaric dry stone fortress of some Munster
pagan king certainly covered it; for very little
work would have to be bestowed on it to render it
an almost impregnable fortress in ancient times.
Some have derived the word Cashel from *cios*,
rent, and *ail*, a rock, making it to mean "rent
rock"; for it is certain that when the kings of

Munster lived in Cashel, it was the place where
they received most of their tributes or rents;
but the best modern Gaelic scholars, including
Dr P. W. Joyce, author of that most useful and
learned book, "Irish Names of Places," maintain
that the word *Caiseal* means simply a circular
building of dry stones, for the name occurs in
scores of places throughout Ireland; and such a
building was no doubt on this rock in pre-
Christian times.

Cashel became a seat of Christian cult at a very
early period, and there are good reasons to think
that St Patrick founded a church there. The
Rock of Cashel has for very many centuries been
known as *Carraig Phadraig*, or Patrick's Rock.
The first Christian Irishman whose writings have
come down to us was Dubhthach, or, as the name
would probably now be Anglicised, Duffy, Mac U
Lugair. In his poem in praise of the prowess of
Leinstermen, he says, that they "unyoked their
horses on the ramparts of clerical Cashel." As
this Duffy was a disciple of St Patrick's, and one
of the first converts made by him in Ireland, we
are forced to think that one of the first Christian
churches ever erected in Ireland was the one
erected in Cashel, as it appears to have been in
existence when Duffy wrote his poem, which could

hardly have been later than the middle of the sixth
century. But no vestige of the church of St
Patrick's time remains. It was probably a wooden
building, and may have disappeared as far back as
thirteen centuries ago. The oldest building on the
Rock of Cashel is the round tower, not Mr Scully's
incongruous edifice, but the original one, built
probably in the ninth century. It is ninety feet
high, and in a fairly good state of preservation.
The cathedral is thought to have been built in
1169 by O'Brien, King of Munster, but there does
not appear to be much of the building he erected
to be seen now, for the ruined cathedral which
exists cannot, from the style of its architecture, be
older than the fourteenth century. We know from
authentic history that one of the Fitzgeralds burned
the cathedral in 1495, because he wanted to burn
Archbishop Creagh, who, he thought, was in it;
but it does not seem to be fully known whether
the building was entirely or only partially destroyed
by Fitzgerald. Divine service is said to have been
celebrated in it so late as 1752, but it must have
been in a semi-ruined condition even then.

But it is Cormac's Chapel that is the real architectural glory of the Rock of Cashel. It is by
some wrongly attributed to the time of Cormac
Mac Cullenann in the ninth century. It was built

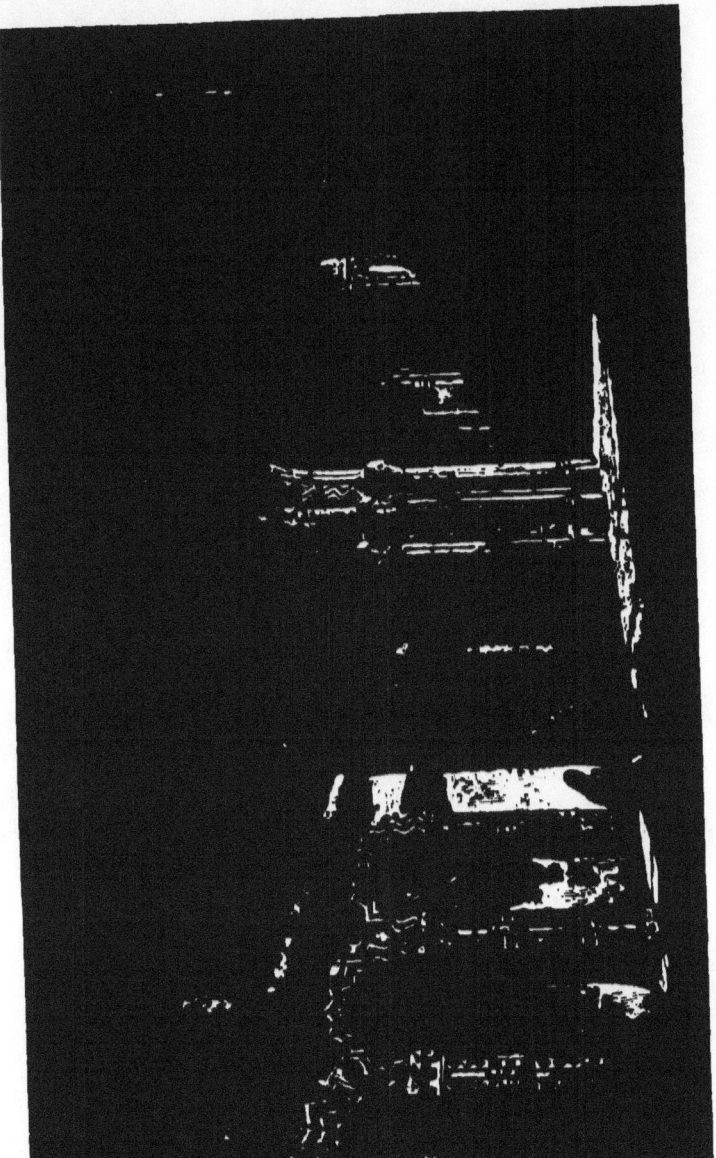

INTERIOR OF CORMAC'S CHAPEL.

by Cormac Mac Carthy, a king of Munster, in the
early part of the twelfth century. The principal
proof that it was built at that time is found in the
Chronicon Scottorum, in which it is stated that
Cormac's Chapel at Cashel was consecrated in 1130.
It is more than probable that the chapel was consecrated very soon after it was finished. It does not
come within the scope of a work like this to enter
into technical details on matters connected with
architecture; but for chaste beauty, for elaborate
carving, and solidity of structure, it may be said
that Cormac's Chapel is one of the most wonderful
ecclesiastical buildings of its age in Christendom.
The practised eye of the trained architectural critic
might notice some signs of decay about it, some
effacement in the gorgeous carvings or designs with
which almost every stone of the interior is more or
less covered; but to the ordinary observer, the
whole building, within and without, seems almost
as perfect as it was the day its architect pronounced it finished. If Cormac's Chapel were
only larger, it would be the noblest and most
remarkable ecclesiastical building of its age in the
British Isles, or probably in Europe. But, unfortunately, it is very small, the nave being only about
thirty feet in length, and the choir only about
eighteen. But what it lacks in size is made up in

elaborate carving, chaste design, and solidity of structure. It looks as if it would last until the day of doom, and as if nothing but an earthquake could destroy it. Its very roof seems as strong and as perfect as its walls. It is of cut stone laid on with geometrical exactness, as sound and as solid as ever it was. However imposing the *coup d'oeil* that "the rock-throned pediments and towers" of Cashel may present from without, it is an examination of this gem of antique architectural beauty that gives one the highest opinion of the artistic skill of those whose appreciation of the unique and beautiful led them to choose this towering rock as a fit place on which to raise edifices dedicated to the Deity.

It is strange how it was that the ancient or rather the mediæval Irish, who knew how to erect such beautiful and enduring stone and mortar structures as the round towers, and such gems of architectural beauty as Cormac's Chapel is, and as Mellifont Abbey certainly was, should have housed their kings and chiefs in dwellings of wood, whose only defence was an earthen rampart surmounted by a palisade of stakes, or in a Cyclopean fortress of dry stones. It is absolutely certain that not a single castle built of stones and mortar existed in Ireland prior to the Anglo-French invasion.

The Irish knew how to build round towers and churches, but seem never to have thought of building castles until their invaders taught them to build them. The thing looks very curious, but, on closer examination, it does not appear so strange, for. it is now pretty well known that none of the Northern nations had castles before the eleventh century. The French seem to have been the first of the Northern nations that had castles. It is very doubtful if there was a castle in Great Britain before the Norman-French conquest. If there were castles in England or Scotland before the battle of Hastings, they were imitations of those on the Continent, and were probably designed and built by Continental architects and mechanics. Neither the Scandinavians nor Northern-Germans appear to have had castles until late in the middle ages, when they copied them from more Southern nations. But it was the Norman-French that brought the art of castle building to its greatest perfection.

The ruins of Hoar Abbey, or St Mary's Abbey, as it is sometimes called, are situated. close to the Rock, but not on it. It is believed to have been founded by the Benedictine order in the thirteenth century.

Cashel is interesting in almost every way. There

is a magnificent view from its ruin-crowned rock over some of the fairest and most fertile land in Ireland. Nor is a mountain view wanting, for the Galtees, the second highest range of mountains in Ireland, are visible, and a noble range they are, not rounded lumps like so many of the Wicklow Hills, but steep, sheer, cloud-piercing heights,—Alps in miniature. It is a pity that the town, or rather the city, of Cashel is not larger and more thriving. It may have been, like Glendaloch and Kildare, much larger in early Christian times than it is at present, but there does not seem to be any statement of the fact in any of the old Gaelic books, so far as is known to the writer. But whatever may have been the past history of the city of Cashel, no one in search of the picturesque, the unique, or the historic in Ireland should fail to see its Rock. It is said that when Scott visited Ireland he was more impressed by the Rock of Cashel than by anything else of its kind that he saw in the country.

Of all the remains of Christian edifices in Ireland, Cashel, Glendaloch, and Clonmacnois are the most interesting. It is not only by the beauty or peculiarity of their situations that they impress us, for their histories go so far back into the past, when the combat of Christianity with Druidism was still going on, that we may regard them as the

advance posts of a purer cult in the ground conquered from paganism. It would be hard to find
in Europe three other places of a similar kind more
antique, more interesting, or more worthy of being
respected. What remains of their hallowed ruins
should be guarded with jealous care, and saved
from any further uprooting or profanation.

Loch Erne and Loch Ree are not only the most beautiful, but the most historic of the great lakes of Ireland. Loch Neagh is larger than either of them, and Loch Dearg and Loch Corrib are probably nearly as large; but none of those three is as picturesque as either of the two first-mentioned lakes. The shores of Loch Dearg are bolder and more mountainous than those of either Loch Erne or Loch Ree, but Loch Dearg lacks the island-studded surface of the two latter, which is their great charm. Whether Loch Erne or Loch Ree is the more beautiful is not easy to decide. Both are as beautiful sheets of water as can be easily found, but both lack mountain scenery in the true sense of the phrase. There are some high lands on the lower part of Loch Erne, but they can hardly be called mountains. In number and variety of its islands, Loch Erne is only surpassed by that famous lake on the vast St Lawrence, known as the Thousand Isles.

Loch Erne is certainly the most peculiar and also the longest lake in Ireland. From where it

may be said to begin, near Belturbet in the
County Cavan, to where it ceases to be a lake, and
pours its waters into the sea through the river
Erne, it is fully thirty-five miles long in a bird
line. Its peculiarity consists in its extraordinary
beginnings, and the number of its islands. Its

VIEW ON UPPER LOCH ERNE.

beginnings are winding, mazy, and, on the map,
almost untraceable water ways, that twist and
turn in almost every direction through swamps
and bogs, with no attraction save for the sports-
man in pursuit of water fowl. As one approaches
Enniskillen the glories of Loch Erne commence.

There is nothing in the shape of mountains to
be seen, but they are not missed; for such is the
beauty of green round hills on both sides, and such
the wondrous number and variety of the islands,
that if there were mountains as lofty as the Alps in
view, one could hardly spare time to look at them.
The islands seem innumerable, and the shores are
so indented with bays, and the lake itself so pierced
by jutting headlands, that on sailing on Loch Erne
it is often impossible to know an island from a
peninsula, or a peninsula from an island. There
is certainly no lake in Ireland or in Great Britain
whose shores are so indented as are those of Loch
Erne. The great charm of its shores and islands
is their roundness and their greenness. They are
not low or swampy, but high and swelling, forming scenes of quiet, and, it might be said, pastoral
beauty, on which one could gaze for days and
weeks without tiring. Variety of the most striking kind is one of the peculiarities of Loch Erne.
It begins in tortuous, narrow, confused bog streams.
It then assumes its fairest aspect, studded with
innumerable islands, and sometimes so narrowed
by far-entering promontories that it is in some
places only a few hundred yards wide; but as it
spreads northwards it gets wider and wider, until
at last it is like a great inland sea, seven or eight

miles wide. If finer views may be had of Loch
Ree than of Loch Erne, in variety of scenery,
number of islands, and startling contrasts, Loch
Erne is without a rival among Irish lakes. If it
and Loch Ree had the mountains of Killarney,
Killarney might well tremble for the fame it enjoys
of being the most beautiful of Irish lakes.

Loch Erne is divided into upper and lower lakes.
The clean and thriving town of Enniskillen is situated on the straight, or narrow river, that joins
the two lakes; but it may be said that there are
not two lakes, but only one, for Enniskillen is situated where the lake narrows into what might be
called a river, but a river full of islands and bays,
just as the upper lake is. Its multitude of islands is
the charm of Loch Erne. The best authorities say
that there are a hundred and nine islands in the
lower lake, and ninety in the upper. It is a shame
that a small steam-boat does not ply regularly,
at least in summer time, from one end of this noble
sheet of water to the other. If Loch Erne, with
its marvellous variety and beauty of scenery, were
in any other European country, there would be
not one but half-a-dozen steam-boats on it. It
is strange that the inhabitants of Enniskillen do
not make an effort to establish a line of light
draft-steamers on Loch Erne that would ply on

both upper and lower lakes. A small steamer does sometimes, according to report, ply in the summer between Enniskillen and Belcek; but it does not appear that any steamer has ever navigated the waters of the upper lake, which is the more picturesque of the two. Nothing could more plainly show the backward condition of Ireland than the fact that there is no regular line of passenger steam-boats either on the Upper Shannon or on Loch Erne. Tourists, or those in search of picturesque localities, will never go to places where there is not proper accommodation for them. No matter how beautiful the scenery may be, it will not be visited by any large number of people unless they can have comforts in travelling and lodging. Switzerland attracts more rich people to visit it in summer-time than any other country in the world; but, with all its marvellous beauties of mountain, lake, and river, it would never attract the multitudes that go there every year if they did not find good travelling and good hotel accommodation. In Switzerland there are steam-boats on every lake and on every river where there are beautiful sights to be seen. There are lakes in it that are visited every year by crowds of tourists, who would find sights as beautiful on Loch Erne or on Loch Ree, and who would visit those lakes if they knew that they could find on their waters, or on their shores, the travelling comforts and the hotel comforts they find in Switzerland. It has to be frankly admitted that the reason why the beauties of Ireland are so comparatively little known is largely owing to the Irish themselves. Let them provide better accommodation for the travelling public, and Ireland will attract people who heretofore have never visited it.

Loch Erne is, as has been already stated, thirty-five miles long, and is navigable, or could with very little expense be made navigable, for light draft steam-boats all that distance. If there is anything in the shape of an aquatic excursion that could be really delightful, it would be a sail on Loch Erne, especially on the narrow waters of the upper lake, where, on the windiest day, the most nervous or the most delicate would have nothing to fear from a rough sea, as they would on Loch Ree or on Loch Dearg, where the water is sometimes very far from smooth, even in summer. On Loch Erne, especially on the upper lake, change of scene takes place every minute. It is a continual surprise of green islands, flowery promontories, swelling hills, and tortuous passages, and is on a fine summer or autumn day something to enchant even the most indifferent to the beauties of nature.

It is really deplorable that not alone the antiquities but the beauties of Ireland are not
better known to people of other countries. They
never can be known as they should be until
better facilities for knowing them are to be had.
Much has been done of late in providing better
hotel accommodation, and much more will be done
in the same line before long. Up to a few years
ago it was impossible to find an hotel where any
respectable person would like to stay in some of
the most beautiful places and amid some of the
grandest scenery of Donegal, Mayo, and Kerry;
but there are now dozens of hotels in those localities where the most fastidious will find all the
comforts they could reasonably expect. But the
internal navigation of the country is fearfully
neglected. The peculiar glory, or at least one of
the principal attractions of Ireland in a scenic
point of view, is its lakes and rivers. No other
country perhaps in the world, of equal size, has
such an abundance of lakes and rivers; but in no
country, except it may be Finnland or Central
Africa, are so few steam-boats to be seen on inland
waters. It was right to move first in the direction
of good hotel accommodation, but the next move
ought to be to provide passenger steam-boats to
ply on the great waters of such noble lakes as Loch

Erne, Loch Corrib, Loch Ree, and Loch Dearg, and on all the waters of the Upper Shannon. It is to be hoped that the present sad want of accommodation on Irish lakes and rivers will be of short duration, for the people of Ireland seem to be awakening to the knowledge not only that they have a country, but that it is one of the most beautiful countries in the world.

But Loch Erne has attractions besides its multitudinous islands, its jutting promontories, winding shores, and encircling hills. It has attractions for the antiquarian as well as for the lover of nature.

One of the most ancient of Ireland's ancient round towers stands on Devinish Island, in the upper lake. It is one of the most perfect, if it is not one of the highest, round towers in the country. There would be no use in speculating on its age, for we are generally left completely in the dark as to the time of the erection of round towers. There are many allusions to them in Irish annals, but the time of the building of them is mentioned only in a few places. The first mention of Devinish by the Four Masters is in A.D. 721, telling of the death of one of its abbots. Devinish, spelled correctly, *Daimhinis*, means "ox island." A Christian church was erected on it at a very early date, probably during the lifetime of St Patrick, for we are told

N

in ancient Annals that Molaise, who appears to
have been the first abbot of the monastery that
was there, died in 563. A Latin life of St Aeden
says that Molaise "ruled many monks in an island
in *Stagno Erne*, called Daimhinis by the Irish."
It was plundered and burnt many times by the
Danes, or some other Northmen, but almost
devastated by them in 836, and at other times; it
was burnt in 1157 and in 1360. It seems, not
like Glendaloch, Monasterboice, and many other
places that were abandoned at an early date, to
have had a church or monastery on it until the
beginning of the seventeenth century. The last
mention of it by the Four Masters is under the
year 1602.

MELLIFONT AND MONASTERBOICE

Of all the ancient remains in the County Louth connected with Christian antiquities, the ruins of Mellifont and Monasterboice are by far the most interesting and important. They are only two miles apart, and only about four from Drogheda. Starting from there both places can easily be seen in one day. There is not, even in the beautiful and picturesque county of Louth, a more beautiful location for a church or monastery than the glen in which all the remains of Mellifont is to be seen. It is not a mountain glen; there is no wildness or savageness about it; it is simply a depression in a rich lowland country, with luxuriant crops of grain and grass all round it, and a clear rushing river flowing through it,—supremely beautiful in summer-time and charming even in winter. In summer and autumn days when the hills around it are radiant with flowers of almost every hue, Mellifont even in its desolation is worth journeying a hundred miles to see.

But in spite of the beauty of the glen in which the ruins are situated, and in spite of the beauty of what remains of the ruins themselves, no right-minded person, no matter what his creed or nationality may be, can look on Mellifont without being not only pained but shocked at the desolation that has been wrought upon it, and the traces of barbarism, hate, and vandalism that stare him in the face. Why such uprooting was done in Mellifont one can easily understand, but *how* it was done is a puzzle. Here stood probably the largest and most beautiful of all Irish monasteries, but hardly a square foot of it remains overground, save the baptistry and chapter house. The walls have been levelled down to their very foundations. A building of such enormous size must have had high walls, but hardly a vestige of them remains. If they were blown up by gunpowder, the material of which they were made would remain, if it had not been carried away. Few traces of the walls are to be seen, consequently one must conclude that the greater part of the very stones of which they were built has been removed to some place of which no one now alive knows anything. A mill was built close by the river about eighty years ago, but it contains in its walls few, if any, of the stones of Mellifont. They had disappeared long before the erection of the mill. The spoilers of Mellifont were not satisfied by uprooting it, for they seem to have removed the greater part of the stones of which it was built. If Mellifont had not been so razed to the ground it would, even in its nakedness and desolation, be one of the most beautiful ecclesiastical ruins in Europe, and would attract a hundred visitors for the one it attracts now.

Mellifont is one of the few Irish ruined abbeys that has a Latin instead of an Irish name. No one seems to have yet found out what its Irish name is, or if it ever had one. Our annalists almost invariably call it the "Drogheda Monastery." The Four Masters call it "Mellifont" only once. In the "Annals of Loch Cé" it is called the "Great Monastery," for there seems no doubt that it was the largest house of the kind in Ireland. The extent of the church itself can now be distinctly traced, thanks to the excavations that were made by the Board of Works some years ago. It was 180 feet in length, with proportional breadth; the entire area covered with buildings was fully an English acre, and there were evidently many outlying buildings connected with, or forming part of the monastery, hardly a trace of which now remains. The small chapel on a hill outside of the monastery is thought to have been founded by St Bernard at the time the monastery was built. There is also about the fourth of what was once a strong castle remaining. It was evidently built after the Anglo-French invasion, but by whom seems not to be definitely known.

Mellifont was founded in 1142, and richly endowed by O'Carrol, Prince of Oriel. He was famed for his generosity and piety. The establishment was built for the Order of Cistercians. From the middle of the eleventh century to the middle of the twelfth was the time when most of the large abbeys and monasteries of Ireland were founded; and many of them, like that of Cong, were built in places that had long been occupied by smaller and plainer ecclesiastical structures like those remaining in Clonmacnois and Monasterboice. The *renaissance* of Irish ecclesiastical architecture in the eleventh and twelfth centuries is, probably, attributable to two things—the cessation of Danish plundering and the conquest of England by the Norman-French. The Danish military power in Ireland got a blow at Clontarf from which it never recovered; after that battle there were comparatively few monasteries raided, and the Irish began to erect large and costly structures in place of the small and often severely plain churches of an earlier period. The Norman-French introduced into England what is called a Romanesque ecclesiastical architecture that was much superior to that of the Saxons; and it seems certain that the Irish copied, to a certain extent, the style of building adopted by the conquerors of the Saxons; but the invasion of Ireland by those same conquerors in the latter half of the twelfth century seems to have arrested the development, not only of architecture, but of almost everything that tended to benefit the country. Most of the great churches and abbeys of Ireland were erected before Strongbow set foot in it. It is strange and hard to be understood how it came to pass that, terrible as were the ravages of the Danes, they put no stop to the development of Art in Ireland. Monasteries would be raided and churches burned by them many times within a few years, but this seems not to have put a stop either to the establishment of monasteries or the building of churches. Lord Dunraven says, in his book on ancient Irish architecture, that "it is remarkable that the fearful struggle with the Norsemen, which lasted for over two hundred years, and ended in their final defeat in 1014 [at Clontarf] does not seem to have materially paralysed the energies of the Irish nation as regards their native arts." It is, however, certain that it was not until the military power of the Norseman was broken that ecclesiastical architecture became a real glory in

Ireland. But the Anglo-French invasion seems
to have put a stop, not only to the development
of architecture, but of art of all kinds. It is a
strange fact that the heathen Dane should have
been less of a curse to Irish art than the Christian
Englishman.

The first mention of Mellifont by the Four
Masters occurs under the year 1152, when a
great synod of three thousand ecclesiastics was
held there. It was in Mellifont that the woman
whose crime is supposed to have been the cause
of the English invasion of Ireland died in the
year 1193. This was Dearvorgil, the faithless
wife of O'Ruarc, whom Moore has called "falsest
of women." It is, however, now thought by most
of those who have studied Irish history closely
that Dermott MacMorrough's relations with this
lady had nothing whatever to do with his banishment. They point out the fact that it was about
ten years after Dearvorgil had been restored to
her people that MacMorrough was banished, and
maintain that the true cause of his banishment
was in order to re-impose the tribute on the
province of Leinster, the Danes being no longer
able to assist the Leinstermen as they were wont
to do. The other provincial rulers wanted to have
the King of Leinster put out of the way, for, as

he was a warlike man, they knew he would fight to the bitter end for the protection of his province. If this version of the matter is true, it goes far to free Dermott MacMorrough from the odium that rests on his memory.

Monasterboice is one of the oldest places connected with Christianity in Ireland. Its foundation may have been as old as the time of St Patrick, for Buite, from whom it takes its name, and by whom it probably was founded, died in the year 524. There seems good reason to believe that "Buite" is the original form of the now very plentiful name "Boyd," but how Monaster Buite got twisted into Monasterboice is a mystery. The situation of this ancient place is not nearly so picturesque as that of Mellifont. There is no rushing river and no deep glen. Still the situation is good, and the country around very fine, and, like most parts of Louth, well cultivated. The peculiar glories of Monasterboice are its crosses and its round tower. There are three crosses, two in good preservation, but one was so broken that it had to be patched or fastened into solid stone work. It is most likely that it was purposely destroyed, for barbarians have done their best to cut down the great cross that stands in the same enclosure—the finest of all ancient

Irish crosses. It must have taken days for a strong man with a heavy sledge-hammer to make such a deep indentation in the hard stone of which the cross is made. It was its extreme hardness that saved it from destruction and de-facement. But hard as the stone of those crosses may be, it cannot resist the action of the elements, for the sculptures with which they are covered are now so effaced by time and weather, that they seem little more than masses of unintelligible tracings; but when those noble crosses were fresh from their makers' hands they must have been magnificent specimens of early Irish art.

The round tower of Monasterboice is one of the finest in Ireland. Its top has been broken off by lightning, but what remains of it is 110 feet in height. It must have been at least 130 feet high when perfect, which would make it one of the highest of the round towers of Ireland. The mason work is of the very best kind, although the stones are uncut, and were evidently found in the immediate neighbourhood of the tower. There is a peculiarity about this tower which is not to be seen in any other structure of the same kind—it is not quite perpendicular. The author of the great book on ancient Irish architecture, already referred to, says that "it leans to one side on the north-west, and has a very peculiar curve. Where the curve commences a distinct change of masonry is visible. When the tower was built to this height the foundation began to settle down, and when this was perceived the builders very skilfully carried up the building in a nearly vertical line, so as to counteract the tendency to lean and to preserve the centre of gravity." It seems a pity that the Board of Works does not repair this splendid structure, and put a new top of antique model on it; it would be, if perfect, the grandest of Irish round towers.

Monasterboice became a ruin many centuries before Mellifont; the latter continued to be a Catholic religious establishment down to the time of Elizabeth, but Monasterboice seems to have been abandoned in the twelfth or thirteenth century. The last notice of it, or any one connected with it, by the Four Masters, is under the year 1122, when they record the death of Fergna, "a wise priest." What caused this famous establishment to be abandoned, or at least to cease to be mentioned in Irish annals at such an early period, seems enveloped in a good deal of mystery. It was plundered more than once by the Danes, and it may be that any wooden buildings it contained were burnt by them and never re-erected, for, like

Clonmacnois, what remains of its two churches shows them to have been so small that they could not accommodate any large number of persons. Being so near Mellifont may also have led to its abandonment when the latter place became one of the greatest religious houses in Ireland. If Monasterboice was not so large as Mellifont, its abbots and professors seem to have been greater scholars and harder workers than those of the great monastery. Flann of Monasterboice was one of the most noted literary men of ancient, or rather of mediæval, Ireland, for he flourished in the eleventh century. He is considered one of the most truthful and correct of Irish annalists, and has left behind him important works that have been preserved to the present day.

The country in the vicinity of Mellifont and Monasterboice is not only very fair to look on, but highly interesting in an archæological point of view. The town of Drogheda, the nearest place to the interesting ruins treated of in this article, is the only place in their vicinity where hotel accommodation can be found. It is full of historic interest and curious remains of the past. But to the antiquarian, to one who wants to see monuments as old as the Pyramids of Egypt, the *Brogha na Bóinne,* or burghs of the Boyne, should be a great

attraction. They are the most colossal things of
the kind known to exist in any part of Europe.
One is known by the name of New Grange, and the
other is called Dowth. Both places are on the
Boyne, and only a few miles west of Drogheda.
They are enormous, partially underground caverns,
lined and roofed with great flag-stones. They are
entirely pre-historic, and are supposed to have been
used as places in which to deposit the ashes of the
dead; but their real use can hardly be more than
guessed at. It is generally thought by archæologists that they were erected by the Tuatha de
Danaans, who occupied Ireland before the Milesians; but authentic history is silent about these
gigantic structures. More than a dozen of such
structures were discovered some years ago in the
Sleeve na Caillighe Hills, near Oldcastle, in the
County Meath. They are just like those in New
Grange and Dowth, but not nearly so large. The
flat stones that form the linings of those curious
caverns or tumuli are covered with incised and
generally semi-circular markings. They bear all
the appearance of being writing of some kind, but
no 'clue to its interpretation has yet been discovered. These markings were certainly not made
for fun; neither could they have been made for
ornament, for they are *not* ornamental. There are

thousands of them, counting what are in the tumuli on the banks of the Boyne and in the same kind of places in the hills near Oldcastle. It is a pity that no one competent for it has ever tried to decipher this curious writing, for writing of some kind it certainly is. When the cuniform inscriptions on the bricks of Assyria have been interpreted, it is strange that no one has tried to find out the meaning of the writing on the stones of these Irish tumuli.

Of all the buildings for defensive purposes that
the Anglo-Normans, or, more correctly, the Anglo-
French, ever raised in Ireland, the castle of Trim
is the largest and most imposing. It has stood
many a siege, and it seems that one wing of it
has entirely disappeared; but what remains of it
still is a gigantic structure. No other Anglo-
French keep in Ireland had such an extensive
enceinte. There cannot be much less than three
acres of enclosed ground round it. The outworks
have been, to a large extent, demolished, but
enough of them remains to show that when the
castle was in repair, when its outward defences
were perfect, and before the invention of gunpowder, it could have defied the largest army
that ever Irish king or chieftain led. The place
chosen for the site of this castle is perfectly
flat. It is not on a hill. Its builder seems to
have known that its six feet thick walls would
be impregnable to any army that could be brought
against it, whether it was on a hill or in a hollow.
Its situation is very fine on the banks of the Boyne,

and in the centre of a country considered by many to be the richest land in Ireland.

Never did any people bring the art of castle-building to such perfection as did the Anglo-French; and, strange as it may appear, it was not in England they raised their finest castles,

TRIM CASTLE.

but in Wales and in Ireland. They must have known almost immediately after the battle of Hastings that no serious resistance would ever be made against them in England, but they were not so sure about Ireland and Wales; there do

not seem, therefore, to have been any castles
erected by them in England during the twelfth
and thirteenth centuries as fine as those they
erected in those parts of their dominions like
Ireland and Wales, that were not fully conquered.
Conway and Caernarvon Castles in Wales, and

TRIM CASTLE.

Trim Castle in Ireland, are thought to be the
finest they ever erected. With all the architectural
skill the Greeks and Romans possessed, it is
very doubtful if they understood the art of castle
building as well as the Norman-French did.

o

The latter built buildings that would last almost as long as the earth itself. That part of the walls of Trim Castle that yet remains is as sound as it was the day it was built; and if let alone and not overturned by an earthquake it will be as sound a thousand years hence as it is to-day.

Trim Castle was built towards the close of the twelfth century by Hugo de Lacy, the greatest castle builder ever the Anglo-French produced. He built the great castle at Clonmacnois, which has been already described. He built another fine one in Carlow, and was building the castle of Durrow, in the King's County, when a young Irishman, who had evidently come prepared to kill him, struck off his head with a blow of an axe as he was stooping down to examine the work. If Hugo de Lacy had not been killed, he would certainly have built many more castles, not only in the English Pale, but throughout Ireland. But Trim Castle was the finest structure of its kind that he ever raised. Lewis' Irish Topography says that the Castle of Trim was built in 1220. This is just such a mistake as one would expect to find in books like it, Hall's, and others of their kind, which were written by persons almost wholly unacquainted with the history of the country about

which they wrote, and entirely unacquainted with
its language and native literature. Trim Castle
must have been built before 1186, for Hugo de
Lacy was killed in that year. The same extraordinary publication says that Trim was burned
by Connor O'Melaghlin in 1108, and that over two
hundred people were burned in the monastery.
It would be interesting to know where Lewis
got his information about this matter. He did
not get it from any authentic source, for the
annals of the Four Masters, the annals of
Clonmacnois, the annals of Inisfallan, the annals
of Ulster, and the *Chronicon Scottorum* are all
silent about it.

Hugo de Lacy was undoubtedly the greatest of
the Anglo-French invaders of Ireland. Although
he was killed, he was not killed for any other
cause except that of his having been an invader;
for in spite of his castle-building propensities, he
was in no way prejudiced against the native Irish.
This is proved by his having married a daughter
of Roderick O'Connor, King of Connacht, and
nominally, but only nominally, King of Ireland.
For having done so, he was recalled from the
nominal government of Ireland with which he
had been entrusted by Henry the Second; but
Henry, probably finding that he could not get

anyone else so well fitted for the office, allowed
him to retain it. But Hugo appears to have
again given offence to Henry on account of
his leniency to the Irish lords who were
under him, and Prince John, who was afterwards King, was sent to Ireland by Henry
because Hugo did not exact any tribute from
the Irish. We are not told how he got out
of this scrape, and he was killed the next year.
He was buried in Bective Abbey, but his body
was afterwards removed to Dublin. Hugo de
Lacy seems to have been as friendly to the
Irish as it was possible for one in his position
to be, and it is almost certain that he cherished
the hope of bringing the whole island under his
rule and making himself King. It was evidently
his ambition, of which Henry appears to have been
fully aware, that caused the trouble between him
and his master. That the Irish petty kings, and
the Irish people of the time, would have accepted
the rule of a stranger who had proved himself a
strong man, is very probable, for the country was
in the very deepest slough of political confusion
and anarchy. Never, during the worst times of
Danish plundering, had Ireland been in such
a state of political chaos as she was in the
twelfth century. The usurpation of the chief

kingship by Brian Boramha was followed by a century and a half of revolution caused by those who aspired to be chief kings. O'Brians, O'Connors, O'Lochlainns, Mac Murroughs, all aspirants for the monarchy, made the island, as the Four Masters so graphically put it, "a shaking sod," and the Irish would have accepted the rule of anyone who would have saved them from themselves. It was the state of political chaos into which the country had fallen that accounts for the slight resistance that Strongbow met in Ireland. The Northmen were met by the sword, and fought for over two hundred years, until they were, if not entirely banished, at least reduced to political powerlessness; but a mere handful of invaders, whose military prowess was in no way superior to that of the Northmen, became, *de facto*, the rulers of the country in a few years after they had landed. It is more than probable that if Hugo de Lacy had lived, he would have risked a war with Henry, and have tried to make himself King of Ireland; and it is more than probable that the Irish would have willingly accepted his rule.

If de Lacy's gigantic castle had never been built in Trim, it would still be an historic place. According to the most authentic annals, St Patrick

founded a church there as early as 432, and
Bishop Erc is the first name that is mentioned
in connection with it after that of St Patrick.
Trim continued to be an important place on
account of its castle and its Church of St Mary's,
until the time of Cromwell.   It was strongly
garrisoned by the Royalists; but after hearing of
the taking of Drogheda, and the shocking massacre
committed there, the garrison surrendered.   Only
one gable of the old Church of St Mary's remains.
Judging by the great height of the part that
remains, the Church must have been a very
large one.   The exact date of the building of the
church or monastery to which the still-standing
tower or steeple belonged, is not known with
certainty, but it could not have formed part of the
original one erected in the time of St Patrick.

The most celebrated place in the immediate
vicinity of Trim is Dangan Castle, where the
Duke of Wellington is said by some to have been
born.   When Dangan passed out of the Duke's
family, it was inhabited by a person who let it
go partially to ruin.   It was burned early in the
present century, and is now an unsightly ruin.
It is curious that there should be such doubt
about the birth-place of one who made such a
figure in the world as Wellington.   Some say

he was born in Dangan Castle; some say he
was born in Dublin; but the people of Trim
maintain that he was born in their town. The
last time the writer was in Trim he was shown
the house in which the Duke was said to have been
born. He was told by a truthful and respectable
resident of Trim that the Duke's mother had
started from Dangan on her way to Dublin so
that she might have the best medical aid during her expected accouchement, but having been
taken ill when she got as far as Trim, she took
lodgings in the town, and that it was there
the Duke of Wellington was born. The exact
truth about the matter will probably never be
known.

A curious story is told in Trim about the early
boyhood of Wellington. It is said that he clomb
the still standing tower or gable of the old church
so high that he found it impossible to get down,
and was in a position of great danger. All the
ropes and ladders in the town were brought out,
but it was found impossible to get him down.
A rough tower like that at Trim might be clomb
easily enough, but it might not be so easy to
get down. The afterwards victor of Waterloo
was told that he could not be saved, and that,
if he had any will to make, to make it without

delay. He is said to have taken the announcement very coolly, and to have willed his tops, balls, and other playthings to the boys that were his favourites, and not to have shed a tear or shown any fear whatever. After having been many hours in his dangerous and far from comfortable situation, he was at length, and with great difficulty, rescued.

The country round Trim is most interesting and full of ruined fanes. The church of Trim was believed to contain an image or picture of the Virgin, at which we are told many and extraordinary miracles were performed. Trim was a sort of Irish Lourdes in the middle ages, to which the sick and suffering used to go in multitudes. There was also the Abbey of Newtown, the ruins of which still stand on the banks of the Boyne close by Trim. It was founded in the year 1206 by Simon Rochefort, Bishop of Meath, the first Englishman that is known to have had so high an ecclesiastical position in Ireland after the invasion. The ruins of Bective Abbey are only a few miles up the river from Trim, in a beautiful situation on the banks of the "clear, bright Boyne," as the old Gaelic poets loved to call it. Bective was founded for the Cistercian order by O'Melachlinn, King of Meath, about the middle of the twelfth century. It is a beautiful ruin, and in a beautiful locality.

There is, perhaps, no part of Ireland more interesting to the antiquarian, the historian, or the lover of rich landscapes than the valley of the Boyne. That little stream is the most historic waterway in Ireland. Its name occurs oftener in Irish history and legend than that of any other river. On its banks are to be seen the pre-historic tumuli of New Grange and Dowth, the oldest monuments of pre-historic civilisation that have yet been discovered on Irish soil. The Boyne may be said to be the river of Tara, for it flows almost at the foot of that hill so celebrated in Irish history, legend, and song.

IT is doubtful if there is in Ireland—there certainly is not in the province of Connacht—a more interesting ruin than Cong Abbey. Its situation is beautiful, between two great lakes, with a background of some of the wildest and ruggedest mountains in Ireland. It would be hard to conceive of a place more suited for a life of religious meditation than this venerable pile, into which he who is called Ireland's last chief king retired to bewail his sins and lament for the power that his own pusillanimity and carelessness had allowed to pass away from him and his family for ever. If Roderick O'Connor was the last of Ireland's monarchs, he was also one of her worst. History hardly tells of a good act of his except the endowment of the Abbey of Cong; and the greater the light is that is thrown on the history of Ireland by the translation of her ancient annals, the weaker and more imbecile the character of Roderick appears, and the more just and merited that which Moore says of him in his history of Ireland:—"The only

feeling the name [of Roderick] awakens is that
of pity for the doomed country which at such a
crisis of its fortunes, when honour, safety, independence, and national existence were all at
stake, was cursed for the crowning of its evil
destiny with a ruler and leader so entirely unworthy of his high calling." If the Anglo-French
invasion of Ireland had occurred in the reign of
his brave and warlike father, Turloch, one of the
greatest of those who claimed the chief sovereignty of Ireland, the invaders would almost
certainly have been all killed within a month
after they landed, and the subsequent history of
Ireland would probably be very different from
what it has been.

Irish annals tell us that the first religious
establishment in Cong was founded by St
Fechin in the year 624; but John O'Donovan
says in a note in his translation of the Four
Masters that Roderick O'Connor founded and
endowed the Abbey of Cong. That a religious
house of some kind was founded in it by St
Fechin there can be no doubt at all, for up
to a recent period it was known as Cunga
Fechin, or Cong of Fechin. O'Donovan may
have meant that Roderick O'Connor endowed
and founded the abbey, the remains of which

exist at present, for not a vestige of the original building founded by St Fechin remains. It was, like most of the very early churches and religious houses of ancient Ireland, built entirely of wood, and has consequently long ago disappeared. Cong was originally a bishopric. There were five bishoprics in the province of Connacht— namely, Tuam, Killala, Clonfert, Ardcharne, and Cong. The Synod that settled the question of the bishoprics of Connacht met at Rathbrassil, in what is now the Queen's County, in 1010. The abbey, the remains of which still exist, was founded in 1128 by the Augustinians, during the reign of Roderick O'Connor's heroic father, Turloch. Roderick subsequently endowed it, and ended his days in it. It is an interesting and suggestive fact that most of the great religious establishments of Ireland were not only founded but built in the material that now remains of them before the Anglo-French invasion, showing clearly that that event put a stop to almost everything that could be called progress. The invaders, although professing the same faith as the invaded, were much more anxious to build castles than churches. There was hardly a castle in Ireland before the time of Strongbow. This was not caused by ignorance of the art of building

among the Irish, for some of the round towers
and churches erected long before the time of
Strongbow are as perfect specimens of architecture as were erected in any country at the same
period.   The native Irish king, or chief, was
contented with a wooden house surrounded by
an embankment, capped with a palisade of wood;
but the Norman raised mighty edifices of stone
to protect him from the wrath of those he had
robbed.

Cong Abbey is a large building nearly 150 feet
in length.   Few of the ancient churches of Ireland
are any longer, and many of them are not nearly so
long.   It would be a mistake to say that the ruins
at Cong are in a good state of preservation, for
traces of violence and vandalism are apparent
almost everywhere on them.   The whole place
has a terribly dilapidated look.   It has been
said that only for ivy and the Guinnesses the
Abbey of Cong would have tumbled down long
ago.   It is true that ivy has prevented great
masses of masonry from falling; and it is true
that the late Sir Benjamin Guinness did a good
deal of mending on the old walls.   But it was
before his time, when religious intolerance was
worse than it is at present, that Cong Abbey
was mutilated and defaced.   It is sad to know

that there is hardly an old religious edifice in Ireland that has not suffered from sectarian animosity. The ruins of Mellifont, near Drogheda, have been torn up from their foundations, so that hardly a trace of that once magnificent abbey now remains except the crypts and the vast walls and fosses by which it was surrounded. Ruthless vandals tried their best with sledges and hammers to overthrow the great cross of Monasterboice in Louth, but the stone of which it consists was too hard for them, for they only succeeded in mutilating what they could not destroy.

In its present dilapidated condition it is hardly possible to form a correct idea of what Cong Abbey was in the days of its splendour. It is almost impossible, also, to form an exact idea of its general plan, for many comparatively modern additions have evidently been made to it. Its having been used as a burying place within recent times has, as the same thing has done at Clonmacnois, sadly interfered with its picturesqueness. But, as at Mellifont, "enough of its glory remains" to show that it must have been a building of exquisite beauty. Some of its floral capitals carved on limestone are as fine specimens of the carver's art as can be found anywhere in the world. Both Sir William Wilde and Doctor Petrie agree in this. There was probably no abbey in Ireland that contained more beautiful specimens of the carver's art than Cong. Vast numbers of its sculptured stones have been defaced by vandalism or carried away to build walls or out-houses. It is not easy to know what was the exact extent of the gardens or mensal grounds of the abbey, for the walls that enclosed them cannot be fully traced, and are not intact like the walls around the Abbey of Boyle in the County Roscommon. The Abbey of Cong seems to have been the great depository for the precious things of the province of Connacht. The Order of Augustinians, to whom it belonged, was very rich, and had vast possessions in the province, and it would seem that no abbey in it was as rich as that of Cong. In it were kept deeds, books, records, and many other precious things, all of which have disappeared save the marvellously beautiful cross now to be seen in the Dublin Museum, and which artists and connoisseurs have pronounced to be "the finest piece of metal work of its age to be found in Europe." It is known from the Gaelic inscription on the Cross of Cong that it was made in Roscommon, for the name of the maker is identified with that town. The fact of such a priceless relic and such a gem of art having been kept in the Abbey of Cong shows that it was considered to be the most important and most secure place in the province. The Cross of Cong was supposed to be formed from part of the real cross. The Irish inscription on it is perfectly legible, and can be easily understood by any one who knows the modern language. The name of the maker is on it, and also that of Turloch O'Connor, who claimed to be chief King of Ireland, and for whom it was made in the year 1123.

The Abbey of Cong was never plundered by the Danes; if it was, no record of its having been plundered is to be found in the Annals of the Four Masters, or in the Annals of Loch Key. This fact of Cong not having suffered from the Danes would seem to show that it did not contain much wealth during the ninth and tenth centuries, when the maraudings of the Norsemen were at their worst. If the Abbey of Cong was worth plundering, it is hard to conceive how it could have been spared by them. It is probable that the church founded there by St Fechin was very small, and that the establishment became important only when the O'Connor family rose to prominence in the province, for it was richly

CROSS OF CONG.

P

endowed by Turloch and by Roderick O'Connor, both of whom claimed to be chief kings of Ireland.

None of our ancient seats of piety and learning will repay a visit better than Cong. In it and around it there is a great deal to interest the antiquarian, the tourist, and the lover of Nature. The neck of land that lies between Loch Corrib and Loch Mask is one of the most curious, varied, and beautiful spots in Ireland. It has rushing, limpid rivers above, and boiling, roaring ones below. The whole country in the vicinity of Cong seems to be honeycombed by subterranean waters. There is probably as much running water underground and overground in the narrow strip of country between Loch Corrib and Loch Mask as would turn all the grist mills in Ireland, but unfortunately there is hardly a wheel moved by it.

There is much in the vicinity of Cong, outside of its glorious old abbey, to interest both the antiquarian and the tourist. It was close to it that the greatest battle history records as having been fought on Irish soil took place—namely, that of Moy Tuireadh, between the Firbolgs and the Tuatha de Danaans, a full account of which will be found in Sir William Wilde's charming

book "Loch Corrib," which should be read by
every one who desires to visit Cong or its
vicinity.

Cong is very nearly on the road to Connemara,
which, with the exception of parts of Donegal,
is the wildest, most savage, and most extraordinary part of Ireland. Those who want to
see all the wildness of Connemara, its chaotic
mountains, its innumerable lakes, far-entering
bays, and illimitable bogs, should drive from Cong,
or from Oughterard to Clifden, and go from there
to Galway by rail. Whoever travels that route
will see some of the most charming as well as
some of the most terrific scenery in Ireland. He
will see more lakes than can be found on an
area of equal size in any part of the known
world. If the visit is made when the heath is
in full bloom, he will have such a world of
flowers to feast his eyes on as can hardly be
seen anywhere else, not even in Ireland.

Loch Corrib, at the head of which Cong is
situated, is one of the great lakes of Ireland.
The traveller going to Cong sails up it from
Galway. There is not very much of antiquarian
interest on its shores or on its islands, save the
ruins of *Caisleán na Ceirce*, or the Hen's Castle.
They are on a promontory on the lake. It is

not a very old building, being probably of the fourteenth century, and was built, it is supposed, by one of the O'Flahertics.

There are the ruins of what antiquarians think are those of one of the oldest churches ever erected in Ireland, on the bleak island of Incha-goile. There are also the ruins of another church on the same island; but judging from the extremely archaic architecture of the one first mentioned, it must be many centuries older than the other. Both churches must have been very small.

But although the lower part of Loch Corrib cannot boast of much scenic beauty, its upper part is magnificent. It thrusts its sinuous arms up into the wildest recesses of the Joyce Country, and among mountains of fantastic forms. The Joyce Country, *Duthaigh Sheoghach* in Gaelic, has ever been remarkable for the gigantic size of its men. There have been scores of Joyces who were from six feet four to six feet six in height, and stout in proportion. There are still some of its men of immense size. It is said that not so very long ago a giant Joyce was going home from a fair or market, and that a faction of ten men who were not on perfectly friendly terms with him, followed him to beat or perhaps kill him. Joyce had no weapons or means of defence of any kind, so he unyoked the horse from the cart or dray on which he was riding, tore it to pieces, armed himself with one of its shafts as a "shillelagh," and awaited his enemies; but they seem not to have liked being hit with the shaft of a cart and retreated. Those who like can believe or not believe this story. It is given as the writer heard it from a very respectable gentleman who knew Joyce.

THIS is another of the great lakes of Ireland. It is over twenty miles long and between two and three miles in average breadth. It is really curious that a small island like Ireland should have so many immense lakes in it. There is, probably, no other country in the world of the same size—there is certainly no island of the same size—on which so much fresh water is to be found. It would seem as if nature intended Ireland for a continent, and not for an island, by giving it lakes so entirely disproportioned to its size.

Loch Derg, anciently called Deirgdheirc, and at present pronounced Dharrig by the peasantry, would be the most beautiful of all the great lakes of Ireland if its islands were as numerous as those of Loch Erne, or even of Loch Ree. It has the defect that almost all lakes have whose shores are mountainous or hilly. Want of islands is the great drawback to the picturesqueness of most of the Scotch lakes and those of the north of England. A few islands do not add much to the beauty of a lake. There must be plenty of them to produce full effect. The few islands in Loch Lomond, because they are so few, hardly add to its beauty. The islands in Loch Derg are very few, and the most picturesque of them are so near the shore that they seem part of it to the voyager on the lake. There is one very large island, Illaunmore—the great island, as its name signifies—but it does not add very much to the scenic attractions. The charms of Loch Derg are its semi-mountainous shores. It would be incorrect to call the bold hills on either side of the lake mountains, for very few of them reach an altitude of more than a thousand feet; but they are most graceful in their outlines, and are, for the most part, covered with luxuriant grass up to their very summits. The lake is by no means straight; its shores are tortuous and full of indentations, so that there is a good deal of change of scene when sailing on it. But if the tourist or traveller who wishes to sail on Loch Derg is not what is usually called a "good sailor," he should consult the barometer before he goes on to this great lake, for sometimes, when the south-west wind sweeps up its twenty or twenty-five miles of water, a sea almost worthy of the Channel will sometimes rise in a very short time. Many a

sea-sick passenger used to be seen in the good
times long ago on Loch Derg, when large side-
wheel passenger boats used to run regularly
between Athlone and Killaloe. Those boats were
large enough to carry over a hundred passengers
without being in the least crowded, and the
cabins were large enough to accommodate fifty
people at dinner. A trip from Athlone to Killaloe
on a fast boat would, on a fine summer day, be
one of the most enjoyable things in the way of
an excursion by water that can be imagined.
It is over thirty years since the writer experienced
the pleasure of it, and the remembrance of its
enjoyableness haunts him still. The shores of
Loch Derg are much wilder than the shores of
Loch Erne or Loch Ree. Very few houses, and
nothing that could be called a town, can be seen
through the whole twenty-five miles of the lake.
The hills that bound it both on the Munster
and on the Connacht sides are almost altogether
grass land, and very little cultivation is therefore
to be seen. But the bold, winding shores and
the green hills form a landscape of a very striking
kind, and there are many who maintain that the
scenery of Loch Derg is finer than that of Loch
Ree. Both lakes are magnificent sheets of water,
and environed with a fair and goodly country;

and were they anywhere else but in Ireland, their waters would be the highway for dozens of steamers, while at present they are almost deserted, and may be said to be

> "As lone and silent
> As the great waters of some desert land."

Loch Derg is full of interest for the antiquarian, especially its lower part. One of the most ancient and important ecclesiastical establishments of ancient Ireland, Iniscealtra, the island of the churches, is on its western shore, close to the land, separated from it only by about a quarter of a mile of water. Iniscealtra was one of the most important places of its kind in the south of Ireland. It was founded by St Cainin certainly not later than the end of the sixth or beginning of the seventh century, for he died in 653. John O'Donovan in his unpublished letters says that he is represented in ancient Irish literature as "A very holy man, a despiser of the world, and an inexorable chastiser of the flesh. He is said to have been author of commentaries on the Psalms. He was buried in Iniscealtra." There is a fine round tower in Iniscealtra which is traditionally supposed to have been built by St Senanus. It is eighty feet in height, and in fairly good preservation, but it wants the top. The ruins of St Cainin's

Church show it to have been a small building.
There are the ruins of two other churches on the
island, one called St Mary's and the other St
Michael's. The establishments on Iniscealtra are
of very great antiquity. It is first mentioned in
the Annals of the Four Masters under the year
548, recording the death of St Colam in the island.
The oldest church in it was dedicated to St Cainin,
who was evidently the founder of the place, and
the first who sought it as a retreat. He is said to
have lived for a long time in a solitary cell, until
the fame for holiness he acquired brought an
immense number of disciples, for whom he erected
a noble monastery - in the island, which afterwards
became famous. The ruins of St Cainin's Church
prove that it must have been a very beautiful
building. It was thought by Petric and other
antiquarians that it and the very beautiful one of
Killaloe were erected during the short time in
the tenth . and eleventh centuries when Brian
Boramha and Malachy the Second, by their victories over the Danes, gave the country some rest
from the plunderings of those marauders.

At the extreme lower end of Loch Derg is the
small but ancient town of Killaloe. Its real name
is Cill Dalua, it was called after an ecclesiastic of
the name of Dalua, sometimes written Malua, who

lived in the sixth century. He placed his disciple, Flannan, over the church. He was made Bishop of Killaloe in the seventh century. The church is known generally as St Flannan's. The Earl of Dunraven, speaking of the beauty of the ruins of this church and the buildings attached to it, says, "These ancient buildings are on a wooded hill which slopes in a gentle incline down to the brink of the Shannon. The cathedral and small stone-roofed church stand side by side, and the walls of the latter are thickly covered with ivy. Nothing can be more impressive than the aspect of this venerable and simple building, surrounded by majestic trees, and hidden in deep shadows of thick foliage. A solemn mystery seems to envelop its ancient walls, and the silence is only broken by the sound of the river that rolls its great volume of water along the base of the hill on which it stands."

But the most historic and probably the most interesting thing about Killaloe is the site of King Brian's palace of Kincora, a place so famed in history and song. Perhaps it will be better to let such a famous man on Irish history and archaeology as O'Donovan tell about Kincora. He says in his unpublished letters while on the Ordnance Survey: "On the summit of the hill opposite the bridge of

Killaloe stood Brian Boramha's palace of Kincora, but not a trace of it is now visible. It must have extended from the verge of the hill over the Shannon, to where the present Roman Catholic chapel stands. I fear that it will be impracticable to show its site on the Ordnance map, as no field works are visible. Of the history of the palace of Kincora little or nothing is known, but from the few references to it we occasionally find, we may safely infer that it was first erected by Brian, *Imperator Scottorum*, and that it was not more than two centuries inhabited by his successors. Kincora was demolished in 1088 by Donnell MacLachlin, king of Aileach (Ulster), and we are told that he took 160 hostages consisting of Danes and Irish." Kincora must have been rebuilt after it was demolished by MacLachlin, for we are told in the Annals of the Four Masters that in 1107 Kincora and Cashel were burned by lightning, and sixty vats of metheglin and beer were destroyed; but it must have been again rebuilt, for the same annals say that in 1118 Turloch O'Connor (King of Connacht), at the head of a great army of Connacht-men, burned Kincora and hurled it, both stones and timber, into the Shannon. Kincora was, like all dwelling-places in those times, built almost entirely of wood; and it is hardly to be wondered at that after having been burned so often by man and by the elements, no vestige of it should remain. It has been completely wiped out.

A description of Kincora would hardly be complete without giving MacLiag's Lament for it, translated by Clarence Mongan. MacLiag was chief poet and secretary to Brian Boramha. The poem is little known even in Ireland; to the English reader it will be absolutely new. The writer gives two prime reasons for reproducing it; one, because it is such a very fine poem; and the other, because it has heretofore never been correctly given.

MacLiag's Lament for Kincora.

" Where, oh Kincora, is Brian the Great ?
    And where is the beauty that once was thine ?
  Oh where are the princes and nobles that sate
    At the feasts in thy halls and drank the red wine,
                    Where, oh Kincora ?

" Where, oh Kincora, are thy valorous lords,
    Oh whither, thou Hospitable, are they gone ?
  Oh where the Dalcassians of cleaving swords,
    And where are the heroes that Brian led on,
                    Where, oh Kincora ?

" And where is Morough, descendant of kings,
    Defeater of hundreds, the daringly brave,
  Who set but light store on jewels and rings,
    Who swam down the torrent and laughed at the wave,
                    Where, oh Kincora ?

" And where is Donagh, King Brian's brave son,
  And where is Conaing, the beautiful chief,
And Cian and Corc ? alas, they are gone !
  They have left me this night all alone in my grief,
                        Alone, oh Kincora !

" And where are the chiefs with whom Brian went forth,
  The ne'er vanquished sons of Evin the Brave,
The great King of Eogh'nacht,* renowned for his
    worth,
  And Baskin's great host from the western wave,
                        Where, oh Kincora ?

" And where is Duvlann of the swift-footed steeds,
  And where is Cian who was son of Molloy,
And where is King Lonergan, the fame of whose
    deeds
  In the red battle-field, no time can destroy ?
                        Where, oh Kincora ?

" And where is the youth of majestic height,
  The faith-keeping prince of the Scotts ?† even he,
As wide as his fame was, as great as his might,
  Was tributary, oh Kincora, to thee,
                        To thee, oh Kincora !

* The Eoghanachts were the posterity of Eoghan Mór,
King of Munster in the third century. Eoghanacht meant a
people of Munster, descendants of Eoghan; and Connacht,
the descendants of Conn,—usually known as Conn of the
Hundred Battles, most of which were fought against Eoghan.

† Prince of Scotts; this was evidently the great Steward,
or *mór maor* of Lennox, who aided the Irish at the battle of
Clontarf, and was killed there.

" They are gone, those heroes of royal birth,
     Who plundered no churches and broke no trust
'Tis weary for me to be living on earth
     When they, oh Kincora, lie low in the dust.
               Low, oh Kincora !

" Oh never again will princes appear
     To rival Dalcassians of cleaving swords !
I can ne'er dream of meeting afar or near,
     In the east or the west, such heroes and lords,
               Never, Kincora !

" Oh dear are the images mem'ry calls up
     Of Brian Boru,* how he never would miss
To give me at banquet the first bright cup,—
     Oh, why did he heap on me honour like this,
               Why, oh Kincora ?

" I am MacLiag, and my home's on the lake ;
     And oft to that palace whose beauty has fled
Came Brian to ask me,—I went for his sake ;—
     Oh my grief ! that I live when Brian is dead !
               Dead, oh Kincora !"

So far the demolished palace of Brian, and the writer, like Brian himself, "returns to Kincora no more."

No lover of the beauties of nature should be on this part of the Shannon and not visit the great rapids of Doonass. They are only about ten miles

---

* This is an incorrect form of the word. It is *Boramha* in the most correct ancient manuscripts, and is a word of three syllables—Borava. It means "of the tribute."

below Killaloe. If seen when the river is full
they are the grandest thing of their kind in the
British Isles. The Shannon here looks like a
continental river, containing ordinarily a volume
of water greater than any river in France. The
country round Doonass, though flat, is superlatively
beautiful. The limpid, rushing river flows on
among meadows and pastures of the brightest
verdure, adorned with stately trees, and bright
in summer-time with innumerable flowers. There
is nothing terrible or awe-inspiring about Doonass.
It is quiet and peaceful in the true sense of the
word. Even the great rushing river, as it glides
down the gentle slope of the rapids, makes no
noise except a deep, musical murmur that would
lull to sleep rather than startle. The rapids of
Doonass form a scene so incomparably lovely, and
so unlike anything to be seen in Great Britain,
or to be seen in any other part of Ireland, that it
is a wonder they are not better known. They can
be reached best from Limerick, being not over three
miles from that city. One of the most curious
things about those grand and beautiful rapids, is
the almost total ignorance which exists about
them, not only in Great Britain, but in Ireland
itself. If they were situated on a wild, hard-to-
be-got-at part of the Shannon, the general ignor-

Q

ance that exists about them among seekers after the beautiful, would not excite so much wonder. A scene of such great beauty and uniqueness, so near a fine and interesting city like Limerick, to be so little known to those who go so far in search of the beautiful, shows how much the world at large, and even the Irish themselves, have to learn about Ireland. If the rapids of Doonass were in England, or even in the United States, there would be not only one, but perhaps three or four hotels on their banks,—hotels which would be full of guests every summer. Let us hope that the beauties of this charming place will be soon better known.

HOLYCROSS ABBEY

THE situation of this abbey, like most places of its kind in Ireland, is very beautiful—on the banks of the gentle-flowing Suir, and surrounded by a fine fertile country. Holycross is thought to have been, with the exception of Mellifont, the largest of the ancient churches of Ireland. There is some doubt as to the exact time of its foundation—some authorities say the year 1182, and others 1208. The probability is that both dates may, in a certain sense, be correct. It may have been begun to be built in 1182, and may not have been finished before 1208. Although founded after the Anglo-French invasion, it was a purely Irish institution, for all authorities say that it was founded by Donagh Cairbreach O'Brian, King of Munster, and that it was founded on account of his having obtained what was believed to be a piece of the cross on which Christ suffered. It is called in Irish annals *Mainister na croiche naoimhe*, or Monastery of the Holy Cross. This relic is said, on good authority, to be at present in the keeping of the nuns of the Presentation Order at Black Rock, near Cork. O'Brian, the founder of the Church, endowed it with a great tract of land, so that it was for many centuries one of the most important places of its kind, not only in the province of Munster, but in Ireland.

Holycross is two miles from the neat and thriv-

HOLYCROSS ABBEY.

ing town of Thurles, in the County Tipperary. Unlike so many ruined shrines of former days, and especially unlike Mellifont in the County Louth, most of the walls of Holycross still remain. The existing ruins show it to have been a large church. Its length is 130 feet; the nave is 58 by 49 feet.

The entire ruins are very beautiful and impressive, and their situation on the banks of the Suir, amid as fine pastoral scenery as can be found in the fine county of Tipperary, make them well worth a visit. Holycross was founded for the Cistercian order, and remained in undamaged condition until the suppression of monasteries in the latter part of the seventeenth century. It appears that it lost its distinctively Irish character soon after English domination became established in Ireland, for in 1267 it was subjected by the abbot of Clairveaux to the abbey of Furness in England. It is the opinion of many antiquarians and judges of ecclesiastical structures that many additions and alterations were made to and in the abbey, and some of them in comparatively recent times. Some judges of church architecture have been loud in their praise of the beauties of the ruins of Holycross, while others have expressed their disappointment.

Here is the testimony of O'Donovan, one of the greatest of Irish antiquarians, on the subject: "The ruins of this abbey entirely disappointed my expectations. The architecture of the choir and side chapel is indeed truly beautiful, but they are not lofty, but the nave and side aisles are contemptible. I am certain, however, that this newer part of the abbey is not more than four centuries old."

The sepulchral monument that was erected to the memory of Elizabeth, daughter of Gerald, Earl of Kildare, who died about the year 1400, is considered one of the most chaste, remarkable, and beautiful things of its kind in Ireland. If nothing remained of Holycross but this remarkable monument, it would be well worth a visit.

There is not so much historical interest connected with Holycross as there is with smaller establishments of its kind throughout Ireland. It was founded too late to be plundered by the Danes, and in all the troublesome times between its foundation and the time when it was abandoned, it does not seem to have been plundered or burned, neither do the vandals seem to have damaged or defaced it much. It is a beautiful and impressive ruin that will for a long time to come attract the notice of lovers of the abandoned fanes that are to be found in almost every parish of Ireland—the land that is richer in ruins than perhaps any other country in the world, Egypt alone excepted.

DUNLUCE CASTLE

If Cashel is the most remarkable ecclesiastical ruin in Ireland owing to its situation, Dunluce Castle is, for the same reason, the most remarkable military one. Cashel has, however, the advantage of being remarkable from whatever side it is looked at; but Dunluce is remarkable only when seen from the sea, or from the strand from which the rock the ruins rest on rises. From the road that goes along the shore, Dunluce looks absolutely disappointing, because the road is as high, apparently somewhat higher, than the castle itself. But seen from a boat on the sea under it, or from the base of the cliffs on which the road to it runs, it forms the grandest and most imposing sight of a Viking's ruined stronghold that is to be seen anywhere in Europe. The rock on which the ruins stand rises sheer from the sea to the height of over a hundred feet. Before the castle was built on it, the rock was completely isolated, and must have been an island, standing about thirty feet from the mainland. Across the profound gulf that separated the rock from the land, a mighty bridge of solid masonry has been erected, over which all who enter the castle must pass. This bridge is only about twenty inches wide, and few, except masons, or those who are accustomed to ascend heights, would care to cross it, for there is not, or at least there was not in

DUNLUCE CASTLE.

1873, a rope, railing, or protection of any kind for those who wanted to visit the ruins of the castle. No one but such as have steady nerves and good heads should think of crossing this bridge, for a fall from it would mean certain death on the jagged rocks more than a hundred feet below.

The first thing that strikes one after examining the ruins is the unusual thinness of the walls. They are no thicker than those of a modern stone-built house. The reason of this is easily under-stood; for when the castle was built, which must have been before cannons were so perfected that they could be used for battering down buildings, it was absolutely impregnable, as no battering-ram, or mediæval siege-engine, could by any pos-sibility approach near enough to the walls to be used against them. There was, therefore, no neces-sity that the walls should be thick. The space on the top of the rock is entirely covered with the ruins of the castle. The walls rise up sheer from the most outward margins of the rock. On look-ing out from one of the narrow windows the sea is straight below one. When the castle was in-habited its inmates must have had an awful experi-ence during the storms that so often sweep over the wild west and north coast of Ireland, when the giant waves of the stormiest ocean in the world beat against the rock on which the ruins stand. If such a place was secure against the assaults of men, it was not secure against the fury of the elements; and it would seem that some of the cliff did at one time give way, for there are some gaps in the walls that appear to have been caused

by rock, upon which they were built, having given
way.

The Giant's Causeway and Dunseverick Castle
are both in the immediate vicinity of Dunluce,
only a few miles west of it; both are well worth
seeing; but nothing on all that magnificent, iron-
bound, cliff-guarded coast of Antrim can compare
in interest with Dunluce. The isolated, almost
sea-surrounded rock on which it stands, the great
bridge that connects it with the mainland, the
narrow and dangerous footpath overlooking horrible depths, and over which the castle can only
be entered, make it one of the grandest and most
suggestive ruins in the world. Dunluce is a revela-
tion. It shows, perched on its storm-beaten, once
impregnable rock, the awful savagery of the time
when might was the only law recognised by
humanity; and that only a few centuries ago life
and property were no safer in Christendom than
they are to-day in the Soudan.

The name Dunluce is a combination of the two
most generally used Irish words to express a military stronghold *dun* and *lios,* and may be translated "strong fort"; and strong it must have
been in olden times, when cannons were either
unknown altogether, or principally remarkable for
the noise they made, and the greater danger they

were to those who used them than to those they were used against. The name of this place is spelled *Dúnlis* or *Dúnlios* in ancient annals. The earliest mention of it by the Four Masters, and in the "Annals of Loch Key," is under the year 1513. It does not appear to be mentioned in any of the other Irish annals, unless it is mentioned in the "Annals of Ulster"; but as they have been as yet translated only down to the year 1375, the question cannot be yet decided.

It is remarkable that so little is known about the early history of such a remarkable place as Dunluce Castle. No trustworthy statement as to when and by whom it was built has, so far, come to light. It was in the possession of the Mac Quillins, spelled *Mac Uidhlin* by the Four Masters, in 1513. It then, by conquest or in some other way, passed into the hands of Sorley Boy, one of the Scotch McDonnells, who kept it until 1584, when it was besieged and taken by Sir John Perrott, Lord Chief Justice of Ireland. Fifty thousand cows, and all his land in Antrim County, of which he had an immense quantity, were taken from Sorley Boy. But he repaired to Dublin, made his submission to Queen Elizabeth, and was reinstated in his possessions in Antrim, but we are not told if he got back his cows. Dunluce seems to have become a ruin early in the seventeenth century, and is becoming more ruined every day, for it is not in the nature of things that the sea is not gradually undermining and weakening the rock on which the ruins stand, exposed as it is to the wrath of the stormiest ocean probably in the world. It is said that long before Dunluce was abandoned, the kitchen and its staff of cooks were swallowed up on a night of a fearful gale of wind. This could only have happened by part of the rock foundations of the castle having been washed away by the sea. The gap in one part of the walls would seem to indicate that some such catastrophe did occur.

Dunluce must have been built before the invention of what is now known as artillery. It is not possible to tell by the style of its architecture in what century it was built, for there was practically no change in the architecture of Irish castles for nearly four centuries. The art of castle-building was just as well understood in the twelfth century as in the fourteenth. Those who pretend to be able to tell within a century of the time when a castle was built, by examining its masonry and architecture, draw greatly on their imaginations. If Dunluce was built after artillery had become so perfected that castles could be destroyed by it at half a mile, or even a quarter of a mile distant, those who built Dunluce were fools, for guns could be brought within fifty yards of it. If it was built to resist artillery, the walls would have been made three times as thick as they are. It was evidently built before artillery began to be used for battering down walls. It must, therefore, have been built before the year 1400, for even at that early date the principal use that was made of artillery was for battering down walls. Half a dozen shots from the very rude and imperfect artillery of the date mentioned would have made a heap of ruins of the thin walls of Dunluce Castle.

BOYLE ABBEY

THERE are very few of the once great abbeys of Ireland of which so little is generally known to the public as of Boyle Abbey. One reason of this may be the remoteness of its situation, and its invisibleness from the town of Boyle. It is not on the track of tourists, and is in a rather uninteresting part of the country in a scenic point of view. Besides, the Abbey is not in the town of Boyle, but over quarter of a mile from it, on a road not so much frequented as some others in the locality. It is a wonder that more is not known about this noble ruin. It may not be so interesting in its architecture as Holycross, or so striking in its situation as Cashel, but it is, nevertheless, one of the finest ecclesiastical ruins in Ireland.

If the country round Boyle Abbey cannot be said to be very interesting or beautiful, the place where the ruins stand is charming. They rise from the banks of the Boyle river, the first large tributary of the Shannon. The river rushes under the very walls of the monastery with a rapid current, and at its highest flood it is generally as clear as crystal, for it rises in, or at least flows through, Loch Ui Gara, which is only a few miles from Boyle, and its waters are filtered in that lake before they reach Boyle. And here it may not be out of place to say that the generally clear waters of most of the rivers of Ireland add greatly to the beauty of its scenery. Scotch rivers are also generally clear,

BOYLE ABBEY.

and the reason they are clear is the reason why the Irish rivers are clear, and that is, because they are filtered in the lakes through which they generally flow. A limpid river is one of the most beautiful things in nature, but a river of dirty water would not be beautiful if it flowed through the Garden of Eden. Almost all rivers that are not filtered by passing through lakes are sure to be dirty. For this reason the St Lawrence may be said to be the only one of the great American rivers the waters of which are clear. To know what an abomination a river of dirty water is, one should see the Missouri. The river that rushes past the ruins of Boyle Monastery is not only clear but limpid. Its pure, rushing waters are one of the principal attractions in the vicinity of the ruins.

The ruins of Boyle Abbey are very fine. The monastery was a large one, one of the largest in Ireland, and was surrounded on almost every side with extensive gardens. The walls of many of those gardens still remain, and seem as sound as they were when first built. The ruins of the Monastery, and the ruins of its adjoining buildings, are covered with the most luxuriant growth of ivy to be seen on any ruins in Ireland. The thickness of its stems, and the size and deep green of its leaves, are remarkable. This extraordinary growth of ivy must eventually tumble down the walls. It may preserve them for a time, but will destroy them in the long run. But without its ivy and its limpid river, the ruined Monastery of Boyle, grand and interesting as it is, would lose a great deal of its attractions.

The ruins of the great church of Boyle, like the
ruins of Cashel, and like the historic hill of Tara,
have been spoiled by the erection of modern buildings near them. Some parson has erected here a
new, intensely vulgar gimcrack house that almost
touches the hoary ruins, it is so close to them. It
entirely spoils their effect, and would disgust any
one with any veneration for the past. In no other
country, perhaps, in the world has the want of
respect for the antique been more manifest among
the masses than in Ireland. In no other country
have so many monuments of the past been more
wantonly destroyed, more defaced, and less respected. If it had not been for the care exercised
by the Board of Works, during the last thirty years,
most of the ruins of Ireland would now be either
entirely uprooted, or so marred, like the Rock of
Cashel, or the Monastery of Boyle, by the erection
of new buildings in their vicinity, that they would
have little attraction for any one in whose soul
there remained the slightest reverence for the past.
There are, however, unmistakable signs that more
patriotic and enlightened ideas about their country,
and everything relating to it, are rapidly gaining
ground among all classes of the Irish people, but
especially among the more educated. Irish history,
Irish antiquities, and even the Irish language get

more of the attention of the upper and middle classes in Ireland now than they ever got before. It seems almost a certainty that the ancient monument-defacing epoch has passed, or is rapidly passing away from a country to which it has been a disgrace so long. It is not enough that the Board of Works should continue to do the good work it has been doing for the last quarter of a century in the preservation of our ruins, it should prevent such outrageous bad taste as the erection of new buildings in the very centre of time-honoured monuments like those on the Rock of Cashel and on the Boyle river.

The ancient name of Boyle was *Ath dá laarg*, that is, the "ford of two forks." It is not easy to understand why such a curious name should have been given to it, for the river at Boyle, even in time of floods, is fordable, and has usually not over six or eight inches of water in it. It has, however, been proved that the rivers of Ireland, and probably of most other countries, had much more water in them in ancient times than at present. The other name for Boyle was *Búil*, whence Boyle. The word *Búil* is entirely obsolete. It is supposed to mean handsome or beautiful. The Monastery, of which the ruins exist, was founded in 1161 by Maurice O'Duffy, a noted ecclesiastic of the

period, but it is known that a smaller and more
ancient monastery occupied the site on which the
larger one was built at the date mentioned. Boyle
Abbey was an offshoot of the great Abbey of
Mellifont in the County Louth, that had been
founded some twenty years before the Abbey of
Boyle. Both abbeys belonged to the Cistercian
order; and it would appear that so many monks
flocked to Mellifont that accommodation could
not be made for them all there, so the Abbey
of Boyle was erected for them. The "Annals of
Boyle," known also as the "Annals of Loch Cé,
or Key," say that the Church of Boyle was consecrated in 1220; but that the church was built
in 1161 there seems no reason to doubt. The
Four Masters mention it under the year 1174.
Their last mention of it is under the year 1602,
and it must have been abandoned very soon
after. It was granted to Sir John King in
1603, when it must have ceased to be a
monastery.

No one should visit Boyle and its grand ruins
and not see the two very beautiful lakes that
are near it, Loch Key and Loch Arrow. Loch
Key is not over a mile from the town, and Loch
Arrow not more than three. The very fine domain
of Rockingham may be said to be almost sur-

rounded by Loch Key. It was on an island in this lake that the McDermotts, chieftains of Moylurg, had a stronghold. The island has a castle on it at present, but, seen from the shore, both island and castle appear very small. The fortress the McDermotts had on the island must have been a sort of *crannióg*, or wooden castle, like so many that have been discovered both in Ireland and Scotland in the tracks of dried-up lakes. Those *cranniógs* were sometimes built entirely on piles, and sometimes on islands, with extensions on piles if the water was not too deep. This last must have been the kind of fortress the McDermotts had on Loch Key, for it must have been much larger than the present island, and must have been large enough to give space to a multitude of people to assemble on it. We read in the annals of Loch Key of the following awful catastrophe that happened on it in 1184: "The Rock of Loch Key was burned by lightning—*i.e.*, the very magnificent, kingly residence of the Muintir Maolruanaigh (the McDermotts) where neither goods nor people of all that were there found protection; where six or seven score of distinguished persons were destroyed, along with fifteen men of the race of kings and chieftains, with the wife of McDermott

. . . and every one of them who was not burned was drowned in that tumultuous consternation in the entrance of the place; so that there escaped not alive therefrom but Connor McDermott with a very small number of the multitude of his people." The same catastrophe is mentioned by the Four Masters, but under the year 1187. This account of the burning of the castle, or, as the annalist calls it, a residence, shows that it was a wooden structure, for it would hardly have been possible to burn a building of stone so quickly that the people in it would not have had time to escape, even if it were on an island.

Loch Arrow is the least known of all the beautiful lakes of Ireland, and beautiful it is in very nearly the highest style of beauty. There are no mountains round Loch Arrow, and none to be seen from its waters; but its numberless attractions in the way of wooded islands, bold promontories, and swelling shores render it one of the lovely lakes of Ireland; and yet, few, except those living in its immediate vicinity, know anything about it, or have ever heard of it. The land near it seems to be, for the most part, in the hands of small farmers; and neater or more attractive peasant homesteads cannot be found in any part of Ireland than on the banks of

Loch Arrow. It is not more than four miles from Boyle; and small as it is, not more than five miles long, and from two to two and a half miles broad, it is a gem of a lake that seems to be forgotten by the world.

THE LAKES OF WESTMEATH

THE lakes of Westmeath, like Loch Arrow in Sligo, are almost unknown to those who go to Ireland in search of the picturesque. These lakes are, for the greater part, in the centre of the County. Loch Ree is not included in them. There may be said to be only four of them worthy of the attention of those who see something to be admired in a lake besides the excellence of the fish that is in it. Those in search of the beautiful very seldom go to see the lakes of Westmeath. The only people who generally visit them are fishermen, very few of whom would turn round their heads to gaze on the fairest prospect the lakes afforded, for seldom, indeed, do those usually styled sportsmen trouble themselves very much to see the beauties of nature, and they are, unfortunately, about the only class of people who come from afar to visit the lake district of Westmeath.

The lakes best worth seeing in Westmeath are Loch Deravarragh, Loch Ouel, Loch Ennel, usually called Belvedere Lake, Loch Iron, and

Loch Sheelin. The last mentioned lake lies on the borders of four counties—Longford, Cavan, Meath, and Westmeath. It cannot be claimed by the most devoted admirer of the Westmeath lakes that there is very much historic interest attached to any of them. It would be hardly possible to find a square mile of Irish soil wholly devoid of historic interest; but while it may truly be said that there is no country in Europe, not excepting even Greece, where so many places of historic interest are to be found as in Ireland, some parts of it are richer than others in memorials of the past. From whatever cause it happened is not very clear, but it is a fact that Westmeath is one of the least historic of Irish counties. The hill of Uisneach is its most historic spot. There are, at the same time, some other places of historic interest in it. Its most beautiful lake, Loch Ouel, anciently called Loch Uair, is the one in which Malachy the First drowned Turgesius the Dane. Turgesius seems to have had what Americans would call "a high old time" in Ireland for some years— robbing churches and monasteries, and living on the fat of the land; until the Irish, under Malachy, at length defeated him in battle, took him prisoner, and drowned him in one of the most beautiful lakes in Ireland. It seems queer that Malachy, instead of giving him a grave in such a beautiful sheet of water, did not fling him into a bog hole, and it is a pity that there should not be any really trustworthy authority for the legend according to which it was love for King Malachy's beautiful daughter that was the means of entrapping Turgesius. Keating gives a very interesting account of the capture of the Danish Viking in his History of Ireland; how Turgesius asked Malachy for his daughter: how Malachy said that the marriage, or rather the *liaison* should not be made public for fear of giving offence to the Irish; and how fifteen beardless youths, dressed as girls, conducted Malachy's daughter to the Dane, overpowered his guard, took himself prisoner, and then drowned him. A great deal of romance has been written about this affair, but it remained for the inimitable Sam Lover to write the funniest thing in the way of a poem about it. He said that the tyranny of the Danes was so heavy on the Irish that the clergy ordered them a long time of prayer and fasting to seek Divine aid to rid themselves of their persecutors. But it would appear that the unfortunate Irish had been keeping a compulsory fast for a long time previous, for the Danes had left them nothing to eat. They could not understand being ordered to fast still more, and said to the clergy :—

"We can't fast faster than we're fastin' now."

The account of the drowning of Turgesius is given with tantalising curtness in the "Book of Leinster": "This is the year, A.D. 843, that Turgesius was taken by Maelseachlainn (Malachy). He was then drowned in Loch Uair." * The "Book of Leinster" does not say that Turgesius was taken in battle, but those who do not believe Keating's story think he was. If he had been taken in battle and defeated, it must be admitted that it is strange that Irish annalists did not say so and give particulars of the battle. This omission makes it appear probable that there is some truth in the version of his capture as given by Keating, although it is altogether discredited by those best read in Irish History.

Loch Ouel can be seen from the train on the Sligo division of the Great Western Railway. Passing as the glimpse of it is from the train, it is enough to reveal some of the beauties of this fairest of Westmeath lakes. But to see it

---

* Is hi seo bliadain ra gabad Tuirgeis la Maelseachlainn. Ra baided ar sain hó il Loch Uair. "Book of Leinster," p. 307.

properly one should wander by its pebbly shores,
for not a yard of them is swampy, or ascend one
of the hills of brilliant green that are on all sides
of it. Loch Ouel has the great defect of being
almost islandless. There are only one or two
small ones in it. If it had proportionately as
many islands in it as Loch Erne, it would be
one of the fairest sheets of water of its size in
Ireland.

Belvedere Lake is a good deal larger than Loch
Ouel, and its shores are better wooded, but part
of them, in fact a very large part of them, is
boggy. Its banks are adorned with gentlemen's
seats, and in spite of the swampy shore on one
side of it, it is a very beautiful lake.

Loch Derravaragh is the most peculiarly-shaped
of all the Westmeath lakes. It is shaped something like a tadpole, only that, unlike a tadpole,
it is its head that is narrow, and its tail, or
lower part, that is wide. It has bolder shores than
any other lake in the county, some of the hills
near it being almost mountains. It has hardly
any islands, and its shores are wilder than any
other of the Westmeath lakes. It wants the
woods that do so much to adorn the swampy
shores of Belvedere Lake; but comparatively bare
as the shores of Loch Derravaragh are, it is a

most picturesque lake, and some think it more
beautiful than Loch Ouel.   Both Loch Derravaragh and Loch Iron are formed by the river
Inny, but it does not, as most rivers do, flow
through the lakes it forms and feeds, for it flows
out of them within a short distance of where it
enters them, and the lakes extend in an opposite
direction from where they receive their water.
This is rather a strange fact in physical geo-
graphy.

The next most important of the Westmeath
lakes is Loch Sheelin, but as three other counties—
Longford, Meath, and Cavan—border it, it cannot
be strictly called a Westmeath lake.   However,
as it is so close to the very picturesque sheets
of water which are the chief scenic attractions
of the county they adorn, it has been thought
best to include it when describing them.   Loch
Sheelin has only a few islands, but its shores,
although low, are very well wooded.   Seen from
the hills in the vicinity of Oldcastle in Meath,
it is as fair a sight as can well be imagined,
with its wood-crowned, indented shores.   If there
are fairer lakes in Ireland than Loch Sheelin,
there are few that have a more beautiful name.
It is euphony itself.   Its name is the original one
of Moore's sweet melody, "Come, rest in this

Bosom." It has often been said, "What's in a name?" There is a great deal. A name so beautiful as Loch Sheelin would give a certain charm to a bog hole. It must be confessed that Celtic, of all European languages, seems to contain the most sonorous place names. Such names as Bassenthwaitewater, Ullswater, Conistonwater, Derwentwater, Thuner See, and Zuger See, sound very tame compared with Loch Lomond, Loch Erne, Loch Awe, Loch Ree, Loch Layn, and Loch Sheelin. There is, however, one continental place-name of wonderful beauty of sound, and that is Lorraine. Its German name is Lothringen, but the French, by eliding its consonants, or by what is generally called aspiration in Gaelic grammar, have turned the harsh German name into one of the most euphonious and beautiful in the world.

Loch Iron and Loch Lene, pronounced Loch Layne, are small sheets of water, but are well worth a visit, even from those who are neither fishers of fish nor of men. The country all round the Westmeath lakes is as beautiful as it is possible for any country to be in which there are neither mountains nor waterfalls. It is never flat, and never uninteresting, covered almost everlastingly with verdure, for although most of the county is hilly, it is one of the most fertile in

Ireland. Its still, clear lakes, undulating surface, and rich soil, make it, even in the absence of mountains (and, unfortunately, in the absence of good hotels in its small towns and villages), one of the most picturesque of the counties of Leinster.

KELLS, the ancient name of which was Ceannanus, and the one by which it is still known in Irish, is one of the most ancient towns in Ireland. According to Irish annalists it was founded by an over-king called Fiacha, 1203 years B.C. If its situation and environs are of no great beauty, it is yet a place of great historic interest. It can boast of the possession of one of the finest round towers in Ireland, a. very ancient cross, and a still more ancient stone-roofed church. If there are no mountains or romantic scenery round Kells, it has the advantage of being situated in the midst of the most generally fertile of Irish counties. It is on the river Blackwater, a tributary of the historic Boyne. Nothing can exceed the fertility of the land round Kells; but that does it no good, for the land is almost all in grass, the rural population sparse, and consequently, of very little outside support to the town. But Kells is no worse off than the other towns of Meath. It is, as far as soil is concerned, the richest county in Ireland, but its towns are either in a state of

271

absolute decay, or at a standstill. There is hardly any tilled land in the county; its herds are large, and its population consequently declining. Where cattle abound, people are generally scarce.

For those who visit Kells merely to see the wondrous luxuriance of its grassy environs, the best thing they can do is to ascend the hill of Lloyd, which is close to the town, and go to the top of the tower that crowns the summit of the hill. It is over a hundred feet high, with a winding flight of stairs, and a turret on top, capable of containing a dozen people. The view from the tower is very fine, and will well repay those who see it. Almost the whole of Meath, Louth, Cavan, and parts of other counties can be seen. The tower was built more than a hundred years ago by the first Earl of Bective. It is sometimes called "Bective's Folly," because it serves for nothing except giving a fine view to those who ascend it. It is generally known as the tower of Lloyd.

To the antiquarian, the neighbourhood of Kells is of supreme interest. Four miles south-east of it, on the banks of the Blackwater, lies the site of what is considered, next to Tara, the most ancient spot of Irish soil—namely, the place where the

games of Tailltean were, for some thousands of
years, celebrated. The place is now called
Telltown, an evident Anglicisation of its Irish
name; but it is still called Tailltean by any old
persons in its vicinity who speak Irish. If any
credence can be given to Irish annals and history,
the antiquity of this place is astounding. The
sceptic has to admit that the mere fact of the
preservation down to the present day of the
name by which it was known from remote antiquity is in itself an extraordinary fact. The
games or sports of Tailltean were somewhat
similar to the Olympic games of Greece, except
that those of Tailltean were celebrated every
year. The whole of Ireland used to assist at
them, and they seem to have been celebrated
every year down to 1168, when they were for
the last time celebrated by the unfortunate and
foolish Roderick O'Connor, the last of those
who were, even in name, chief kings of Ireland.
In spite of internal wars, Danish invasions and
plunderings, a single year does not appear to
have elapsed from the time they were first established down to the twelfth century in which
they were not celebrated. It would also seem
that no matter what wars or troubles were dis-
tracting the country, the games of Tailltean were

never omitted. They took place at the beginning
of August, as has been mentioned in the article
on Tara, and from them the Irish name of the
month of August—*Lughnasa*—is derived. The
name Tailltean is the genitive case of Tailtte, the
woman in whose memory they were established by
her son, Lugh, who lived and reigned in Tara,
according to the chronology of the Four Masters,
which differs only slightly from that of other
annalists, 1824 years B.C. ! It is no matter how
we may smile or shake our heads when this
astounding antiquity is mentioned, the preservation of those two names, *Lughnasa* and *Tailltean*,
down to the present day, drives away the smile
and makes us look serious. Such collateral proofs
of the existence of historic personages of such
antiquity cannot be furnished by any other nation
in the world, not even by Egypt or by Greece.

We must not pooh-pooh the statement of Irish
annalists as to the enormous antiquity they give
to persons who figure in early Irish history. Here
is what the late Sir William Wilde says in his
book, "Loch Corrib": "With respect to Irish
chronology, we believe it will be found to approach the truth as near as that of most other
countries; and the more we investigate it and
endeavour to synchronise it with that of other

lands, the less reason we shall have to find fault with the accounts of our native annalists."

There are not many monuments of the past to be seen at Tailltean save an earthen fort of about a hundred paces in diameter, and two small lakes that bear evidence of having been formed artificially. To show how long traditions live in countries that even partially preserve their ancient language, it need only be said that up to about a hundred years ago, the peasantry of the neighbourhood used to meet on the first of *Lughnasa*, or August, at Tailltean to have games and athletic sports of different kinds. The meeting was called a *pattern*, but it was not held on any patron saint's day. It was merely the traditional remembrance of the old games that had not been celebrated for seven hundred years previously, that caused the peasantry to meet at Tailltean. It is said that on account of the drinking and consequent fighting that used to take place, the clergy forbid the people to assemble. Irish history and annals, while they constantly mention the games of Tailltean, leave us a good deal in the dark about the nature of the sports that used to take place. But they do say that marriages, or, rather, alliances of a somewhat evanescent kind used to be contracted; and to this day, all through the part of the country in the neighbourhood of Tailltean, when a matrimonial alliance turns out badly, or when the parties separate, it is called "a Telltown marriage." No one who has ever written about Telltown, not even such profound archæologists as O'Donovan and Petrie, has ever had any doubt about its being the exact place where the games of Tailltean were held in ancient times.

There cannot be said to be any very ancient monuments of Christian times to be seen in Kells save a very fine round tower, the top of which is gone; a very ancient cross in the market-place, two in the churchyard, and a stone-roofed church or oratory. The last is the oldest and most interesting ancient monument in Kells. It is a small building, only nineteen feet long, fifteen broad, and twenty-five high. It is one of the most ancient edifices built with cement that exists in Ireland. Its foundation is attributed to St Columba; and it is considered to be at least of his time, or the middle of the sixth century. It is apparently as sound and as solid as it was the day it was built. Everything that could with any certainty be believed to have been part of the great monastery that was in Kells has disappeared. Its stones were probably taken to build the present church that stands near to where the monastery was. The stones of the ancient building that has been described would also probably have been used for some purpose if they could have been easily removed, but it is so solid, and the stones are so firmly bound together by grouting, that the labour of tearing it down deterred the vandals from destroying it.

Kells was so often burned and so often plundered by the Northmen that it is a wonder how anything in it remains. According to the annals it was burned twenty-one times, and plundered seven times, before the twelfth century! Every vestige of the great castle, that was built either by Hugo de Lacy or John de Courcy, has disappeared. This castle must have been nearly as large as that of Trim, for it was built for the protection of some of the most valuable country conquered by the invaders. It is said that the monastery was in a ruined condition at the close of the twelfth century, and that de Lacy renovated it and richly-endowed it.

That wondrous manuscript known as the Book of Kells, although it is not believed to have been written in that town, has been named from it, and consequently should be mentioned in connection with it. That the book found its way to

Kells, and that it was there for many centuries, there cannot be any doubt. Neither can there be any doubt that it belonged to the Church of Kells, for there are curious charters in it, written in Irish of a very archaic kind, relating to the clergy of that town. It seems to have been in Kildare in the twelfth century, for it is evidently of it that Giraldus Cambrensis speaks when he says, "Of all the wonders of Kildare, I found nothing more wonderful than the marvellous book that was written in the time of St Brigit." It was in the church of Kells until 1620, when Archbishop Ussher saved it from being destroyed. It is a Latin version of the Gospels, with some Gaelic charters, relating to the Church of Kells, that were bound into it many centuries after it was written. It was taken by the Danes, it is believed, and the golden cover torn off it; it was found buried in the ground some time after. This is recorded to have happened in 1006. It is the most wonderful work· of art of its kind known to exist in any country, and it is no wonder that in a credulous age it should have been believed to be the work of angels. Westwood, an Englishman, and author of the greatest work on illuminated manuscripts ever written, says of it: "It is unquestionably the most elaborately executed

manuscripts of so early a date now in existence."
Doctor Waagen, Conservator of the Royal
Museum of Berlin, says of it: "The ornamental
pages, borders, and initial letters exhibit such a
rich variety of beautiful and peculiar designs, so
admirable a taste in the arrangement of colours,
and such an uncommon perfection of finish, that
one feels absolutely struck with amazement."
Where and when the Book of Kells was executed,
and by whom, will probably never be known; but
it must have been written as early as the sixth
century. Tradition attributes it to Columba, or,
as he is usually called, Columb Cille. The late
Dr Todd, one of the most learned archæologists,
and one of the best Gaelic scholars that ever
Ireland produced, believed that it was as early as
the time of Columba. The author of *Topographia
Hiberniae* says of it: "The more frequently I behold it, the more diligently I examine it, the more
I am lost in admiration of it." No one who has
not seen the Book of Kells can form an idea of its
beauty. In the pages that have not been soiled
the colours are as pure and as bright as if they
were laid on only yesterday. The naked eye cannot follow all its delicate and minute tracings;
to see it aright, it should be seen through a
microscope. It is beyond any doubt the most

wonderful book of its kind in the world. In it and in the Tara Brooch Ireland possesses two works of ancient art, two gems of artistic beauty which are unequalled of their kind and of their age. The art treasures of metallurgy exhumed in Pompeii, and all that have been found in Greece and Asia Minor by Schliemann, contain nothing equal in exquisite finish to the Tara Brooch; and in all the treasures of illuminated manuscripts in the libraries of the world, there is nothing of its kind equal to the Book of Kells. The Tara Brooch can be seen in the Museum, Kildare Street, Dublin, and the Book of Kells in Trinity College, in the same city.

All the ecclesiastical establishments that have been described owed their origin to native piety, benevolence, and enterprise.

CUCHULAINN'S DUN AND CUCHU-
LAINN'S COUNTRY

No one, whether an Irishman or a stranger, can
look on the vast mound and vast earthen ramparts
that mark the home of him whom the most trustworthy of Irish annalists, Tighearnach, calls *fortis-
simus heros Scottorum*, without feelings of indignation and shame—indignation at the way one of
the greatest and most interesting monuments of
Irish antiquity has been profaned, and shame
that so little reverence for their country's past
should be found among the Irish people. If the
Copts and Arabs of Egypt sell and uproot the
antiquities of that country, they can, at least,
say that they are not the descendants of the men
who lived under the sway of the Pharaos; but
those who have, in recent times, done most to
obliterate and profane the most historic monuments
of Ireland are the lineal descendants of the men
who raised them. Nothing that ancient Irish
monuments have suffered, and they have suffered
a great deal, can exceed the wrong committed by
him who built a horrible, modern, vulgar, gewgaw

house on top of the *dun* of Cuchulainn!   To show
how utterly obtuse, and how unsympathetic with
his country's past the person was who built the
vulgar structure on one of the most curious and
interesting historic monuments in Ireland, he has
actually engraved his name and the date of the

CUCHULAINN'S DESECRATED DUN.

erection of the house on its front wall! seeming
to glory in the vandalism he committed.   The
legend on the wall says that the house was built
in 1780 by a person named Patrick Byrne for his
nephew.

About a mile from the Dundalk railway station,

crowning the summit of a hill that rises amid green
fields and rich pastures, stands all that remains of
the *dun* on which the wooden dwelling of Cuchulainn stood wellnigh two thousand years ago.
Before it was partially levelled to build the gewgaw house that now stands on it, it must have
been the finest monument of its kind in Ireland.
It is quite different from the remains of Tara,
Knock Aillinn, Emania, or Dinrigh. Those places
were evidently intended to accommodate large
numbers of people; but Cuchulainn's *dun* was
evidently that of one person or one family. It
answered to the Norman keep that some lords
of the soil built for their own private protection
in later times. Cuchulainn's *dun* was immense,
and its remains are even still immense in spite of
the way it has been ruined. It is yet over forty
feet in perpendicular height, and, like most structures of its kind, is perfectly round. It has an
area of over half an acre on its summit. The
enceinte outside the central *dun* encloses fully
two acres, and where-it has not been levelled, is
still colossal, being thirty feet high in some parts.
The immense labour it must have taken to raise
such a gigantic mound, and to dig such vast en-
trenchments on so high a hill, strikes one with
astonishment. If it had not been ruined and

partially levelled by the utterly denationalised and soulless person who built the vulgar structure on it, it would be the finest thing of its kind in Ireland, and would attract antiquarians from all parts of these islands and from the Continent.

The existence of this fort is another collateral proof of the general truth of what has been called Irish bardic history. It says that Cuchulainn lived at Dundealgan, or Dundalk, and there his *dun* is found. He can hardly be said to figure in what are generally known as Irish authentic annals. The "Annals of the Four Masters" do not mention him at all, although they do mention some of his contemporaries. Tighearnach, who lived in the eleventh century, is the only one of the Irish annalists who mentions him. His annals have not yet been translated or published; but the following passage occurs in them: "Death of Cuchulainn, the most renowned champion of Ireland, by Lughaidh, the son of Cairbre Niafer [chief king of Ireland]. He was seven years old when he began to be a champion, and seventeen when he fought in the Cattle Spoil of Cooley, and twenty-seven when he died." Tighearnach makes Cuchulainn and Virgil contemporary. He and Queen Meave are the two great central figures in the longest and greatest prose epic in the Irish language, the Tain Bo Cuailgne, or Cattle Spoil of Cooley, which Sir Samuel Ferguson has made familiar to the English reader in his poem, "The Foray of Meave."

Cuchulainn is the Hercules of Irish romantic history; but in spite of all the fabulous tales of which he is the hero, there cannot be any doubt that he was an historic personage, that his dwelling-place was on the *dun* that has been described, and that he lived shortly before the Christian era. The name Cuchulainn is a sobriquet; it means "the hound Culann." This Culann was chief smith to Connor, King of Ulster. He had a fierce dog that he used to let out every night to watch and guard his premises, which were in the vicinity of Emania, the palace of the Ulster kings. Cuchulainn, who was nephew to Connor, was going to some entertainment at his uncle's; but having been out later than usual, was attacked by Culann's fierce hound. He had no weapon with which to defend himself save his hurling ball; but he cast it with such force at the dog that he killed him on the spot. Culann complained to King Connor about the loss of his great watch dog, and Cuchulainn, who was then only a boy of eight or nine years old, said that he would act as watch dog for the smith and be Culann's hound, or dog. Whether he did so or not is left untold.

It is very curious that in all the romantic tales in which Cuchulainn figures, and in spite of his incredible strength and prowess, there does not seem to be a passage in any tract that has been translated about him up to the present where anything is mentioned about his size or stature. We are left under the impression that he was no bigger than ordinary men; and it may have been that he was not. Size and strength do not always go together. Some of the feats that he is said to have performed are utterly incredible; such as flinging his spear haftwise, and killing nine men with the cast; and pulling the arm from its socket out of a giant whom he was unable to get the better of with weapons. It is very natural that such impossible feats would, in a credulous age, be attributed to any one who was possessed of more than ordinary prowess. Things quite as impossible are found in the classics relative to Hercules. The Irish had just as good a right to relate impossibilities about Cuchulainn as the Greeks had to do the same about Hercules. But Cuchulainn figures in Celtic legend and romance in a manner in which Hercules does not figure in the legends of Greece, for the

Irish hero was more of a ladies' man than was the giant of the Greeks.

If Cuchulainn did not fill such an important place in what may be called classic Gaelic literature, the total ignorance about him in the very place where he was born and where he lived would not be such a national disgrace as it is. The mere remnant of Gaelic literature in which he is the central figure is immense. No other race in Europe would have so totally lost sight of a personage that was the hero of so many tracts and stories, and who was, besides, an historic character, and not a myth. Even sixty years ago, during the Ordnance Survey of Louth, the parties employed on it found that no one in the neighbourhood of Castletown, the modern name of the place in which Cuchulainn's fort is situated, knew or heard anything about him. They were told by the peasantry that the fort was made by the Danes! Some said it was the work of Finn Mac Cool; but of the real owner of it, they knew nothing.

It is evident that the Irish monks of early mediæval times were much more broad-minded and liberal than their countrymen of the same class of more recent years. It is to monks and inmates of monasteries that we owe nine-tenths of the Gaelic literature that has come down to us. They produced more books in proportion to their numbers than perhaps any class of men of their kind that lived in ancient times. They were sincere Christians, but, like patriots, they loved to record the deeds of their pagan ancestors. Just as soon as national decay set in they were succeeded by men of their own calling, who appear to have thought little worth recording except the works of saints, or at least of those who professed Christianity. If the monks of the early centuries of Christian Ireland were as narrow-minded as the Four Masters, we never, probably, would know anything about Cuchulainn, Queen Meave, Conall Carnach, or any of the heroes of pagan Ireland, round whom there is woven such a wondrous web of legend, romance, and song. Every patriotic Irishman should revere the memories of those liberal-minded monks who handed down to us the doings of their pagan forefathers. To show how much those men valued the literature, and loved to recount the exploits of their pagan ancestors, it will only be necessary to give the words of the dear old soul who copied the *Tain Bó Cuailgne*, the great epic of pagan times, into the "Book of Leinster": "A blessing on every one who will faithfully remember the *Tain* as it is [written] here, and who will not put another shape on it."

Cuchulainn, above all men who figure in ancient Irish literature, seems to have been "*grádh ban Eireann*," the darling of the women of Ireland. While yet in his teens, the nobles of Ulster came together to determine who should be a fitting wife for him. After a long search they found a lady named Eimir, accomplished in all the feminine education of the time; but her father, a wealthy chief or noble who lived near Lusk, in the present County of Dublin, did not like to give his daughter to a professional champion. Cuchulainn had seen her, and had succeeded in gaining her love. She was guarded for a year in her father's *dun;* and during all that time, Cuchulainn vainly strove to see her. At last he lost patience and became desperate, scaled the three fences that encircled her father's fort, had a terrible fight for her; killed three of her brothers; half killed half-a-dozen others who opposed him, and carried her and her maid northward in his chariot to his home in Dundalk.

Like all violent love, Cuchulainn's love for Eimir seems soon to have cooled, for we find that a lady called Fann, the wife of Manannan MacLir, King of the Isle of Man, or some place

T

east of Ireland, fell in love with him. She came
to see her father, a man of rank and wealth,
who lived somewhere on the east coast of Ireland.
She eloped with Cuchulainn, and Eimir, finding
that she and her erring husband were staying at
Newry, in the present County of Down, followed
him, attended by fifty maids armed with knives,
in order to kill Fann. This lady, in spite of her
errors, must have been an intellectual woman, for
her speech when leaving Cuchulainn and going
home with MacLir is very fine, and would be
a credit to the literature of any language. The
tract in which it occurs is in the Book of the
Dun Cow, an Irish manuscript compiled in the
eleventh century, and is entitled "The Sick Bed
of Cuchulainn and only Jealousy of Eimir." It
was admirably translated nearly forty years ago
by Eugene O'Curry, and was published in the
long since dead periodical, the *Atlantis*. None
but a few Celtic savants have ever read it.
To the general public it will be absolutely new.
Fann, finding that she must leave Cuchulainn,
says :—

> "It is I who shall go on a journey ;
> I give consent with great affliction ;
> Though there is a man of equal fame,
> I would prefer to remain [here].

" I would rather be here
  To be subject to thee without grief,
  Than go, though it may wonder thee,
  To the sunny palace of Aed Abrat.*

" Woe to the one who gives love to a person,
  If he does not take notice of it !
  It is better for one to be turned away,
  Unless he is loved as he is loved."

It seems that by some occult means it was
revealed to Manannan MacLir that his wife,
Fann, was in trouble between the jealous women
of Ulster and Cuchulainn. So he came from the
east to seek his eloped spouse. When Fann
found out that Manannan had found *her* out,
she utters the following very quaint, extraordinary,
and touching rhapsody :—

" Behold ye the valiant son of Lir
  From the plains of Eoghan of Inver,—
  Manannan, lord of the world's fair hills,
  There was a time when he was dear to me.

" Even to-day if he were nobly constant,—
  My mind loves not jealousy ;
  Affection is a subtle thing ;
  It makes its way without labour.

" When Manannan the Great me espoused
  I was a spouse worthy of him ;
  He could not win from me for his life
  A game in excess at chess.

        * Aed Abrat was Fann's father.

"When Manannan the Great me espoused
I was a spouse of him worthy;
A bracelet of doubly tested gold
He gave me as the price of my blushes.

"I had with me going over the sea
Fifty maidens of varied beauty;
I gave them unto fifty men
Without reproach,—the fifty maidens.

"As for me I would have cause [to be grieved]
Because the minds of women are silly;
The person whom I loved exceedingly
Has placed me here at a disadvantage.

"I bid thee adieu, O beautiful Cu;
Hence we depart from thee with a good heart;
Though we return not, be thy good will with us;
Every condition is noble in comparison with
    that of going away."

It would appear that Cuchulainn was as much distracted about Fann as she was about him; for when he found that she had gone home with Manannan MacLir, he became desperate, and the tale says, with extraordinary grotesqueness and apparent inconsequence, that "It was then Cuchulainn leaped the three high leaps and the three south leaps of Luachair; and he remained for a long time without drink, without food, among the mountains; and where he slept each night was on the road of Midhluachair." But what good did the jumping do him, or why did he jump?

Connor, King of Ulster, and the nobles and Druids of the province, had a hard time with Cuchulainn after Fann left him, as he seems to have gone downright crazy. The tale says that Connor had to send poets and professional men to seek him out in his mountain retreat, and that when they found him he was going to kill them. At last the Druids managed to give him a drink of forgetfulness, so that he remembered no more about Fann.

The death of Cuchulainn in the "Book of Leinster" is one of the finest things in ancient literature. It has not yet been fully translated, but a partial translation of it by Mr Whitley Stokes appeared in the *Revue Celtique* in 1876. An epitome of it here can hardly be out of place: When Cuchulainn's foes came against him for the last time, signs and portents showed that he was near his end. One of his horses would not allow himself to be yoked to the war chariot, and shed tears of blood. But Cuchulainn goes to the battle, performs prodigies of valour; but at last he receives his death wound. Though dying, his foes are afraid to approach him. He asks to be allowed to go to a lake that was close by to get a drink. He is allowed to go, but he does not want a drink, he merely wants to die like a hero, standing up;

for there is a pillar-stone close by, and he throws
his breast-girdle round it, so that he might die
standing up, and not lying down.   His friend
Conall determines to avenge his death.   Here the
literal translation is so fine that it must be given:
"Now there was a comrades' covenant between
Cuchulainn and Conall—namely, that whichever of
them was first killed, should be avenged by the
other.   'And if I be first killed,' said Cuchulainn,
'how soon wilt thou avenge me?' 'The day on
which thou shalt be slain,' says Conall; 'I will
avenge thee before that evening.' 'And if I be
slain,' says Conall, 'how soon wilt thou avenge
me?' 'Thy blood will not be cold on earth,' says
Cuchulainn, 'when I shall avenge thee.'"   Lugaid,
the slayer of Cuchulainn, had lost his right hand
in the fight.   He goes south in his chariot to a
river to rest and drink.   His charioteer says, "One
horseman is coming to us, and great are the speed
and swiftness with which he comes.   Thou wouldst
deem that all the ravens of Erin were above him,
and that flakes of snow were specking the plain
before him."   "Unbeloved is the horseman that
comes there," says Lugaid.   "It is Conall mounted
on [his steed] the Dewy-Red.   The birds thou
sawest above him are sods from that horse's hoofs.
The snowflakes thou sawest specking the plain

before him are foam from that horse's lips and nostrils." Conall and Lugaid fight, of course; but as Lugaid has but one hand, Conall has one of his hands bound to his side with ropes, so that he should have no advantage over his foe. They fight for hours, until at last Lugaid falls by Conall, and Cuchulainn is avenged. The tale winds up thus: "And Conall and the Ulstermen returned to Emain Macha (Emania). That week they entered it not in triumph. But the soul of Cuchulainn appeared there to the fifty queens who had loved him; and they saw him floating in his spirit-chariot over Emain Macha, and they heard him chaunt a mystic song of the coming of Christ and the Day of Doom."

There are few views in Ireland more beautiful than that from the summit of the mound on which Cuchulainn's mansion stood. It may not be so extensive as other views in the locality, but for beauty and variety it can hardly be exceeded. If admittance is obtained into the house that is built on the track of Cuchulainn's, the view will be still finer. It is said by some that that house is haunted. It is to be hoped that it is; and that Cuchulainn's ghost will drive away sleep from the eyes of every one of Patrick Byrne's descendants who stop in it.

The ancient name of the country round Dundalk

was Muirimhne; but it has not been called by that
name for some centuries. It appears to have been
the patrimony of Cuchulainn; for in the tale, in the
"Book of the Dun Cow," from which extracts
have been given, Fann calls him, "Great chief of
the plain of Muirimhne." He, probably, or the
clan of which he was the head, owned all that
part of northern Louth where the land is level,
and up to the foot of the Cooley hills. All the
County Louth is fairly studded with ruins of one
sort or another. It is one of the most interesting
counties in Ireland in an antiquarian point of view.
It contains the remains of nearly thirty castles in
almost all stages of preservation. One of the finest
of them is only a few hundred yards from the *dun*
of Cuchulainn. It is not in the least ruined, but
its architecture shows it to be one of the oldest
castles erected by the Anglo-Normans in Ireland.
Its style is almost exactly that of the castle at
Trim, which we know was built before the end of
the twelfth century. Like Dunsochly Castle, near
Finglas, in the County Dublin, the one near
Cuchulainn's *dun* must have been inhabited at a
comparatively recent date, for modern windows
have been opened on its front. The only light
that was admitted into those old castles was what
came through the narrow slits in the walls, about

three feet long and six or eight inches wide. These served the double purpose of letting in light and discharging arrows through them. It does not seem to be known by whom the very fine Norman Keep at Castletown, County Louth, was built. There are many larger castles of the same kind in different parts of Ireland, but there are not many of its age in such a good state of preservation. There is a church in the immediate proximity of the castle, and the exact date of its erection seems also unknown. It is in a state of almost utter ruin. The County Louth can boast of having been the birth-place of St Brigit. She was born at Fachart, only a few miles from Castletown, but it was in Kildare she spent almost all her life, and it was there she died and was buried.

There are few parts of Ireland more beautiful than the country round the ancient *dun* of Cuchulainn, and few parts less generally visited by tourists. Carlingford Loch is only a few miles from Dundalk, and except Clew Bay, and one or two others, there is nothing finer on all the coasts of Ireland. But the grandest and most striking scenery in this part of the country are the Mourne mountains in the County Down. There are higher mountain ranges in Ireland, but there are not any more bold, or more truly Alpine. Seen from the central parts of the County Louth, they and the Cooley mountains seem to form a continuous range of "sky-pointing peaks," forming one of the finest, if not the very finest, mountain view in Ireland. The ancient name of the Mourne mountains was the Beanna Boirche. They were called the Mourne mountains from being in a territory anciently called Crioch Mughorna. It gave a title to Lord Cremorne, from whom, it is generally believed, the Cremorne Gardens in London derive their name. It has to be admitted that, in this instance, the Anglicised form of the name is the more euphonious.

The County Louth, and all that part of the County Down bordering on it, have not had their due share of attention from those who go in search of the picturesque and beautiful. Although the direct route between the two largest cities in Ireland, northern Louth and southern Down are not at all known as well as they should be. There are, even in Kerry or Connemara, few places in which finer views of mountain, bay, and plain can be had, and all within less than two hours by rail from Dublin or Belfast. And as for antiquities, no county of its size in Ireland possesses so many as Louth.

THE WILD WEST COAST

By the west coast is meant the whole of that wondrous succession of far-penetrating fiords and bays, cliff-guarded shores, and sea-washed mountains from Bantry Bay to Malin Head, a distance of over four hundred miles. There may be wilder scenery on the coasts of Norway, Labrador, or Scotland, but for wildness, sublimity, and beauty combined, there is hardly in Europe, or in the world, another four hundred miles of coast equal to it. Its variety is one of its principal charms. There is the grandeur and wildness of Norwegian coast scenery, together with scenes of radiant beauty which cannot be found on the coasts of Norway or of Scotland. The more southern latitude of the Irish west coast, and its consequently milder climate, give it a great advantage over the coasts of Norway or of Scotland. Its grass is greener and more luxuriant, and its flowers bloom earlier in spring and later in autumn than those of more northern climes. The mild climate of the southern part of the Irish west coast is almost phenomenal. Winter, in its real sense, or as it generally is on the coasts of Norway, or even of Scotland, may be said to be unknown on the west coast of Munster. Snow is seldom seen, and frost still less frequently. Rain and wind are about all the climatic disagreeableness that those living on the south-west coasts of Ireland have to contend against. It is, however, a fact that the rainfall is not so heavy immediately on the coast as it is some ten or twenty miles inland. This is owing to the fact that the higher mountains are generally some distance from the sea; and it is well-known that mountains are great attractors of rain.

Bantry Bay is the first great sea loch of the south-western coast. It is one of the finest natural harbours in Europe, but, unfortunately, ships are seldom seen in it except when they take shelter from the "wild west wind," which blows on these storm-beaten shores with a fury hardly known anywhere else in the world. The whole of the coast of Kerry, up to the mouth of the Shannon, is a succession of the wildest and grandest scenery, with here and there land of only slight elevation, with level meads and pastures of perennial green. Still further north, we come to the mouth of the Shannon, which forms another very fine harbour. About twenty miles north of the Shannon the famous cliffs of Moher appear. There are higher isolated cliffs than those on the west coast, but there is no long range of cliffs so high. They average between six and seven hundred feet in perpendicular height above the sea. To be seen in all their grandeur they should be seen from the sea, but to be seen in all their terribleness, they should be seen in a storm. Such is the force of the west wind on these coasts, sweeping over three thousand miles of unbroken, islandless sea, that the waves sometimes break over the cliffs of Moher in spite of their nearly seven hundred feet of perpendicular height. In no other part of the world is the force of the sea, when driven before a gale from the west, more terrific than on the west coast of Ireland. Old men who lived close to this iron-bound coast on the night of the great storm of January 6, 1839, known over the most of Ireland as the "Night of the Big Wind," say that none but those who were near these coasts on that awful night could have even a faint idea of what the Atlantic is when a storm from the south-west drives it against the rocky barriers that seem to have been placed where they are to prevent it from overwhelming the whole island. They say that when some gigantic wave of millions of tons of water was hurled against these cliffs, the noise made was so loud that it could be heard miles inland above the roar and din of the storm; and that the very earth would tremble at every assault of the waves on those tremendous barriers to their fury.

Recent soundings taken off the west and south-west coast of Ireland have fully proved that a very large part of the island has been washed away by the fury of the west wind and the sea, and that at some far-back epoch it extended nearly three hundred miles further towards the south-west. The sea, for some two or three hundred miles west and south-west of Ireland, is shallow—hardly deeper than the Channel between Great Britain and Ireland—but at that distance there is a sudden increase of over two thousand feet in the depth of the sea. Scientists think that this submerged mountain was once the south-west coast of Ireland, and that the shallow sea between the present coast and the deep sea, about three hundred miles south-west, was once dry land, and, of course, part of Ireland. There do not seem to be any reasonable grounds to doubt this theory, for the fury of the sea is every year washing away both land and rock on these western coasts, and the way it has encroached, even in the memory of living

persons, is very remarkable. Not a year passes
during which hundreds of thousands of tons of
rocks are not washed away from cliff and mountain by the ceaseless assaults of the stormy sea
that beats with such force on the western coast
of Ireland. Were it not for the cliffs and
mountains that guard the whole of the west
coast, the probability is that thousands of acres
would be submerged every year, until there would
be very little of the country left in the long run.
It may be said that there must be a time coming
when those barriers of cliff and mountain that
now guard almost the entire west coast will be
swept away, seeing that they are being constantly
broken down and washed into the sea. Such a
time must certainly come, unless some unforeseen
event should alter the course of the Gulf Stream,
or change the prevailing west and south-west
winds to opposite points of the compass. The
question is, How long will it be until there is
real danger from the encroachment of the sea on
the west coast of Ireland? This is a question
which the most profound geologist living could
not answer with even approximation to correctness.
It is impossible to know what 'amount of erosion
takes place every year, or what amount has
taken place in any given number of years; but

that not only the cliffs of Moher, but the still more gigantic ones of Slieve More in Achill, and Slieve League in Donegal, must finally succumb to the fury of the Atlantic's waves there can hardly be a doubt. Thousands of years may elapse before the cliff barriers on the western coast become so weakened that the island will be in danger from the assaults of the sea.

From the cliffs of Moher to the Killaries, or Killary Bay, or Harbour, for it is known by all these names, there are many scenes of very great beauty; but to take even passing notice of all of them would be entirely beyond the scope of a work of the size of this. The coasts of Connemara, if not remarkable for very striking cliff scenery, are wild, sea-indented, strange, and interesting in a very high degree. But Killary Bay is one of the glories of the wild west coast. It has more the character of a Norwegian fiord than any other sea loch in Ireland. It divides the counties of Galway and Mayo. Some put it before the famed Clew Bay, and Inglis said, over half a century ago, that if the shores of the Killaries were as well wooded as Killarney, the latter might tremble for the supremacy it enjoys of being the fairest lake either of fresh or salt water in Ireland. The Killaries run some ten

or fifteen miles inland, between some of the
highest hills in the province of Connacht, with
Maolrca, the king of Connacht mountains, on its
northern side.   This fiord, or narrow sea loch, is
one of the most splendid harbours, not only in
Ireland, but in the world, with not only complete
shelter from winds from all points, but with depth
of water enough to float the biggest ship that ever
has been or ever will be built.   But, unfortunately,
there is little to attract commerce to these desolate
shores, where there are no large towns, and only a
sparse population.   It has been said by some who
have seen almost all the fiords of Norway, that
there are few of them superior to the Killaries
in everything that constitutes beauty, sublimity,
and wildness.   That this sea loch is, in a certain
degree, dark and gloomy has to be admitted,
because the mountains come so close to it that
they seem in some places to rise almost perpendicularly out of the water.   But Killary harbour
is a glorious place on a clear, sunny mid-day,
when its sombre mountains cast but little shade
on its ever calm waters; for no matter how rough
the sea may be outside, this mountain fiord is ever
calm, as it is sheltered on all sides by towering
heights.   As an enchanting bay it is the only one
on all the Irish coasts of which Clew Bay or

U

Dublin Bay, were they living things and tormented with human passions, could possibly feel jealous.

We now approach the queen, not alone of Irish bays, but of all bays in these islands, and, according to its most ardent admirers, of all bays in Europe. This is the glorious sheet of salt water, presided over by the most symmetrical and beautiful of Irish mountains, Croagh Patrick, and guarded from the stormy Atlantic by the rocky shores of Clare Island. This is Clew Bay, the radiant beauty, the "matchless wonder of a bay," that not one in a hundred of those in search of the beautiful know anything about. It is indeed strange that this gem of sea lochs is not better known, now that a railway brings one to its very shores.

It is almost impossible to draw a comparison between Clew Bay and the many magnificent arms of the sea that penetrate the west coasts of Ireland and Scotland, for it is so unlike most of them : Dublin Bay, while less grand and not so beautiful as Clew Bay, is the one that is most like it. Howth has somewhat the same position with regard to Dublin Bay that Clare Island occupies with regard to Clew Bay, and Slieve Coolan—in the name of all that's decent

let that abominable name "Sugarloaf" be dropped
for ever—is the presiding mountain genius of
Dublin Bay, just as Croagh Patrick is the presiding mountain genius of Clew Bay. Both bays
are beautiful rather than sublime ; they are
bright and cheerful rather than dark and frowning.
With all the wildness and grandeur of the many
far-entering fiords of the coast of Scotland, with
all the Alpine glories of their shores, there is not
one of them that for beauty alone can be compared with Clew Bay. It is shrouded by no
terror-striking precipices. No cataracts pour into
it even in flood time. No mountains overhang
it. It seems to have been made to cheer and
to delight, and not to terrify or to startle. It
seems to have said to the mountains round it—
"Stand back ; come not too near me lest your
shadows should fall on me and hide, even for
an instant, one gleam of my radiant loveliness."
So the mountains round it do stand back, and
this is the one cause of its winsomeness, bright-
ness, and cheerfulness. When the tide is full on
a sunny day, Clew Bay seems absolutely to laugh.
No shadow of surrounding hills can fall upon
it, for they are too far away. It is as bright and
as radiant a bay as there is in the world, and the
glory of the coasts of Connacht.

Clew Bay has a great advantage over the greater part of the bays on the Irish coast on account of its size. Killary Bay is in no place more than a mile wide, but Clew Bay is fully seven miles wide at its narrowest part, and about sixteen miles long—that is from Clare Island to the quay at Westport. Those who desire to see this splendid bay aright should not attempt to look at it from the town of Westport, for it cannot be seen to advantage from there. Neither can it be seen to advantage except during high tide, when all its multitude of islands are clearly defined. Let them ascend the high lands east of the town of Westport for about a mile, and then look back on the scene beneath them. If the day is fine, if there is plenty of sunlight, they will have to be the least sensitive of mortals if they can gaze on such a scene unmoved. Scenes sublimer and grander, and views more extensive, can be found in other countries; but for pure beauty—a beauty that seems to laugh and rejoice at its own matchless charms—Clew Bay may challenge anything of its kind on earth.

North of the bay rises that most symmetrical of Irish mountains, Croagh Patrick, or the Reek, as it is frequently called. It seems to have been made to order, it is so regular and at the same time so graceful and grand in its outlines. There are few mountains of its height that look so high as Croagh Patrick. It is somewhat less than three thousand feet high, but owing to its symmetry and its steepness it looks higher and more imposing than many mountains of double its altitude. Exactly at the mouth of the bay, stretching almost straight across it, and almost completely shutting it in from the Atlantic, rises the great mass of Clare Island, making the bay a safe harbour as well as adding in a most extraordinary degree to its beauty. Clare Island is almost a mountain; its highest point cannot be less than fifteen hundred feet above the sea level, and it rises sheer from the water. It is almost as beautiful an object as Croagh Patrick itself. The hills on the north side of the bay are rather tame, but the beauty of the famous Reek is such that almost any other mountain would appear tame in comparison with it. The number of islands in Clew Bay is said to be three hundred and sixty-five—one for every day in the year. There seem not to be any exact details as to the number of these islands, but it cannot be much less than the number stated. They seem so numerous as to be uncountable. The reason that those wishing to see this wondrous

bay at its best are advised to see it when the tide
is full is because all the islands do not appear at
low water. This is certainly a defect, but no sea
loch looks so well at low water as when the tide
is full. The citizens of Dublin know what a
difference the tide being in or out makes in the
appearance of their own magnificent bay. But in
Clew Bay the difference in its appearance caused
by the tide being full or low is much greater than
in the bay of Dublin, for the reason that has been
already stated. However much the difference the
state of the tide may make in Clew Bay, it is
beyond all doubt the most beautiful bay, not only
in Ireland, but in all those countries known as the
British Isles.

Those who go to this part of the west coast in
search of the sublime and beautiful should not
omit to ascend Croagh Patrick, and gaze from
its top on one of the grandest and most extensive
views to be seen in Ireland. The mountain, seen
from Westport or its environs, appears wellnigh inaccessible, but it is not so steep on its south side,
and can be ascended with no great amount of difficulty. The view from Croagh Patrick is one of
the most sublime that can be imagined. The whole
of that wild, storm-beaten, cliff-guarded coast of
Connacht, from Slyne Head in Connemara to the

most northern part of Mayo, lies before one; and
Clew Bay, beautiful as it is from wherever it is
seen, seems fairer than ever when seen from the
summit of Croagh Patrick.

Going north from Clew Bay the next most
interesting and wild spot is the island of Achill,
and the grandest things there are the cliffs of
Minnaun and Slieve More.   As we are going
north, Minnaun Cliffs, which are on the southern
side of Achill, must be spoken about first.   They
are seven hundred feet in height, and will, therefore, average higher than the cliffs of Moher in
the County Clare, but they do not rise perpendicularly from the sea as those of Moher do.
But their sea sides are so steep as to be quite
inaccessible even to the wild goats which still
haunt the cliffs of Achill.   The cliffs of Minnaun
are magnificent, but if they rose sheer from the
sea they would form a much more grand and
impressive sight.

But the cliffs of Minnaun, gigantic as they are,
are only insignificant · things compared with the
great sea wall on the northern shores of the
island, formed by Slieve More and Croghan.
The whole northern shore of Achill, from Achill
head in the extreme west of the island to the
narrow straight that separates it from the main-

land on the east, a distance of some thirteen miles, may be said to be a terrific barrier of cliffs, rising to the height of over two thousand feet at the hills Croghan and Slieve More. It is generally allowed that the north shore of Achill has the most stupendous mural cliffs that are to be seen anywhere nearer than Norway, and that even Norway has not very much cliff scenery more magnificent. There is nothing in the shape of cliffs or sea walls in these islands that can compare with the cliffs of Achill in grandeur except Slieve League in Donegal, of which mention will soon be made. A geologist has said, speaking of the cliffs of Achill, that it appeared to him as if part of the mountain which forms the western extremity of the island, and terminates in the noted cape of Achill head, had suffered dis-severance from a sunken continent by some convulsion of Nature. These gigantic cliffs can only be seen to advantage from the sea, but in the almost entire absence of passenger steam-boats on these coasts, it is very difficult for those who visit them to get a proper means of seeing them as they ought to be seen. They rise from out of one of the stormiest oceans in the world, that even in summer-time is often rough and dangerous; and very few would care to risk their

lives in the cockle-shell boats, or *currachs*, of
fishermen to see the stupendous cliffs of Achill
from where they look best. In far distant Norway there are plenty of large and commodious
steamboats to take tourists all round its coasts;
but if they want to see some of the grandest
and most beautiful scenery of their own country
to its best advantage, they must trust to a
fisherman's cot.

It would take at least a week of the longest
summer days to see all the wonders and grandeur
of these tremendous cliffs, or rather cliff mountains,
of Achill. In the interior of the island there is
not anything of great interest to be seen, but
it has more cliff scenery of the stupendous sort
to boast of than perhaps any other island of its
size in the world.

It is a "far cry" from Achill to Slieve League
in Donegal—considerably over a hundred miles
if the coast is followed; but between the giant
sea walls of that island and Slieve League there is
nothing of their kind that will in any way bear comparison with them. There is, however, much magnificent scenery on the northern coast of Connacht,
and also a great many things of antiquarian interest.
There is the extraordinary Druid remains of Car-
rowmore, only three miles from Sligo town, where

there are almost, if not quite, half a hundred cromlechs to be seen on about half a dozen acres. They are of almost all sizes. Some of them are baby cromlechs, the top stones of which are not much more than a hundredweight. This place must have been a sort of Stonehenge at one time. In no other known spot of either these islands or France are so many cromlechs to be seen in so small a space, and very few seem to know anything about it. Sir Samuel Ferguson seems to have been the only person who has written anything about it. But here the same disrespect for monuments of antiquity that has been so long prevalent all over the country may be noticed. Many of the cromlechs have been torn down, and some of them have been actually made to serve as road walls and have been built over. Fully half of them have been either utterly torn down or in some way mutilated. Their generally small size has made them an easy prey for those who wanted stones to build walls or houses. These curious relics of far-back ages should not be allowed to be any further ruined.

The country in the vicinity of Sligo is one of the most interesting and beautiful in Ireland. Close to it is the famous Loch Gill, the queen of the fresh water lakes of Connacht. It is so

LOCH GILL.

near the coast that it is not improper to say
something about it in treating of the scenery of
the coast. It is connected with the sea by a
river only a few miles in length that passes
through the town of Sligo, consequently it is
only three or four miles in a direct line from
the sea. There is no other large fresh water
lake in Ireland, except Loch Corrib, so near
the sea as Loch Gill. It is fully ten miles in
extreme length, and from three to four in
breadth. Its shores cannot be said to be mountainous, but the hills around it are so bold, and
their lower parts are so well wooded, that Loch
Gill, in spite of its having comparatively few
islands, is yet one of the most beautiful lakes
in Ireland, and no one in search of the beautiful
should omit to see it. There is no other town
in Ireland that has more objects of scenic and
archæological interest in its vicinity than Sligo.
There is the immense cairn on top of Knocknarea,
sixteen hundred feet above the level of the sea.
There are four or five other immense cairns close
to the town, and there is the extraordinary mountain of Ben Bulben, anciently Ben Gulban, that
is shaped like a gigantic rick of turf. It is a
couple of miles long, and some sixteen hundred
feet above the level of the sea. Its summit is

perfectly flat. It can be ascended in a carriage from the south side; but on the north side, facing the sea, it is not only perpendicular, but overhangs its base in some places. If not the highest or most beautiful mountain in Ireland, it is certainly the most extraordinary.

We now approach the famous Slieve League, the grandest, the boldest, the steepest, if not the highest, of all the cliff barriers on the coasts of these islands, and one of the most remarkable in the known world. It can be seen from the shore near Sligo, rising almost perpendicularly from the sea. The cliff-mountains of Achill, colossal as they are, seem to shun the full fury of the western gales, for they face the northwest; but Slieve League looks almost due southwest, and thrusts itself out into the ocean as if to court the most tremendous shock of the Atlantic's billows. It forms the culminating point of a range of cliffs that are over six miles in extent, extending from Carrigan Head to Teelin Head, the lowest cliff of which is over seven hundred feet in height. Slieve League is two thousand feet high, and almost perpendicular. It is two hundred feet lower than the highest of the cliff-mountains of Achill, but it is bolder, nearer being perpendicular, grander, and more rugged than they. Those who have not been on the sea at the base of Slieve League cannot form a true idea of its awful grandeur. Its summit is almost as sharp as a knife blade; and he who could look from the jagged rocks that form its cone down on to the seething ocean under him without feeling giddy should have a steady head and strong nerves. Those who go from these islands to Norway in search of the sublime should first see this king Irish cliff-mountains, and know how grand and beautiful are the sights that may be seen at home.

The whole of the coast of Donegal is magnificent. There is no other cliff on it as high or as grand as Slieve League, but there are hundreds of places along its nearly a hundred miles of iron-bound, storm-beaten coast that are well worth seeing. It has nothing like Clew Bay, but it has gigantic cliffs, narrow arms of the sea, some of which are nearly as wild and as grand as the famous Killary Bay that has already been described. There may be certain places in the more southern coasts that are finer and fairer than anything on the coasts of Donegal with the exception of Slieve League, but for general wildness and cliff scenery there is hardly any sea-coast county in Ireland can equal it. It has the longest sea loch in the island on its coast—namely, Loch Swilly. Following its windings from its mouth to where it begins must be over five' and twenty miles. It is a beautiful lake also, and hardly known at all to tourists, and never can be known until better means are supplied for seeing it from a steamer on its waters. The "wild west coast" may be said to end at the mouth of Loch Swilly. From there eastward it is the northern coast. There is much of the grand, beautiful, and curious to be seen on the northern coast from Inishowen to Fair Head, including the celebrated Giant's Causeway, and "high Dunluce's castle walls." The latter have been already described.

It would be hard to find anywhere in the world another sea coast of the same length as that from Cape Clear in the south to Inishowen in the north, where there is so much to be seen of the grand, the terrible, and the beautiful. If the mountains on the coasts of Norway are higher, if its fiords penetrate further inland, and if in some places the shining glacier may be seen from them, there is not such astonishing variety of scenery on the coasts of Norway as there is in the west coast of Ireland. The climate of Norway does not permit the growth of many species

of wild flowers which add so much to the beauty
of even the wildest and most sterile parts of
Ireland. In Norway there are no mountains
radiant with purple heather and golden furze,—
mountains that may be unsightly and sombre for
ten months out of the twelve, but are, in autumn,
turned into living bouquets, thousands of feet in
height, and with areas of tens of thousands of
acres. Moisture and mildness of climate are the
parents of flowers. If rain and mist hide for
days and weeks the most beautiful scenery in
Ireland, there is ample compensation afterwards
in the bloom of wild flowers more luxuriant and
more plentiful than can be found where there is
more sunlight and less moisture.

It is a curious and humiliating fact that, so far as
can be learned from the sources at command, there
are ten people who go from these islands to the
coasts of Norway every year for the one that visits
the west coast of Ireland. It may be that many
people go to Norway just because it has become
fashionable to go there, but all the fashion in the
world would not send people five or six hundred
miles across a stormy sea if there was not good
accommodation for them to go to that distant
country, and good means for seeing its beauties.
Let there be the same means for seeing the

x

beauties of the west coast of Ireland as there are
for seeing the coast of Norway, and thousands
will visit the former every year. Those who
want to see the grandeur of the Norwegian coast
go in large and well-equipped steamers, and live
in them, eat and sleep in them for weeks together,
while they are brought from fiord to fiord and from
town to town. Let similar means be had for those
who desire to see the west coast of Ireland, and it
will not be long unknown.

There is no way to see coast scenery properly
except from the sea. One might be looking at
Slieve League or the Cliffs of Moher all his life
from the land, but he could never have a full
idea of their grandeur unless he saw them from
the sea at their base. Those who see the cliffs
and cliff-mountains of Norway from the deck of
a commodious steamer see them aright. Most
of those who make the trip to Norway are loud
in praise of its magnificent coast scenery; but if
they had to go by land from fiord to fiord, as
they would have to do on the west coast of
Ireland did they want to see its beauties, would
they be so enchanted? They certainly would not.
When tourists go to see the Norwegian fiords,
they need not trouble themselves about engaging
beds, or worry themselves by fearing that the

hotel in such a place will be full, for they have
an hotel on board the steamer, are carried from
place to place, and are given ample time to see
the beauties of each place. If there were the
best hotels in the world at every romantic spot
on the west coast of Ireland it would never
attract visitors, and never would be known as
it should be, and as its wondrous grandeur and
beauty entitle it to be, until large and commodious steamers were provided in which people
could live, if they chose, while being brought
from one place of attraction to another, or from
one town to another. There are few coasts in
the world better provided with harbours than the
west coast of Ireland. It could hardly happen
that a steamer like those that take tourists from
Leith to the coasts of Norway could be caught
by a gale on any part of the coast from Cape
Clear to Malin Head, ten miles from a harbour
in which she could not take shelter. The danger
of shipwreck would be so small as to be infinitesi-
mal. The trip from Cape Clear to Malin Head,
or even to the Giant's Causeway, could be made
in two weeks, and give sufficient time to stop a
day or more at such remarkable places as Clew
Bay or the Arran Islands, where things of more
than ordinary interest are to be seen, such as the

view of Clew Bay from the high lands east of it,
and the cyclopean ruins in the islands Arran,
the most colossal and extraordinary things of their
kind in Europe.   There ought to be enterprise
enough in Ireland to put a steamer, like those
that take tourists to Norway every summer, on
the Irish west coast for three or four months
every year.   Without such means of seeing the
beauties of the west coast, as only a large, commodious steamer could furnish, the beauties and
the grandeur of the cliffs of Moher, Clew Bay,
Slieve More, and Slieve League will never be
known as they should be.

There is only one part of the Irish west coast
where harbours for large craft are scarce, and that
is the Donegal coast.   It is said that there is no
safe harbour between Killybegs and Loch Swilly,
a distance of nearly a hundred miles.   This is
unfortunate; but stormy as the north-west coast
is, there are always many days in summer when
steamers could go from harbour to harbour in a
calm sea.

DUBLIN AND ITS ENVIRONS

Some may think, especially natives of Ireland, that writing about Dublin and its environs is mere waste of time, ink, and paper, seeing that there is so much known about them already. It should, however, be remembered that this book is intended for people who are not Irish, as well as for the Irish themselves. But even the Irish, and above all, the natives of Dublin, want to be told something that may be new to some of them about a city which so many of them seem neither to love nor admire as they should. 'There is, unfortunately, a certain class of people in Dublin who, although many of them were born there, think that it is one of the most backward and unpleasant places in Europe. They do not admire the beauty of its environs, and will not acknowledge willingly that it has been improved so much as it has been during the last twenty-five years. It has been improved and beautified in spite of them. 'Those citizens of Dublin who take no pride in it should go abroad and see as many cities as the author of this book has seen, and they would come back

with more just ideas about Dublin. ⸣If there is
any other city in Europe as large as Dublin, with
environs more beautiful, where life is more enjoyable, and where life and property are more secure,
it would be interesting to know where that city is.
Dublin is a great deal too good for a good many
who live in it.⸣

The history of Dublin may be said to commence
with the Danish invasions of Ireland. It is rarely
mentioned in Irish annals before the time when the
Danes took it, and first settled in it in the year
836, according to the Four Masters. It probably existed as a small city long before the Danes
got possession of it, and there is reason to believe
that it was a place of some maritime trade at a
remote period. It is stated on legendary more
than on historic authority, that when Conn of the
Hundred Battles and Eoghan Mór divided the
island between them in the third century, the
Liffey was, for a certain part of its length, the
boundary between their dominions; and that the
fact of more ships landing on the north side of
the river than on the south side gave offence to
Eoghan, who owned the southern shore of the
Liffey, and caused a war between the two poten-
tates. It is, however, hardly probable that Dublin
was a place of much importance before its occupa-

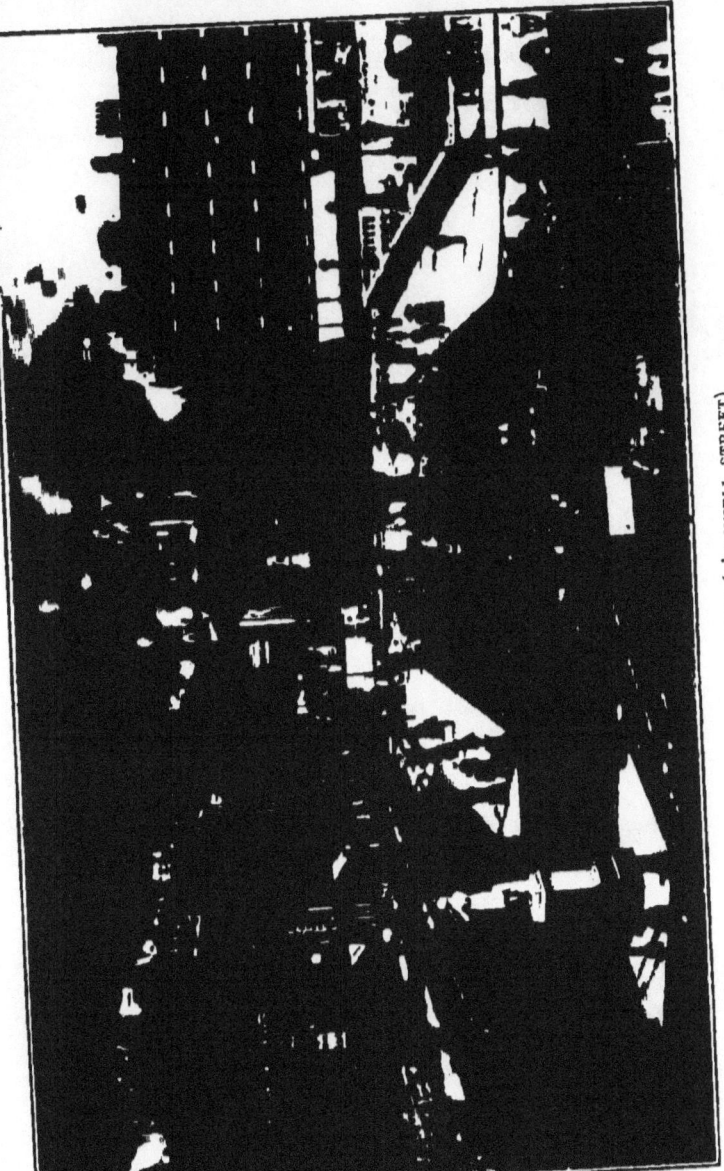

SACKVILLE STREET (O'CONNELL STREET).

tion by the Scandinavians in the first half of the ninth century.

The Irish name of Dublin is, perhaps, the longest one by which any city in Europe is called. It is *Baile Atha Cliath Dubhlinne,* and means the town of the ford of hurdles of black pool. In ancient Irish documents it is generally shortened to *Ath Cliath,* and sometimes to *Dubhlinn.* We have no means of knowing what was the size or population of Dublin in Danish times; but long after it became the seat of English government in Ireland, it extended east no further than where the city hall now stands in Dame Street, no further west than James Street, and no further south than the lower part of Patrick Street; both Patrick's cathedral and the Comb having been outside the city walls.

We have no account of the first siege of Dublin by the Danes in 836. The annals merely say that a fleet of sixty ships of Northmen came to the Liffey, and that that was the first occupation of the city by them. The Irish captured and plundered Dublin a great many times, but do not appear to have ever tried to banish the Danes permanently out of it. It is probable that the Irish found them useful as carriers of merchandise to them from foreign countries; for seeing how often the city was captured and plundered by the Irish, it is incredible that they could not have held it had they chosen to do so. The Four Masters record its capture and plunder by the Irish in A.D. 942, 945, 988, and 998. In 994 Malachy II. sacked Dublin and carried off two Danish trophies, the ring of Tomar and the sword of Karl; and in 988 he besieged it for twenty days and twenty nights, captured it, and carried off an immense booty; and issued the famous edict, "Every Irishman that is in slavery and oppression in the country of the foreigners (Danes) let him go to his own country in peace and delight." But the Irish were not always lucky in their attacks on the Danes of Dublin, for in 917 Niall Glundubh, King of Ireland, was killed by them, and his army defeated at Killmashogue, beyond Rathfarnham. He evidently intended to take Dublin from the south, because it was so well defended on the north by the Liffey. The battle usually known as the battle of Clontarf was not fought in the locality now called by that name, but between the Liffey and the Tolka. Where Amien Street is now was probably the very centre of the battle-field. Here it may not be out of place to make a remark on the curious fact that the Danes never made any serious attempt to conquer Ireland after the battle of Clontarf, although they were at the height of their power some six or eight years after by the terrible defeat they gave the Saxons at Ashington, in Essex, which gave Canute the crown of England. He thus became not only King of England, but was King of Denmark and Norway as well—the most powerful potentate in Christendom in his time. It is strange that historians have not taken any notice of this extraordinary fact. There was comparatively little fighting between the Irish and the Danes after the battle of Clontarf, although the foreign people held Dublin until the arrival of Strongbow, and made a very poor stand against him, for he captured the city with very little difficulty. Dublin has hardly suffered what could be called a siege since 988, when Malachy II. took it from the Danes. When Strongbow held it, the Irish under the wretched Roderick O'Connor marched a great army under its walls, and were going to take it; but before they began siege operations, and while they were amusing themselves by swimming in the Liffey, Strongbow sallied out on them and totally defeated them. That was the last serious attempt to besiege Dublin.

Dublin does not appear to have grown much until after the wretched, and for Ireland terribly

unfortunate, Jacobite wars were over. It grew
and prospered rapidly almost all through the eigh-
teenth century when a native parliament sat there;
but from about 1820 until about 1870 there was
not very much either of growth or improvement
in it. Since then, in spite of what the census
may show, it has grown considerably, and has been
improved immensely. It is not easy to see what
has caused such improvement in Dublin since 1870.
The only way that the improvement in the state
of the streets, the pulling down of old buildings
and the erection of new ones, can be accounted
for, is by the fact that the local government of
the city is in the hands of a different class of men
from those who ruled it so long and so badly up
to about the time mentioned. When one considers all that has been done since then in the
paving of streets, the laying down of new side
walks, the tearing down of old buildings, the
erection of cottages for the working classes where
rotten and pestiferous houses had stood, the
deepening of the river so that the largest ships
can now enter it, the extension and perfecting
of the tram-car system, and other improvements
too numerous to mention, it strikes him as something astonishing; but when it is remembered that
all these improvements have taken place in the

face of declining trade, declining population, and declining wealth in the country at large, what has been accomplished becomes absolutely sublime. It shows clearly that there is a class of the Irish people who, with all their faults, possess hearts and souls

"that sorrows have frowned on in vain,
  Whose spirit outlives them, unfading and warm";

and that they never give up and never despair. Never has any city been so much improved in so short a time, and in the face of such difficulties. The improvements are still being carried on. If they are carried on for another quarter of a century at the same rate at which they were carried on during the last quarter of a century, Dublin will be one of the cleanest, pleasantest, healthiest, and most beautiful cities in the world.

In an educational point of view, there are very few cities either in these islands or on the Continent that offer more facilities for culture than Dublin. Its new National Library is, for its size, one of the finest and best organised and best managed in Europe. It is not a British Museum, nor is it a Bibliothèque Nationale; and the citizens of Dublin who have children who are fond of reading, and who wish to add to their store of knowledge, ought to feel very well satisfied that their National Library is *not* like either the monstrous and little-good-to-the-masses institution in London, or the still more monstrous and still less good-to-the-masses institution in Paris. Those to whom time is of little value can afford to wait during a considerable part of the day to get a book from the great libraries of London and Paris; but for any one to whom time is really valuable, to visit the great libraries mentioned as a reader of their books, should, in most cases, be the last thing he should think of.

There are three libraries in Dublin, of which two are free to any one known as a respectable person—these are the National Library and the Royal Irish Academy. To become a reader in Trinity College Library costs, to a person known to be respectable, only a couple of shillings a year. Seeing the facilities that are in Dublin for cultured people, or for those who wish to become cultured, it is strange that it does not stand higher as an educational centre. The three great libraries it contains—that is, the National Library, Trinity College Library and the Royal Irish Academy—contain almost every sort of book required for the most complete education in every art and science known to civilised men. But one of the grand advantages of these institutions, an advantage almost as great to the people at large as the treasures they contain, is the fact that they are not controlled by "red tapeism." The amount of trouble and downright humiliation one has to go through to become a reader in the British Museum of London, or in the Bibliothèque Nationale in Paris, is enough to deter any but a person of nerve from seeking admittance to them as a reader. The British Museum is not so bad in the matter of "red tapeism" as it might perhaps be; but the Bibliothèque Nationale puts so many obstacles in the way of those who desire to become readers, that it is little else than a disgrace to Paris and to France. For ridiculous red tapeism it beats any institution of its kind on earth. There are probably not three libraries in the world more easy of access than the three Dublin ones that have been mentioned, and in which there is less red tapeism, or more courtesy shown to readers.

The buildings that have been recently erected in Kildare Street, Dublin, the Library and the Museum, would be considered chaste and elegant in any city in the world; and it is questionable if any buildings of their kind can be found in any city to surpass them in architectural beauty. Even the Picture Gallery and the Natural History Gallery, close to them in Leinster Lawn, are very handsome buildings. If the front of Leinster House, facing Kildare Street, were brightened up and made to look like its rear, the whole group of buildings, including Leinster House itself, would form an architectural panorama hardly to be surpassed anywhere; and if Dublin contained nothing else worthy of being seen, it would make Dublin worth travelling hundreds of miles to see.

But it is the Museum of Irish Antiquities that is, or that ought to be, the glory of this splendid group of buildings, and it is the only one of them with the management of which fault can be justly found. The way it has been managed ever since the articles it contains were removed from the Royal Irish. Academy in Dawson Street is a disgrace to all Ireland, and a blot on the Irish people. There is not room to show the public much more than half the objects of antiquity. They are stowed away in drawers, and have been so for nearly ten long years. They might as well be in the earth from which they were recovered as be packed into drawers in a back room where none but officials can see them. If there was a decent and proper national spirit among the Irish people, such treatment of Ireland's wonderful and unique antiquities would not be tolerated for a single week. Her antiquities are among the chief glories of Ireland. In monuments of the past she stands ahead of almost all countries save Greece and Egypt. It is not alone in her ruined fanes, round towers, gigantic *raths*, sepulchral mounds, and Cyclopean fortresses that she can boast of antiquarian curiosities more numerous and more unique than those of almost any other country, but also in her multitudinous articles in gold, bronze, and iron. A good many of these—the greater part of them, perhaps—are in positions where they can be seen; but thousands of them are where no one but an official can see them. If the Irish antiquarian department were properly arranged, and if *all* the objects it possesses that have been dug up from Irish soil were properly exhibited, Ireland could boast of an exhibition of national antiquities greater, more entirely her own, and more unique than that possessed by any other country in Europe.

Some may think that this statement is not true. They may point to the enormous collection of antiquities in the museum in Naples. It is, however, hardly fair to class the treasures of that museum with the objects found in Ireland. It was the accidental calamity that befel Herculaneum and Pompeii that stocked the museum in Naples. If that calamity had not happened, it is all but certain that not a single object in the Neapolitan

Y

museum would now be extant. It was by no
accidental calamity that the enormous number of
Irish antique objects were brought to light. They
were found from time to time all over the country.
There are many private collections in the hands of
private individuals in almost all the large towns in
Ireland, and a very large percentage of the bronze
objects in the British Museum were found in
Ireland. No other country of its size has yielded
so many objects of a far-back antiquity. It seems
a pity that those who have so many private collections of antique objects in so many parts of Ireland
do not send them all to the Royal Irish Academy;
but if they are to lie there, stowed away in drawers
in a back room, they might better remain in the
hands of private collectors. If there was a real
national press in Ireland, there would be such wide-
spread indignation awakened at the way Irish antiquities have been treated since they were removed
to the Museum in Kildare Street that those who
manage it would be *forced* to treat one of the
finest collections of its kind in the world in a very
different manner. Hardly a word has appeared in
the Dublin press protesting against the way the
department of Irish antiquities has been managed.

With all the advantages Dublin possesses over
most of the European capitals in great facilities for

education, in cheap house rent as compared with
many other cities, in uncommon beauty of environs,
very few rich, retired people with families to
educate, choose it for a residence.   It is not to be
wondered at that wealthy English and Scotch
people should prefer to live in their own countries,
but wealthy Irish people seem not to desire to live
in Dublin unless it is their native place.   Ireland,
unfortunately, does not possess very many rich
people, but she has at least some outside of
Dublin ; but very few of these, even if they have
young, growing-up families, go to reside in the
capital in order to educate them.   Some seem to
think that outside of Trinity College, Dublin has
no advantages in an educational point of view
worth speaking of.   This is not now the case.   It
is true that some years ago Trinity College was the
only institution in Dublin where high-class education could be obtained, but it is not so any longer,
since the rise of other educational institutions.
But it is in the excellence of its libraries, and the
easy access that there is to them, that Dublin
offers such great advantages to those who do not
desire to enter Trinity College.   There is, of
course, a much larger collection of books in the
British Museum, and in many of the Continental
libraries, than there is in the libraries of Dublin ;

but between red tapeism, and the greater number of readers that frequent those places as compared with the Dublin libraries, it is safe to say that more reading could be done and more knowledge gained by a student in one week in a Dublin library than in two weeks in any of those enormous places where there are such crowds and consequently such loss of time.

It is, however, hardly to be wondered at that Dublin has heretofore attracted so few rich people to it. It got a name for being dirty and ill-governed; and it has to be confessed that the name was, in a large measure, deserved. Dublin *was* dirty and *was* badly governed, but it is not now. A bad name lasts a long time, and is not easily got rid of; and the improvements made in Dublin are of such recent origin that it is only natural that outsiders should think it is still what it was thirty years ago. Let Dublin continue to be improved for the next twenty years as it has been during the twenty years that have elapsed, and it will be one of the most attractive of the European capitals. It is not yet what it should be; there are many things of many kinds in it which require improvement or alteration; but so much good has been done already that it is only reasonable to expect that still more will be done, and that the time cannot be far distant when the city "of the black pool," badly as its English translation may appear, will attract not only visitors from all parts of the world, but rich people who will take up permanent abode there, attracted by the educational advantages it will afford, by the beauty and cleanliness of the city itself, and by the superlative beauty of the country around it.

The situation of Dublin can hardly be called romantic. It is built at the mouth of a river, and consequently not on high ground; but the site is good, for the ground rises on both sides of the Liffey, making the drainage easy. When the system of main drainage that is now being carried out is finished, it will be one of the best drained cities in the world. Dublin has not such a picturesque site as Edinburgh has, neither has any other city in Europe; but outside of Edinburgh there are no objects of scenic interest unless one goes forty or fifty miles away to see them. But if the site of Dublin cannot be called picturesque, it can boast of having some of the most beautiful, if not the largest, public buildings in the world. For chasteness, harmony, symmetry, and grace, the Bank of Ireland, if it has any equals at all in modern architecture, has very few. The Custom

House is one of the finest buildings in Europe. The new public buildings, containing the National Library and the Museum, are gems of architectural beauty; so are some of the banks, and so is the Great Southern Railway Terminus, and so are many other public buildings. Dublin cannot boast of possessing any building as large as St Paul's or the Tuileries; but size and beauty are two different things.

But it is in its environs that Dublin stands ahead of all the capitals in Europe, or, perhaps, of any other city of equal size in any country. Because the beauties around Dublin were not described in the first chapters of this work does not imply that they are much inferior to what may be seen in other parts of the country. There is nothing like the Lakes of Killarney in the environs of Dublin, and Dublin Bay is hardly equal to Clew Bay; but barring those two gems of scenic loveliness, it is questionable if there is, for beauty alone, leaving sublimity aside, anything in Ireland that surpasses the immediate environs of Dublin, without going further north than Howth, or further south than Bray. Every inch of the country round Dublin has some peculiar scenic charm of its own. The Botanic Gardens of Glasnevin are the most interesting and beautiful in Europe; not so much for the care that has been taken of them, or the quantity and variety of the plants that are in them, but principally on account of the charming locality in which they are situated. It is not meant to be implied that they are not well taken care of, or that their collection of plants is not both rare and large. What is meant is that had they the rarest and largest collection of plants to be seen in any gardens in the world, they would not have the same attraction were they situated in a less picturesque locality. If ever there was a place made to spend a hot summer day in, it is these gardens, with their murmuring river, their shaded, sunless walks, their gigantic trees and deep glens. The place where the flower gardens of Glasnevin are would still be beautiful if there wasn't a flower in it.

Its bay is the great scenic attraction round Dublin. It cannot be seen to real advantage but from the south-west side of the hill of Howth. The bay has very few islands, but its background of mountains on one side and woodland on the other is so wonderfully fair, that were there myriads of islands to be seen, they could hardly add to the wondrous beauty of the view. What a Scotch mechanic said about the view of Dublin Bay from the high land on the south-west of Howth the first

time he was there will give the reader a better
idea of Dublin Bay than a whole chapter of descriptions, and loses nothing by being expressed
in the strong doric of the north : " Ech, mon, I
seed mony a bonny sicht in Scótland, but this
beats a'." There are many who think the view
from Killiney Hill finer than that from Howth.
The view from the former takes in Sorrento Bay,
which is in reality part of the Bay of Dublin that
can hardly be seen from Howth, and also takes in
many valleys in Wicklow and plains in the interior
that are not visible from Howth. It is not easy to
say which of the views is the finer ; but either is
worth travelling not only ten miles, but a hundred
miles, afoot to see.

In describing the beauties of Dublin Bay, it
cannot be out of place to give the finest poetic
address to it that was ever written. It will be
new to most English and many Irish readers. The
poem is by the late D. F. M'Carthy :—

> " My native Bay, for many a year
> I've loved thee with a trembling fear,
> Lest thou, though dear and very dear,
>   And beauteous as a vision,
> Shouldst have some rival far away,
> Some matchless wonder of a bay,
> Whose sparkling waters ever play
>   'Neath azure skies elysian.

" 'Tis love, methought, blind love that pours
  The rippling magic round these shores,
  For whatsoever love adores
      Becomes what love desireth ;
  'Tis ignorance of aught beside
  That throws enchantment o'er the tide,
  And makes my heart respond with pride
      To what mine eye admireth.

" And thus unto our mutual loss,
  Whene'er I paced the sloping moss
  Of green Killiney, or across
      The intervening waters ;
  Up Howth's brown side my feet would wend
  To see thy sinuous bosom bend,
  Or view thine outstretched arms extend
      To clasp thine islet daughters.

" My doubt was thus a moral mist,—
  Even on the hills when morning kissed
  The granite peaks to amethyst,
      I felt its fatal shadow ;
  It darkened o'er the brightest rills,
  It lowered upon the sunniest hills,
  And hid the wingèd song that fills
      The moorland and the meadow.

" But now that I have been to view
  All that Nature's self could do,
  And from Gaeta's arch of blue
      Borne many a fond memento ;
  And gazed upon each glorious scene,
  Where beauty is and power has been,
  Along the golden shores between
      Misenum and Sorrento ;

" I can look proudly on thy face,
  Fair daughter of a hardier race,
  And feel thy winning well-known grace,
       Without my old misgiving ;
  And as I kneel upon thy strand,
  And clasp thy once unhonoured hand,
  Proclaim earth holds no lovelier land
       Where life is worth the living."

One great charm of the country around Dublin,
like one of the great charms of Killarney, is its
diversity.   There are mountain, bay, woodland, and
river.   There is a variety of scenery in the immediate vicinity of Dublin such as cannot be
found so near any other European capital, and
such as not even Naples itself can boast of.   Great
indeed is the difference in the style of scenery
between the cliffs of Howth and the green lanes
of Clontarf, although both places are hardly more
than four miles apart.   To go a few miles further
from the city, Bray is reached.   It is only twenty-
five minutes by train from Dublin.   There one finds
himself almost within a gunshot of some of the
most picturesque and peculiar scenery in the world.
The Dargle and Powerscourt Waterfall are in the
same locality.   They are gems of loveliness that
surpass anything of their kind in these islands.
Even Killarney has nothing like them.   Their very
smallness adds to their charms.   The Dargle is

exactly what its name, *Dair-gleann*, signifies, an oak-glen. It is a chasm some two or three hundred feet deep, every inch of the sides of which is covered in summer-time with some sort of tree, shrub, or flower. In its depths laughs or murmurs a limpid stream that can rarely be noticed, such is the thickness and luxuriance of the trees and shrubs that overhang it. Powerscourt Waterfall is close by the Dargle. The river that forms it leaps down a rock nearly three hundred feet in height, into a valley of brightest verdure, covered with a thick growth of primeval oak-trees. An enchanting spot—which it is gross folly to attempt to describe—in a land of towering hills and flower-crowned rocks. Its wildness, winsomeness, and loveliness must be seen in order to form anything like a just idea of it. And all within about twelve miles of Dublin!

Then there is Howth on the north side, and only nine miles from Dublin, one of the most wonderful spots of earth for its size in Europe. It is a hill-promontory that juts out into nearly the middle of the bay, about three miles in width and nearly the same in length. It is over five hundred feet high, and in autumn is a pyramid of crimson and gold; for wherever there are not trees or cultivation, there are furze and heath. A place of wondrous beauty of its own, in no way like the Dargle or Powerscourt. From the summit of Howth there is one of the most enchanting and extensive views conceivable, reaching north to the Mourne Mountains and east to Wales. And all this about nine miles from Dublin! Yet with all these glories at her very feet, Dublin is still the Cinderella among the capitals of Europe.

There is beauty of a "truly rural" kind within half-an-hour's walk from the Dublin General Post Office, or from the centre of the city. Thackeray said in his "Irish Sketch Book," half a century ago, that it was curious how some of the streets of Dublin so suddenly ended in potato fields; but the potato fields Thackeray saw there are all covered with houses now. It is true, however, that on the north side of Dublin one gets into the real country by walking only a quarter of an hour from the city limits; no sham country of cabbage gardens, but real fields of grass and grain growing from soil of the most exuberant fertility. Trees and hedgerows abound; so do some of the best and most thrifty farmers in Ireland, who generally pay enormous rents for their land. The country north of Dublin is almost perfectly flat, while on the south side the mountains commence within a few miles of the city limits. But flat as the country north of

Dublin is, it is one of the finest and most fertile parts of Ireland, and was known in ancient times as Fingall, because some *Finn Galls*, or fair-haired foreigners from Scandinavia settled in it when they ceased to plunder churches and monasteries. Those who prefer a flat, well-wooded, and very fertile country to a land of mountains and valleys, like that on the south side of Dublin, should see the plains of Fingall.

It has been said that the gentle and refined are ever fond of flowers. If this be so, the gentle and refined ought to be very plentiful in Dublin and its environs, for in no other part of this planet known to man are there as many wild flowers to be seen so near a great city as in the environs of Dublin. This statement is made in sober earnestness, and with absolute certainty as to its truth. It may be asked, if this is so, how is it to be accounted for? It is easy of explanation. To begin, Ireland is, *par excellence,* the land of wild flowers because of its moist, mild climate and generally rich soil. Sunlight, when it is the burning sunlight of southern climes, is death to flowers. Dublin enjoys a milder climate than any city in Great Britain, although not so mild as Cork or some other Irish southern cities. It is only a few miles from the mountains on the south of

Dublin to Howth on the north. Between Howth and the mountains, if the whole of the mountains of Wicklow are counted and taking inequalities of surface into account, for government surveys always mean level surfaces, there are every autumn at least a hundred thousand acres of wild flowers within half a day's journey of Dublin. It may be said that these wild flowers are nearly all of one species—heath. That is true ; but heath, or heather as it is more frequently called, is a wild flower, and one of the most beautiful that grows. The reason the Irish mountains produce so much more heath than those of Great Britain is because they are less rocky and more boggy, and are in a milder climate. The mountains of Wales, being so stony, have hardly any heath on them. Then there is the furze or gorse, as it is generally called in England. Heath and gorse bloom side by side over thousands of acres in Howth and on the Dublin and Wicklow mountains. Then there is the hawthorn. Where in these islands, or on the continent of Europe, are there as many hawthorns to be seen on an equal space of ground as in the Phœnix Park, Dublin ? Let those who have seen them in their snowy glory of white blossoms in the early summer answer. But there are still other flowers that do certainly bloom in greater luxuriance, and are more plentiful round Dublin than round any other city in these islands—one of these is laburnum.   Florists have said that no-where else does it bloom with such luxuriance as around the Irish capital.   Dublin is indeed seated in a flowery land, for it is well known that even the rich soil of Ireland produces more wild flowers than the rich soil of Great Britain.   It is true that not only the flora but the fauna of Ireland are less numerous in species than those of Great Britain.   There are a great many species of flower-ing plants that are common in the larger island but unknown in the smaller one except in gardens. It is not easy to account for this ; but if there are fewer indigenous flowering plants in Ireland than in Great Britain, the former country produces those that are natural to it in much greater abundance than the latter.   The reason of this is easily under-stood.   It is because the climate of Ireland is milder and moister than that of Great Britain ; and it is probable that the soil is of a different quality in Ireland.   But one thing is certain, that not in England or in any European country are there such a quantity of wild flowers to be seen as in Ireland.   It is not alone on Irish bogs and mountains that wild flowers are more abundant than in most other countries, for the most fertile soil in Ireland, the best fattening land, generally grows wild flowers in such abundance that pastures become parterres.

Dublin and its vicinity are not quite so rich in antiquities as some other parts of Ireland. Very few traces of the old Danish city have been left. Its walls can be traced in some few places. But what sort of houses the people lived in can only be guessed at. They were probably, for the most part, built of wood; for it cannot be too often impressed on those who have a taste for antiquarian studies, that in ancient, and even what is generally known as mediæval times, almost the entire populations of northern countries lived in houses of wood or of mud, and sometimes in houses made of both materials. For centuries after the art of building with stone and mortar was well understood, stone houses were rarely used by the masses either in towns or country places. They had stone-built churches and round towers, and sometimes castles, but the people lived in wooden or in mud houses. Dublin has more round towers in its immediate vicinity than any other Irish city. There are three of them within a few miles' distance. That of Clondalkin is on the Great Southern Railway; that of Lusk is on the Great Northern; and that of Swords is only seven miles from Dublin by road, and only two miles from Malahide Station on the Great Northern. All these towers are in a good state of preservation; but the one at Swords will soon be a ruin if the ivy, with which it has been foolishly allowed to become completely covered, is not removed from it. Ivy holds up for a time a building that is in a state of decay, but in the long run it is sure to ruin it completely; for when the ivy becomes strong enough, it forces its way between the stones, gradually displaces them, and the building then tumbles down. If it is the Board of Works that has charge of the Swords round tower, they are greatly to blame for allowing the ivy to be gradually but surely bringing it to certain ruin. If it is under the control of a private person, public opinion should compel him to have the ivy removed from what was not long ago one of the most perfect and best preserved of Irish round towers.

There is something connected with the census of Dublin published in Thom's directory from official documents which may be more interesting to some than any description of the Irish capital, however graphic. This something is an evident error that has, by some means, been made in enumeration of its inhabitants. According to the published census, there were in round numbers 13,000 more people in Dublin in 1851 than in 1891; and only 14,000 more in county and city included in 1891 than in 1851. There is a gross error here, for between the two epochs mentioned, the increase in what is generally known as the metropolitan district has been so great that it is visible to anyone who has been familiar with Dublin for forty years. It is known that since 1851 nearly 25,000 houses have been erected in city and county. That number of houses would represent at least 100,000 people, but it only represents 14,000 according to the census, or two-thirds of a person to each house! It may be said that a great many houses have been pulled down in the city since 1851. True, there have; but ten have been built since then for the one that has been pulled down. There are at least a dozen streets, large and small, in Dublin, the population of which is four times greater than it was in 1851; for there were no tenement houses in those streets then, whereas they are all tenement houses now, and consequently there are four or five families instead of one in each house. The great increase in the population of Dublin during the last forty or forty-five years is quite apparent in the more crowded state of the thoroughfares. It seems not only probable, but

certain, from all the data that can be got at outside
the census, that there are from fifty to one hundred
thousand more people in what is known as the
metropolitan district of Dublin than is shown by
the published census. This will go far to account
for the weekly death-rate of Dublin being generally
higher than that of any other city in these islands ;
for if the weekly number of deaths is based on a
population less than what it is, it will make the
weekly death-rate per thousand higher than it
should be. This is a very serious matter for
Dublin, for nothing has a more detrimental effect
on the welfare of a city than getting the name of
being unhealthy.

It is to be hoped that the reader will not set
down either to national bigotry or private advantage what has been said in praise of Dublin and its
environs. The writer may be national in the broad
sense of the word, but he has no sentimental love
for Dublin beyond any other Irish city. He is not
influenced by the *genius loci;* he has no personal
interest whatever in Dublin. What he has said in
its praise, and in praise of its environs, would be
said of Timbuctoo had he the same knowledge of
the African city that he has of Dublin, and were
Timbuctoo and its environs as worthy of laudation.
Dublin is not his native city ; but even if it were

he would be perfectly justified in telling the truth about it. If what he has said about Dublin be untrue, it can easily be shown to be untrue. If that city has not been improved and beautified in a most remarkable manner during the last twenty-five years; if some of its public buildings are not remarkable specimens of architectural excellence; if its environs are not beautiful beyond those of any other European capital; if any of these statements be untrue, let them be proved to be so at the very earliest opportunity.

BELFAST AND ITS ENVIRONS

BELFAST is not only the second city in Ireland in population and wealth, but the second in beauty of environs. Its growth has been, during the last three-quarters of a century, greater than that of any city in these islands. It is an immense jump in population from 37,000 in 1821 to 273,000 in 1891. In splendour of public buildings, cleanliness of streets, and general appearance, Belfast can be favourably compared with any city of equal size in any country. Its citizens are proud of it, and so they ought to be, for it was their own enterprise that made it what it is. The extraordinarily rapid growth of Belfast shows what manufactures can do for a city, for without them it would still be hardly more important than any of the provincial towns of Ulster. It has an excellent harbour, and besides its linen manufactures, it has become one of the most important ship-building places in the world. But it was its linen manufactures that gave Belfast the start. It is the largest linen mart in the world ; but unfortunately for it, and every other place in which the manu-

facture of linen is carried on, the competition of
cotton fabrics is rapidly making the manufacture
of linen less profitable, and threatens to drive it
out of use almost entirely in the long run.   If
cotton were unknown, Belfast would be now, in
all probability, a place of a million of inhabitants,
and Ireland would be one of the richest, if not the
very richest, country of its size in the world.   It
is well known that for flax growing and for linen
bleaching Ireland is ahead of all countries.
Experts say that in no other country can flax be
grown with a fibre so strong and yet so fine as
in Ireland.   It seems to be the country of all
others that is best suited for the growth of flax
out of which the finest linen fabrics can be made.
It would almost seem as if Ireland was fated to
be for ever suffering some sort of ill-luck, and that
things which are blessings to humanity at large
are often misfortunes to her.   There cannot be
any doubt but that the cotton plant has proved
one of the greatest of blessings to mankind in
general, but it has been a great misfortune to
Ireland.   Were it not for cotton, three-fourths of
the land of Ireland would now be growing flax,
and it would most likely contain a dozen linen
manufacturing centres as large as Belfast.   Whatever the future of the linen trade may be, it is

hardly possible that Belfast can ever sink into insignificance, for its people have so much of the true commercial spirit in them that if linen became as useless as the chain armour of the middle ages, they would turn their energies to some other branch of manufacture and make it a success.

Belfast hardly figures at all in ancient Irish history or annals. It is a comparatively new place. It is first mentioned in the Annals of the Four Masters under the year 1476, where it is said, "A great army was led by O'Neill against the son of Hugh Boy O'Neill; and he attacked the castle of Bel-feiriste, which he took and demolished, and then returned to his house." The name Belfast is a corruption of *Bél-feiriste*, or as it would probably be written in modern Irish, Beul-fearsaide, the mouth or pass of the spindle. This seems nonsense, but the following, from Joyce's "Irish Names of Places," will explain it : "The word *fearsad* is applied to a sand-bank formed near the mouth of a river by the opposing currents of tide and stream, which at low water often formed a firm and comparatively safe passage across. The term is pretty common, especially in the west, where these *fearsets* are of considerable importance; as in many places they serve the inhabitants instead of bridges. A sand-bank of

this kind across the mouth of the Lagan gave
name to Belfast, which is called in Irish authorities Bel-feirisde, the ford of the *farset;* and the
same name in the uncontracted form, Belfarsad,
occurs in Mayo." The Irish name for a spindle
is *fearsaid;* it also means a sand-bank, as described
above, probably because the shape of such sand-
banks is generally something like that of a spindle.
According to the orthography of the Four Masters,
whose spelling of place names is generally correct,
feiriste is the genitive singular of *fearsaid;* while
in the name "Belfarsad," mentioned by Joyce,
forsad seems to be the genitive plural.

Belfast and its environs cannot be said to be
very rich in monuments of antiquity. There are,
however, two round towers not far from it; one
at Antrim, some fifteen miles away, in excellent
preservation; and one at Drumbo, in the County
Down, about five miles from the city. The last
is in a ruined condition—not much more than
thirty feet of it remains. But Belfast can
boast of the most extraordinary monument of
antiquity of its kind in Ireland being in its immediate vicinity. This is the vast *rath* known
as the Giant's Ring. There is nothing in Ireland
so fine as it. The *rath* on the summit of Knock
Aillinn, in the County Kildare, which has been

already described in the article on that hill, is
much larger, and encloses three times the space;
but the earthen ramparts are not nearly so high
as those of the Giant's Ring. The space enclosed
by this gigantic rath is seven statute acres. When
standing in the centre of this ancient fortress,
nothing is seen but the sky above and the vast
earthworks all around. The centre is as level
and almost as smooth as a billiard table, and
exactly in the centre stands a cromlech. Old
men living in the locality say that the ramparts
were for many years planted with potatoes. This
must have reduced their height by many feet;
but they are still nearly, if not quite, twenty
feet high. Like most ancient raths, it has
two entrances, one exactly opposite the other.
It would give ample room to a population of
some thousands, and was evidently an ancient
city. But one of the most extraordinary things
connected with the Giant's Ring is that annals,
history, and legend are silent about it. So far,
there seems to be no-more known about those
who built the Giant's Ring than about the
builders of the temples of Central America. It
is the same with many of the vast Cyclopean
forts along the west coast, of which the Stague
fort in Kerry and the forts in the islands of

Arran in Galway are the most remarkable. There are, however, very few large earthen forts in any part of Ireland about which annals and history are alike silent. The Giant's Ring is by far the most remarkable structure of its kind in Ireland, and the most remarkable of all the ancient remains in the vicinity of Belfast. It has been much better preserved than most of the remains of its kind in Ireland, for the landlord on whose property it is has built a stone wall round it, so it is safe from spoliation.

The environs of Belfast are finer and more interesting than those of any Irish city, Dublin alone excepted. It is really curious that so little notice has been taken of them. The view from Devis Mountain, the top of which is hardly more than four miles from the centre of the city, is one of the finest and most extensive that can be seen in any part of Ireland. The greater part of the north of Eastern Ulster can be seen from it. Ailsa Craig in the Firth of Clyde seems almost at one's feet when standing on the summit of Devis Mountain. To know the immensity of Loch Neagh, it should be seen from there. It appears like a vast inland sea, out of all proportion to the size of the island to which it is a curse rather than an adornment;

BELFAST LOCH.

for it is one of the most utterly uninteresting of Irish lakes. The view from Cave Hill is also very fine. This hill is only three or four miles from Belfast.

Belfast Loch, as it is called, if not as picturesque as Dublin Bay, is, nevertheless, a very fine bay, and has most beautiful and sumptuous residences on its shores, particularly on the southern side. It is on this side of the loch that Hollywood is situated. There are more fine, well-kept residences in Hollywood than there are in the neighbourhood of any other Irish city. The people of Belfast are proud of Hollywood, and they ought to be. There are few places in the immediate vicinity of any city of the size of Belfast in England or Scotland where so many fine, well-kept, and sumptuous residences can be seen as in Hollywood. The greater part of them are owned by Belfast merchants.

Few go to Belfast in search of the picturesque. It has got such a commercial name that those who have never been there think that it has no attractions save for the business man. But if Belfast is visited in the summer time, if the views from its hills are seen, and if its beautiful suburb of Hollywood is seen, it will be found that there are scenic attractions of a very high order in the neighbourhood of the northern capital.

CORK, like Dublin, is a place of considerable antiquity. It does not figure in the annals or history of pagan Ireland, but Christian establishments were founded there very soon after the time of St Patrick. Its Irish name, and the one by which it is mentioned in all ancient Irish annals and history is *Corcach Mór Mumhan*, literally, the great swamp of Munster. A very inappropriate name seemingly, for, although the place where the city is built might have been a swamp, it never could have been a big one, as it is a narrow, and by no means a long, valley. It is, however, clear that the word *mór*—big —was not intended to relate to the size of the swamp, but to the greatness of either the town or ecclesiastical establishments that grew up in it.

The earliest notice of Cork that appears in Irish annals is in the still unpublished "Annals of Inisfallen," where it is stated, under the year 617, that "In this year died Fionnbarre, first bishop of Cork, at Cloyne. He was buried in his own church at Cork." Under the year 795, the following curious entry occurs in the same annals:—"In this year the Danes first appeared cruising on the coast [of Ireland] spying out the country. Their first attacks were on the ships of the Irish, which they plundered." The same annals say that Cork, Lismore, and Kill Molaïse were plundered by the Danes in the year 832, and that in 839 they burned Cork; and that in 915 they plundered Cork, Lismore, and Aghabo. They also state that in 978 Cork was plundered twice, presumably by the Danes. The *Chronicon Scottorum* says that Cork was also plundered by the Danes in 822. It was so often plundered by them that it is hardly to be wondered at that the annalists should not have been able to keep account of every time it was harried by the Northmen. But the Danes were not the only parties by whom the south of Ireland suffered, for we read in the Four Masters, that in the year 847 Flann, over-king of Ireland, for what reason does not appear, harried Munster from Killaloe to Cork. They say also that a great fleet of foreigners (Northmen) arrived in Munster in 1012 and burned Cork. They were, however, defeated by Cahall, son of Donnell. This fleet had evidently come to Cork for the purpose of making a diversion in the south of Ireland, so that the great Danish army, whose headquarters were in Dublin, and who contemplated the entire conquest of the country, should not have the men of Munster to oppose them. The Danish army that came to Cork in 1012 (the correct date seems to be 1013), were not able to give any assistance to their countrymen at the battle of Clontarf by making a diversion in Munster, for it would appear that they were wholly destroyed. There is no record in the Irish annals of the Danes making any attack on Cork after the battle of Clontarf.

The situation of Cork, like that of Dublin and Belfast, is at the mouth of a river, and on low-lying land. While the country round the city is exceedingly fine, it has not, like the country in the neighbourhood of Dublin and Belfast, any places from which extensive views can be had. The country round Cork is by no means flat, but there is nothing near it that could be called a mountain, or even a high hill. It is, however, as beautiful as any country of its kind could be, with green, rounded eminences, but not as much wood on them as there should be to make them look to best advantage. The river between Cork and the Cove, or Queenstown, as it is now called, is one of the finest six or eight miles of river scenery to be found anywhere. The people of Cork are proud of it, as they may well be.

Cork, unfortunately, is not growing as Dublin and Belfast are. There is a curious belief, partly a prophecy, that it will yet be the capital of Ireland. "Limerick was, Dublin is, but Cork will be the capital," is frequently heard in the south of Ireland. So far, there is not much sign that the southern city will overtake Dublin, nor is it quite clear that Limerick was ever the principal city of Ireland. It was, however, a very important place during the greater part of the eleventh century. Limerick seems to have been in the possession of the Danes for nearly a hundred years, until Brian Boramha took it from them about the year 970. It continued to grow as long as his descendants retained political power, which they did for nearly a century after his death. Giraldus Cambrensis calls Limerick "a magnificent city," but it must have begun to decline even before he saw it, about the year 1190, for the O'Briens, or descendants of Brian Boramha, had by that time lost a great deal of their political power. Cork has, for at least two centuries, been a more important place than Limerick.

Some of the streets and public buildings in Cork are very fine, and will compare favourably with

2 A

those of any city. But it is evident that the city was built too far up the river. Cork should be where Queenstown is. If it were, there would be a chance of its becoming at some future day the capital of Ireland. It is curious that almost all cities that are built on rivers, and that were founded in ancient times, are generally at the head of navigation. This habit of building cities as far up rivers as ships could go was followed in order to give greater security from attacks by sea. The farther up a river a city was, the more easily it could be defended from attacks by sea. In olden times, when the largest ships drew no more than eight or ten feet of water, Cork was as advantageously situated for trade where it is as if it were where Queenstown is. But such is not the case now. This defect of being too far up the river is the only thing in its situation that is not favourable. It has one of the finest harbours in Europe, and one of the finest in the world, but the harbour is too far from the city.

If there is a single place on the whole of the west coast of Europe especially adapted for the site of a great city, it is the spot on which Queenstown is built. It was nothing but the constant warfare of ancient times that prevented Cork from being built there. There is that magnificent harbour

that the mightiest ironclad leviathan that floats
can enter at any state of the tide and be in it
in five minutes from the time she leaves the main
ocean. Then there is that splendid site for a
great city on a gentle ascent, where street behind
street and terrace behind terrace could deck the
hill-side, and all look down on that glorious land-
locked bay where a thousand ships could anchor.

There cannot be any doubt that with the ever-
growing trade and passenger traffic between Europe
and America, both Cork and Queenstown must be
benefitted. Even if an American packet station
were established at Galway, it would hardly
interfere seriously with Queenstown or Cork, for
harbours like the Cove are too scarce on the
coasts of Europe, and the trade between Europe
and America is too great and increasing too fast
to leave Loch Mahon * in the slightest danger of
being deserted. As long as ships navigate the
Atlantic they must enter it. Nothing but the
establishment of aërial traffic between Europe and
America can ever leave the Cove of Cork shipless.

The country round Cork is very fine, and there
are many splendid and well-kept gentlemen's seats
in its suburbs. It would be hard to find any city
more picturesque in its situation, although built

* The old name of what is now called Queenstown Harbour.

very nearly at the mouth of a river. It is, more than any large place in Ireland, a city of hills and hollows. Some of its streets are very steep, rather too much so for pleasant walking. But this hillyness makes it all the more picturesque, and makes the drainage all the better. Cork is a beautiful city, and—surrounded by a beautiful country. If it has not the busy appearance of Belfast, or the metropolitan appearance of Dublin, it is, nevertheless, a fine city, and on account of its magnificent harbour, it has, in all probability, a great and prosperous future before it.

The antiquities of Cork have almost entirely disappeared. It suffered so much from the Northmen and was so often plundered and burned by them that it is not to be wondered at that so few of its ancient monuments exist. It had a fine round tower, of which nothing is left but the foundation. It was, presumbly, the Northmen who destroyed it. Every vestige of the old church founded by St Finnbar has disappeared long ago. The fact that Cork was so often plundered by the Danes and other Northmen shows that it must have been an important place, at least in the matter of churches and monasteries. The Danes knew that wherever the largest religious establishments were the most wealth was. This is proved by history and annals telling us that Armagh, Kildare, Cork, Glendaloch, Downpatrick, Clonmacnois, and other important religious centres, were most frequently plundered by them. Just in proportion to the importance of a place in an ecclesiastical point of view, the more frequently it was plundered by the Danes. When they began their attacks on Ireland, they seem to have known, as well as the Irish themselves, where the principal wealth of the country would be found.

As Cork is the last large place that suffered greatly from the Danes that shall be mentioned in this work, it cannot be uninteresting or out of place to give an extract from the Earl of Dunraven's book on ancient Irish architecture about those terrible Vikings, and the causes that made them a terror to all the maritime nations of Europe for so many years, more especially as such an expensive work is not generally read, and not within reach of the masses: "Dense as is the obscurity in which the cause of the wanderings and ravages of the Scandinavian Vikings is enveloped, yet the result of the investigations hitherto made on the subject is, that they were, in a great measure, consequent on the conquests of Charlemagne in the north of

Germany, and on the barrier which he thereby—
as well as by the introduction of Christianity—
set on their onward march. It can hardly be
attributed to accident that, with the gradual
strengthening of the Frankish dominions, the
hordes of Northmen descended on the British
Isles in ever-increasing numbers. The policy
of Charlemagne in his invasion of Saxony, and
the energy by which he succeeded in driving his
enemies beyond the Elbe and the German Ocean,
were manifestly intensified by religious zeal. The
Saxons were still heathens ; and the first attack
made by the Frankish King was on the fortress
of Eresbourg, where stood the temple of Irminsul,
the great idol of the nation. We read that he
·laid waste their temples and broke their idols to
pieces. . . . However it may appear from ancient
authorities that for some centuries before then,
the Scandinavians had occasionally infested the
southern shores of Europe ; yet in the added
light that is cast by the Irish annals on the
subject, we perceive that from this date their
piratical incursions afford evidence not before
met with of preconcerted plan and incessant
energy; and these events in the reign of Charles
may lead us to discover what was the strong
impulse that thus tended, in some measure, to

condense and concentrate their desultory warfare. Impelled by some strong, overmastering passion, these hordes of northern warriors held on from year to year their avenging march; and such was the fury of their arms that even now, after the lapse of a thousand years, their deeds are in appalling remembrance throughout Europe, not only in every city on the sea-shore, or on river, but even in the peasant traditions of the smallest village."

It is curious, and for the Irish a source of very legitimate pride, that of all the countries attacked by the Northmen, they got the hardest blows and the most terrible, as well as the most frequent, defeats in Ireland. They seem to have made more frequent attacks on it than on any other country, and to have poured more men into it than into any other country. This appears not only from Irish annals and history, but from Icelandic literature, which was the common property of all the Scandinavian nations, and the only literature in which the doings of the Vikings are recorded by writers who were nearly contemporary with them. There appears to be more written about Ireland and its people in the Icelandic Sagas than about any other country or people the Vikings harried. The

terrible defeat the Northmen suffered at Clontarf
in 1014 is fully acknowledged in the Icelandic
Sagas. It must, however, in truth be admitted
that that battle, while it turned out to be a
national one, originated in a family quarrel, and
was brought about, as many battles had been
brought about before, by a bad and beautiful
woman. If Gormfhlaith and King Brian had
not quarrelled, if Broder had not been desperately
enamoured of her, and if she had not been of
the royal blood of the terribly maltreated and
so often ravaged province of Leinster, the battle
of Clontarf never would have been fought. Brian
was an elderly man when he became over-king,
and was quite willing to allow the Danes to
hold Dublin and other sea-ports as trading points,
for after a time they became traders and carriers.
He was willing to let them alone provided that
they let him alone. This is proved by his having
given one of his daughters in marriage to Sitric,
the Danish King or Governor of Dublin. The
Danes, knowing they had the entire strength of
the province of Leinster at their back by Brian's
quarrel with Gormfhlaith, who was sister to the
King of Leinster, seem, probably for the first
time, to have seriously contemplated the complete
conquest of Ireland.

That the Irish suffered some terrible defeats from the Northmen has to be admitted. In justice to those who compiled the various Irish annals, it must be said that they always freely acknowledge when the invaders had the best of it in a battle. It is, however, evident that, taking the almost continuous fighting between the invaders and the invaded for two hundred years, or from about the year 814 to the time of the battle of Clontarf in 1014, the net gains of the fighting was decidedly on the side of the Irish. Many of those well-versed in Irish history think that if Ireland had been really under the dominion of one sovereign, even as England was under the later Saxon Kings, the Northmen would certainly have conquered Ireland and held it as they held, for a time, England, Normandy, and other countries. Very few of those called Irish chief kings were such except in name. Their vassals used to lick them as frequently as they licked their vassals. The Northmen defeated in battle and killed more than one Irish chief king, but that does not seem to have brought them any nearer the conquest of the island, for the provincial kings used to fight them on their own account. The Northmen had too many heads to cut off, and none of the heads controlled the destinies of the country. The most terrible defeat that was probably ever inflicted on the Irish by the Northmen was at the battle of Dublin in 917. The over-king, Niall Glundubh, was killed in it, and from what the Irish annals say, it would seem that his whole army was cut to pieces; but the victory was of little use to the invaders, for the very next year they suffered a defeat from the Irish in Meath, in which their whole army was destroyed and almost all their leaders slain. We are told that only enough of the Danes were left alive to bear tidings of their defeat. How the Irish managed to get the better of the Danes and at the same time do so much fighting amongst themselves is one of those historic puzzles the solution of which seems hopeless.

Many thoughtful persons among the Irish regret that Ireland had not been thoroughly conquered by the Northmen. They say that had it been conquered by them it would have been united under one supreme ruler, the provincial divisions would have been obliterated, a strong central government formed, and intestine wars brought to an end. Such a state of things might have come to pass; but it seems clear that the Northmen were not capable of building up a nation. They failed to do it whenever they tried. They had complete control in England for two generations when they were at the height of their power, but they failed to keep their grip on England, although having had ·the advantage of a large, and what might be called an indigenous, Scandinavian population north of the Humber. Hardly a trace of their nearly three hundred years' rule in some Irish cities remain, and in the entire island all the traces left of their language is to be ·found in less than a dozen place names. They became great in Normandy only when they ceased to be Northmen and mingled their blood with that of the people whom they had conquered, and became French.

Whatever benefit other countries may have received from the Danes or Northmen, Ireland received none. ·To her they were nothing but a curse. If they had conquered her, they might, in the long run, have benefitted her. It would be not only difficult, but absolutely impossible, to point out a single way, except, perhaps, by an admixture of a little new blood, in which Ireland was benefitted by the visits of the Northmen. In spite of their very great skill in ship-building and navigation, they introduced not a single art into Ireland. Confused as the political state of the country was before they came to it, it was still more confused when they ceased to be plunderers and became merchants. They had nothing themselves that could be called literature, and were the greatest enemies that Irish literature had ever encountered, for the number of books they must have destroyed is beyond calculation. Not a monastery or church from one end of Ireland to the other escaped being plundered by them, and most of the monasteries were plundered *ten times* during the two hundred years their plunderings lasted. Iona, though not in Ireland, was an Irish establishment; it was so often plundered by them, and its entire population so often killed, that it had to be entirely abandoned in the ninth century. It became a ruin, and remained such until the Northmen ceased their raids; its treasures, or what remained of them, were removed to Kells in Ireland. Nothing can show more plainly the knowledge the Northmen possessed of the country, and their determination to leave nothing in it unplundered, than their having plundered the anchorites' cells on the Skelligs rocks, off the coast of Kerry. It is said that there is but one spot at which a boat can land on these rocks, and then only on the very finest and calmest day; but the Northmen found out the landing-place, plundered the cells, and, of course, killed every one they found in them.

It is very curious how it came to pass that a people so very brave as the Northmen undoubtedly were should be so lacking in almost every quality that goes to form a great, conquering people and builders up of nations. They never impressed themselves on any nation or province they conquered. A very large part of the north of England was not only conquered but settled by them, and three Danish kings reigned in England, yet it remained Saxon England until the battle of Hastings. In France they not only lost their language, but lost their identity in less than three generations, and became absolutely French. They did not even call themselves Northmen, or Normans; for on the Bayeux Tapestry we find the legend, *Hic Franci pugnant*, showing plainly that they regarded themselves as nothing but French. They conquered the greater part of the island of Sicily, but, as usual, have left hardly a trace of their occupation in it. It need hardly be repeated that in Ireland, in spite of their having held and ruled some of its chief cities for three hundred years, and in spite of their many alliances with Irish chiefs and nobles, all they have left that in any way shows that they

ever set foot on Irish soil are less than a dozen
place names. The Northmen might well be for-
given for their plunderings and burnings if it
were not for the quantity of books they burned.
But for them, ancient Celtic literature would be
so immense that it would be regarded with
respect even by those who would be most hostile
to the nation that produced it.

The successful resistance of the Irish against the
Northmen is a very curious historic fact. Of all
countries in Europe in the middle ages, it ought
to have been, no matter what might be the valour
of its inhabitants, the most easy of subjugation on
account of its political divisions, and the consequent state of almost continual war that existed
among the provinces. Yet in spite of all, in no
part of Europe which the Northmen attacked, did
they encounter such strong and such long-sustained
resistance as in Ireland, in spite of the fact that
for many years before the battle of Clontarf, the
province of Leinster, whose soldiers from time
immemorial had been considered the bravest in
Ireland, was in alliance with the invaders. The
successful resistance the Irish made against the
Northmen is proved from sources that are neither
Scandinavian nor Irish ; for the Norman Chronicle
says, "that the Franks, or French, were grateful to

the Irish for the successful resistance they made against the Danes; and that in the year 848 the Northmen captured Bordeaux and other places which they burned and laid waste; but that the Scotts (Irish) breaking in on the Northmen drove them victoriously from their borders." It is absolutely sickening to read of all the plunderings, murderings, and burnings committed by the Northmen in Ireland. When we think of all the similar sort of work the Irish practised on one another, we wonder how it happened that there were any people left in the island; and we are almost driven to the conclusion that if it had not been for the extraordinary fecundity of the race, it would have become depopulated. It was not only the numbers of Irish that were killed by the Northmen, but also the numbers that were brought into captivity by them that tended to depopulate the country.

Under the year 949 the Annals of the Four Masters state that Godfrey, a Danish king or general, plundered Kells and other places in Meath, and carried off three thousand persons into captivity, and robbed the country of an enormous quantity of gold, silver, and wealth of all kinds. That sort of work had been carried on for nearly two hundred years, and it is a wonder that the entire country was not utterly ruined.

An interesting as well as gruesome illustration of what Ireland suffered from Danish raids was revealed some few years ago while workmen were levelling ground for the erection of a house at Donnybrook, near Dublin. They unearthed the skeletons of over six hundred people, of almost all ages; from those of full-grown men to those of babies, all buried in one grave, and only about eighteen inches under the surface. This vast grave was close to the banks of the little river Dodder. The Northmen had evidently gone up the river in their galleys, for at full tide it had enough of water to float them. By some chance the leader, or one of the leaders, of the Danes was killed in the foray, for his body was found a little distance from the grave of the victims. His sword was buried with him; it was of recognised Danish make, and had a splendid hilt inlaid with silver. Not a vestige of clothing or ornaments was found on the bodies of the slain, save a common bronze ring on the finger of one of them. Everything they had seems to have been taken. A village had evidently stood in the locality; it was raided by the Danes, the inhabitants all killed, and everything of value they possessed, even to their clothing, taken; for if they had been buried in their clothing, which must have been almost entirely of woollen material, which

resists decay for a long time, some vestige of it
would have been discovered. The remains of the
victims of the massacre were carefully examined
by the most eminent scientists and archæologists
of Dublin, among them Dr Wm. Fraser, who wrote
an article on the discovery that may be seen in the
transactions of the Royal Irish Academy. Irish
history and annals are silent about this terrible
massacre, and it is hardly to be wondered at that
they should not have mentioned it, for such things
were of such frequent occurrence in Ireland during
the time of the Northmen that it was impossible
to keep track of them all.

It is hard to agree with the Earl of Dunraven
in what he says in the passage that has been
quoted a few pages back, as to the cause of the
invasions and plunderings of the Northmen. The
victories of Charlemagne over the Saxons could
scarcely have caused the vast outpourings of
Northmen on southern and western Europe. The
Saxons were Germans, pure and simple; but there
seems to have been a very great difference beween
Northmen and Germans. They may both have
belonged originally to the same race, and their
languages may have been, and undoubtedly were,
closely allied, but they seem to have had very
little in common. One was an essentially sea-

2 B

faring people, and keeps up a love for the sea
to the present day. The other was not a seafaring people, and hardly yet takes kindly to
maritime life. The Norse and German races lived
side by side in England for some centuries, but
they lived apart, quite as much apart as the Celts
and Scandinavians lived apart in Ireland. It
would rather seem as if it was want, added to
a bold and restless nature, that was the primary
cause of Norsemen's raids on the south-western
coasts of Europe. Their own country was barren,
and cold, and unable to support a dense population. It sometimes happens that people multiply
faster than they can be supported. Such a state
of things occurred in Ireland in the early part of
the present century. Not that Ireland could not
have supported a much larger population than
it ever contained, provided the social condition
of the country was different; but under the conditions that existed, the people multiplied beyond
their means of support. The same thing may
have occurred in Scandinavia. The people may
have been forced by hunger to seek a living by
foul means or fair, somewhere else than in their
own country. Cruel as they were, they were
probably not more cruel than any other people
of their time would have been under the same

circumstances. It would seem that it was ex-
haustion of population in Scandinavia that put
an end to Scandinavian raidings. Its people
having become Christians may have had some
effect in softening their manners; but it is certain
that it was not hatred of Christianity that
prompted them to plunder Christian nations. It
was love of plunder, intensified, in all probability,
by want and semi-starvation at home. It is, however, very curious that the people who were once
the terror of southern Europe should have become
what they are to-day, and what they have been
for some centuries, as peaceable and as law-abiding
nations as there are in the world.

GALWAY AND ITS ENVIRONS

GALWAY is one of the most modern of the Irish provincial capitals. It does not figure at all in ancient annals. The first mention of it in the annals of the Four Masters is under the year 1124, when it is stated that the men of Connacht erected a castle in Galway. The first mention of it in the annals of Loch Key is under the year 1191, when it is stated that the river Gaillimh, from which the town takes its name, was dried up. The cause of this phenomenon is not stated. Galway was at one time a place of considerable wealth and trade. It was, in the fifteenth and sixteenth centuries, the port to which most of the Spanish wine destined for Ireland used to come; and it is generally believed that a Spanish type of features can still be noticed on some of its inhabitants. But whatever mercantile prosperity Galway enjoyed some centuries ago, very little of it unfortunately remains; for of all Irish towns the decrease of its population has been the most terrible. In 1845 it contained very close on 35,000 inhabitants, in 1891 it had only 14,000! It is painful to walk

388

OLD HOUSES IN GALWAY.

in the outskirts of the town and pass through whole streets in which nothing remains save the ruins of cottages. Galway ought to be a prosperous place, for it is situated on a noble bay that forms a spacious harbour, sheltered from the fury of the Atlantic by the Isles of Arran. It is pleasant to be able to state that the condition of this once fine city is improving.

In spite of the signs of decay that are only too visible in Galway, it is a very quaint and interesting town. It contains many buildings that were erected centuries ago, in the days of its prosperity, that are evidences of its former wealth and trade. In what may be called mediæval remains, it is, perhaps, richer than any other town in Ireland, and will well repay a visit. It is one of the few large towns in Ireland in which a majority of the people are bilingual, using both the English and Irish languages.

There is not much either of scenic or antiquarian interest in the immediate vicinity of Galway; but if those who wish to see the most ancient and gigantic cyclopean remains in Europe, or perhaps in the world, go to the Isles of Arran, to which a small steamer sails from Galway, they will be well repaid for a two hours' trip. The Arran Islands contain more antique monuments of the

pre-historic past and of a more interesting kind
than any other places of equal extent in these
Islands.   These monuments consist of vast drystone
fortresses that were raised by some pre-historic race.
There is what may be called historic tradition that
they were built by a remnant of the Firbolgs in the
century preceding the Christian era ; but those
most learned in things pertaining to Irish antiquities, do not think there is any reliable historic
evidence as to where or by whom they were
erected.   The principal fortresses are, Dun Aengus,
Dun Connor, Dun Onacht and Dun Eochla.   They
are all in the Great Island, or Arran Mór, except
Dun Connor, which is in the Middle Island, or
Inis Maan.   Dun Connor is the largest.   It is
considerably over two hundred feet long, and over
a hundred feet wide.   Its treble walls are still
twenty feet high in some places, and from sixteen
to eighteen feet in thickness.   These vast fortresses
look as if they were the work of giants.   Like
almost every relic of the past, they seem to have
been more marred by men than by time.   They
have evidently been injured by people looking for
treasure ; and a good deal of their stones have
been removed to build cabins and outhouses.   Miss
Margaret Stokes, who has devoted almost all her
life to the study of Irish antiquities, and who

consequently knows more about them, perhaps, than any one in Ireland, says of these vast fortresses in Arran: "They are the remains of the earliest examples of architecture known to exist in Western Europe." There is something awfully grand and grim in the aspect of these ruined fortresses. To gaze on their colossal dimensions and barbaric rudeness seems to carry us back almost to the beginning of time, when the earth was inhabited by beings unlike ourselves. But however old the forts in Arran may be, it is evident that they were the strongholds of a seafaring people; for the whole products of the barren islands on which they stand would not be worth the labour of erecting such gigantic fortresses for their protection. These islands support a good many people now, thanks to the potato; but in ancient times, when it was unknown, it is hard to understand how the multitude of men it must have taken to build so many vast fortresses could have found sustenance on these barren isles; and we are, therefore, almost driven to the conclusion that the fortresses in the Isles of Arran were built by pirates or seafaring men of some kind.

THE CLOUD SCENERY OF IRELAND

It is only those who have lived a long time in continental countries that can fully appreciate the beauty of Irish cloud scenery. As a rule, insular countries are richer in cloud scenery than continents. Any one who has lived even in the western part of continental Europe knows that Great Britain, owing to its being an island, is much richer in cloud scenery than France; and the further east one goes, the drier the climate will be found to be, the fewer the clouds, and consequently the less attractive the sky.

Ireland being situated so far out in the "melancholy ocean" is, beyond all European countries, a land of clouds, and it has to be admitted that she very often has too much of them. But if these clouds frequently pour down more rain than is necessary for the growth of crops, there is a certain amount of compensation given by skyey glories they create; and marvellous these glories sometimes are. It is not only at sunset or sunrise that Irish cloud scenery is fine; for often during even a wet summer, when the rain ceases for a time, and the sun appears, the sky becomes what it is hardly incorrect to call a wonderland of beauty, with its "temples of vapour and hills of storm." But the real glories of Irish cloud scenery are its sunsets. Ireland is, beyond any other country perhaps in the world, the land of gorgeous sunsets. Sometimes they are such wonders of golden glory that even the most stolid peasant gazes on them with emotion. As a rule, it is only in the latter part of summer and the first half of autumn that Irish sunsets can be seen in their greatest beauty. Sometimes, when the summer is very wet, fine sunsets are seldom seen ; but in fine weather they are generally such as can be seen in no other country. For months during the fine summer and autumn of 1893, every sunset was a wonder of indescribable beauty, with almost half the heavens a blaze of golden clouds.

SOMETHING ABOUT IRISH PLACE NAMES

IT has been said that almost everything connected with Irish history and topography is peculiar. The truth of this can hardly be doubted. If the ancient Irish were a non-Aryan race, the strange phases of their history and the abundance of Irish place names might not strike us as so curious. But it is well known that the Irish are Aryans, and that they are substantially the same people as the ancient Britons were; yet nothing in the history of England or of Great Britain will satisfactorily account for the fewness of place names in the latter country as compared with Ireland. British, but especially English, place names are, in a vast majority of cases, either of Saxon, Norse, or Celtic origin. Their fewness as compared with Irish place names is what strikes a native of Ireland with astonishment. There are probably as many place names in a single Irish province as there are in the whole of England. The townland nomenclature of Ireland is almost unknown in England. The names of all the townlands in Ireland can be seen in the Government

Survey of 1871. They number, exclusive of the names of cities, towns, and villages, about 37,000. But it is only the place names that mean human habitations, places erected by men, and where men dwelt, that shall be mentioned here. Let five denominations of place names suffice to show their immensity—namely, *ballys, kills, raths, duns* and *lises*. The first means towns or steads; the second, churches or cells; and the three last mean fortified habitations of some kind. Of *ballys* there are 6700, of *kills* 3420, of *lises* 1420, of raths 1300, and of *duns* 760, making altogether 13,600 place names meaning habitations of some kind. But this is not the half of them! The place names in the subdivisions of townlands are not mentioned at all. There is a parish in Westmeath in which there are three place names beginning with *rath*, and three with *kill*, none of which is mentioned in the printed list of townlands. Multitudes of names in which some one of the five words mentioned is included have been translated or changed; just as Ballyboher has been made Booterstown, and Dunleary made Kingstown. Many place names in which *bally, kill, dun, rath*, and *liss* occur are not included in the numbers given, for very often the adjective goes before the noun, as in such names as Shanbally, Shankill,

Shanlis, Shandun, &c. Taking everything into consideration, it would seem fair to estimate that not more than half the place names formed from the five words that have been mentioned appear in the printed list of Irish townlands; then we have the astounding total of over *twenty-seven thousand* place names in Ireland formed from five words that mean human habitations.

The only explanation of the astonishing number of ancient place names found in Ireland, as compared with England, seems to be the dense rural population that must have existed in the former country in ancient times. That an enormous percentage of ancient place names have totally faded away owing to the disuse of the Gaelic language, the consolidation of farms, and the decline of population, there cannot be any doubt at all. The puzzle about Irish place names is, if their extraordinary numbers were caused by a more dense population in Ireland than in England—why was Ireland more densely peopled than England in ancient times? The soil of Ireland is hardly more fertile than the soil of England, and the climate of Ireland is not as good, for it is much wetter than that of the larger island. England is nearer to the Continent, and therefore was more easy of access to continental traders. The situation as well as the soil and climate of England were rather more favourable to the growth of a large population than were those of Ireland. It is now generally conceded that the ancient Britons and Irish were of the same race, and spoke a language that was substantially the same. But why should there seem to have been such a difference in the political and social condition of the Irish and the ancient Britons who were their contemporaries? Why are there so comparatively few ancient place names in Great Britain and such an overwhelming number of them in Ireland? Why should Ireland have a history that goes so far back into the dim twilight of the past, and England have no history beyond the time of Cæsar? These are most interesting and important questions, but how can they be answered? It is to be hoped that some future savant will succeed in solving them.

THE END.